The Corporation in the American Economy

The
Corporation
in the
American
Economy

Edited with an Introduction by
Harry M. Trebing

❦ a New York Times Book

Quadrangle Books
CHICAGO

Contents

3. Ownership and Control of the Modern Corporation

4. Dimensions of Social Responsibility

5. Corporate Size, Performance, and Public Policy

The Corporation in the American Economy

Introduction

BECAUSE OF its superiority as a means for organizing economic activity, the corporation is pre-eminent among the major institutions of modern capitalism. No other form of business enterprise matches it as a device for marshalling resources to produce goods and services to satisfy consumer wants.

To appreciate the importance of the corporate form, one has only to note its general significance in the American economy. In 1965 there were 11,416,000 business enterprises in the United States. Of this total, 9,078,000 were sole proprietorships, 914,000 were partnerships, and 1,424,000 were corporations. When one considers these three types of enterprises in terms of total receipts or gross revenues, the dominant position of the corporation becomes evident. Of the total receipts or gross revenues of all business enterprises, 14 per cent were accounted for by proprietorships, 5 per cent by partnerships, and 81 per cent by corporations. As more than half of all the proprietorships were engaged in agriculture and service activities, the dominance of the corporate form would have been even greater if these fields had been excluded and consideration limited to manufacturing, mining, construction, public utilities, trades, and finance. In manufacturing, for example, the world's largest enterprises are organized exclusively along corporate lines, and the brand names used by many of these firms tend to become synonymous with the products themselves (Kleenex, Frigidaire, Coke, and so on).

Also, the giant corporation emerges as a major factor in the

American economy when one considers concentration at the aggregate or overall level and at individual industry levels. For example, in 1967 the largest one hundred corporations held 47.6 per cent of all manufacturing assets. The two hundred largest corporations held 58.7 per cent of all manufacturing assets, and the largest five hundred controlled nearly 75 per cent. Concentration in individual industries (sometimes called market concentration) is measured by a "concentration ratio," which indicates the percentage of the value of all shipments accounted for by the top four and top eight firms respectively. In 1966 the concentration ratio for the top four firms in the aircraft industry was 67 per cent; for the top eight it was 88 per cent. In motor vehicles, the top four accounted for 79 per cent and the top eight for 83 per cent. In computing and related machines, the top four accounted for 63 per cent and the top eight for 78 per cent. In tires, the top four accounted for 71 per cent and the top eight for 90 per cent. In cigarettes, the top four accounted for 81 per cent and the top eight for 100 per cent. In soaps and detergents, the top four accounted for 72 per cent and the top eight for 80 per cent. In photographic equipment, the top four accounted for 67 per cent and the top eight for 79 per cent. And this list can be expanded.

The adaptability of the corporate concept has been another intriguing feature of its existence. While the corporation is normally associated with privately owned enterprises, publicly owned corporations have been established by the federal and state governments to provide goods and services that can be organized as enterprise functions. The Tennessee Valley Authority and the New York Port Authority are examples of well-known government corporations. In other instances, public and private capital have been comingled in joint ventures and mixed corporations. The corporation has also demonstrated a versatility with respect to size, having been adopted not only by giant enterprises but by small and medium-scale firms as well. Only in those areas where capital requirements are negligible, where the scale of organization is small and localized, or where professional skills alone are necessary, does the corporate form not predominate.

The corporation has achieved its position of eminence for three major reasons. First, the corporate concept emerged at a time when it could be easily adapted to the burgeoning industrial revolution of the nineteenth and early twentieth centuries. Second, the corporation had features that were inherently superior to alternative forms of organization (such as the sole proprietorship and partnership) for attracting labor, capital, and management skills for the production of goods and services. Third, the corporate form was readily adaptable to diverse requirements. One can appreciate these advantages by reviewing the historical development of the corporate form.

Historical Development of the Corporation

The corporation can trace its origin to English legal traditions and to the common law. The first corporations were chartered by the British and the Americans in order to authorize a selected number of enterprises to perform public-service functions. Formal incorporation was confined primarily to firms that operated turnpikes, canals, bridges, docks, banks, and insurance companies. For example, 335 corporate charters had been issued in the United States up to 1800. Of that number, 219 were granted for highway-transportation companies, 36 were for local public-service functions, and 67 were for banking and insurance. Only 13 were awarded for strictly private business activities.

Government restrictions on incorporation were gradually relaxed. General acts of incorporation were passed by Massachusetts in 1799, by New York in 1811, and subsequently by other states. These acts permitted a firm to acquire full corporate powers, including limited liability, in order to pursue business activities. In the 1840's and 1850's, state laws were liberalized and the pace of incorporation increased. The liberalization of the incorporation laws was particularly important because it gave a firm greater freedom in structuring its charter and therefore the scope of its activities and powers. In a landmark decision in the Dartmouth College case, Chief Justice John Marshall emphasized the importance of the charter in defining the concept of the corporation:

> A corporation is an artificial being, invisible, intangible and existing only in contemplation of law. Being a mere creature of the law it possesses only those properties which the charter of its creation confers upon it, either expressly or as

incidental to its very existence. (*Dartmouth College v. Woodward,* 4 Wheat [U.S.] 518, 636 [1819])

The number of new corporate formations continued to increase through the end of the nineteenth century and into the twentieth. The benefits of the corporate form were extended to more and more areas of business and, as part of this process, the business corporation began to acquire its modern features. The degree of superiority of the corporate form can be seen by comparing these features with those of the proprietorship and the partnership.

The sole proprietorship is a business owned and controlled by a single individual who risks his property in the enterprise and receives all of the profits. The proprietorship is subject to unlimited liability, and the life of the enterprise is limited to the life of the owner. A partnership is a more advanced form of business organization, embodying the idea of an association. Essentially, it is an extension of the sole proprietorship resulting from the pooling of resources and abilities of two or more people. These people, or partners, associate themselves by means of a contract. All partners have unlimited liability to creditors; the partnership cannot sue or be sued in its own name, nor can it own property; it is not recognized as a legal entity.

By contrast, the corporation enjoys the status of a person or entity with an unlimited life span. As a legal entity, the corporation can sue or be sued in its own name, buy and sell commodities, hire and discharge employees, enter into contracts with others, and pledge its property to lenders. The corporation also has economic features which help it to attract capital. The liability of each investor is limited to his capital commitment in the enterprise. And the corporation can issue a wide variety of securities, thereby enhancing its appeal to various classes or groups of investors. It can raise debt capital (i.e., bonds) by pledging its property or revenues, or it can raise equity capital (i.e., common stock), which gives proportionate ownership and a claim to residual earnings. Hence the corporation can appeal to all segments of the capital market, offering a range of risks and varying degrees of participation in management decision-making. It also facilitates a division of labor between the professional manager on the one hand and the owner on the other.

Clearly, the corporate form was ideally suited to the challenge of the industrial revolution. It fulfilled the need for an economic institution that would give flexibility and a division of responsibility as well as create an opportunity for involvement by a variety of participants.

Corporate Concentration and Discretionary Power

Despite its advantages, the corporation has also given rise to a number of major problems, and it is not uncommon to find that much of the fury for social and economic reform has centered around corporate structures and corporate behavior.

One of the most significant problems has been the corporation's tendency to concentrate economic and political power. The American economy is highly concentrated, and the danger is that such concentration tends to increase the discretionary power of the firm by minimizing the constraints of the competitive market. Reduced competition will increase the opportunities for the firm to restrict output and raise prices. It may also tend to aggravate price discrimination; that is, the firm will have a greater opportunity to charge different prices for essentially the same service or product. Less competitive markets will pay higher prices, and more competitive markets will pay lower prices for the same units of output. Of course, reduced competition may also be reflected in other areas than final product markets. For example, a firm with enhanced discretionary power may be able to depress the prices it pays for labor, materials, and capital. In either case, an increase in corporate power and a reduction in competition will adversely affect the allocation and use of resources, as well as the distribution of income. Monopoly restricts output, distorts consumer wants, misallocates resources, and redistributes income in favor of the monopoly enterprise. Under these conditions, the maintenance of the public interest requires that the government take appropriate action.

The giant corporation, discretionary power, and economic concentration are all interrelated. Under certain conditions, increased concentration may be the result of greater efficiency, as when the economies of large-scale production are great relative to a given market. That is, if an expansion of output reduces unit costs, there will be a trend toward fewer and fewer firms in that market. But increased concentration or the emergence of the giant corporation may stem from factors other than those related to efficiency. For example, both industry and overall concentration may increase if the firms in an industry are able to employ strategies which foreclose the entry of new firms. Similarly, concentration and corporate growth may stem from aggressive efforts at merger and acquisition. If a firm is successful in acquiring control of direct competitors (horizontal mergers), then aggregate or overall concentration, industry concentration, and the size of the firm will increase. If the firm is able to gain control of sources of supply or sales outlets (vertical integration), then aggregate concentration and the size of the firm will increase. If the firm diversifies by acquiring companies in other unrelated lines of activity (conglomerate mergers), then aggregate concentration and the size of the firm will increase.

Where corporate size and concentration are related to increased efficiency, then public policy may call for direct government regulation, since increased competition would result in inefficiency. But if concentration and corporate size are the result of mergers and various efforts to restrict competition, then public policy should vigorously seek to restore competition.

Concentration, Merger Trends, and Public Policy

The growth of the giant corporation and concentration in the economy may be examined in some detail by reviewing the historical development of big business, the three major merger movements, and the present state of the argument regarding economic concentration. This review will also allow us to comment on the development of public policies toward business.

The problems of corporate size and concentration did not begin to make themselves felt until after the Civil War. Before that time there was little concentration in the United States. Two-thirds of the labor force was engaged in agriculture, and the family farm was the typical form of organization. Railroad consolidation was just beginning, and most manufacturing was carried on in small plants or local shops. The United States was indeed an economy of small-scale enterprises.

The first giant corporation to appear on the national scene was the Western Union Telegraph Company. Originally telegraph service had been provided by the government on an experimental basis, but the Western Union Company, chartered in 1851, rapidly established itself as the dominant firm in the field. Western Union's position was the result of an aggressive program of merger and acquisition, implemented by a favorable settlement of war claims with the federal government at the close of the Civil War. In the 1870's and 1880's, Western Union treated the country to a display of monopolistic practices through price discrimination, poor service, and an avoidance of innovation and change. But Western Union was not the only monopoly power during this period; the nation's small businessmen and farmers undoubtedly suffered much more grievously at the hands of the railroads. The railroads had overexpanded and were plagued by rivalry and excess capacity between major traffic centers. As a result, rate wars were common, and the industry took steps to insure price stability by semi-conspiratorial and cartel-like measures. Such efforts to restrict competition were not successful, and price fluctuations continued. Nevertheless, the carriers had sufficient economic power to practice aggressive price and service discrimination on the basis of commodities, places, and persons. Only the largest shippers were able to extract price concessions from the rail carriers.

Manufacturing also grew in the years following the Civil War, though its monopoly impact on the consumer tended to lag behind that of the telegraph carrier and the railroads. The newly established manufacturing corporations soon perceived the virtues of curbing rivalry, and they developed the "trust" as a means of limiting competition. Under the trust arrangement, the owners of controlling shares of stock in competing corporations transferred legal title to these shares to a group of trustees. The shareholders received trust certificates in return, and were entitled to participate in the profits of the combination. The trustees voted all of the stock of the participating companies, thereby administering them as a single enterprise. This form of organization was first applied on a massive scale by the promoters of the Standard Oil Combination in 1879. Its adoption became widespread in the next several decades.

Public resentment against monopoly and increased concentration was kindled by the Populist movement. The Populists served as spokesmen for farmers and small businessmen, and sought to redress the imbalance in power by political means. That is, the Populists sought to use the power of the state legislature as a countervailing force against growing corporate concentration and wealth. In a number of cases they were successful in pushing through state regulation of prices and conditions of service for such lines of activity as grain elevators, railroads, slaughter houses, and public utilities. In the pioneering case of *Munn v. Illinois* in 1876, the Supreme Court upheld the right of the State of Illinois to regulate a grain elevator, thereby establishing a precedent which would reinforce all subsequent efforts on the part of state legislatures to impose direct regulations on businesses declared to be affected with the public interest. Various states also passed anti-trust laws designed to curb the power of the combinations and trusts, without recourse to direct regulation.

The power of the state legislature was, of course, limited to intra-state activities. It became abundantly evident therefore that the federal government would have to intervene in order to curb the growing extortionist powers of the large corporations, the trusts, and the railroads operating in interstate commerce. The government moved in two directions. First, it imposed direct economic regulations on the railroads through the passage of the Interstate Commerce Act of 1887. Second, it passed the Sherman Anti-Trust Act of 1890, forbidding conspiracies in restraint of trade and authorizing the Department of Justice to prosecute such conspiratorial practices. In the Interstate Commerce Act, Congress had created an independent administrative agency charged with fixing reasonable rates for the nation's railroads. The agency was given authority to curb abusive price discrimination and limit extortionist earnings. In the Sherman Act, Congress took an alternative route. Rather than create an agency which would impose direct regulations on the corporations, it sought to restrain combinations, trusts, and other forms of agreement that would monopolize business and diminish competition.

The early efforts of the states and the federal government

toward the social control of business did not meet with any appreciable success. The United States Supreme Court was a major stumbling block. The Court emasculated the efforts of the Interstate Commerce Commission to curb price discrimination. It also sought to circumscribe the powers of the state agencies to regulate business by holding for itself the right to establish substantive guidelines for economic regulation. In so far as the Sherman Act was concerned, the Department of Justice had very limited resources with which to prosecute violations. During the first thirteen years after the passage of the Act, no separate appropriation was made for work undertaken by the Department of Justice as part of its anti-trust responsibilities. Vigorous enforcement of the Sherman Act did not begin until the administration of Theodore Roosevelt.

By the end of the nineteenth century, efforts at acquisition and consolidation, which had begun with the Standard Oil Company, gained momentum, and the nation was faced with its first major merger movement. This wave of mergers was marked by the formation of horizontal combinations in mining and manufacturing. The United States Steel Corporation was formed during this period as the nation's first billion-dollar company, and more than two hundred large combinations were organized with a consequent massive increase in concentration in many of the nation's basic industries. The first merger movement ended with the depression of 1903. Whether its termination can be attributed to the efforts of the Roosevelt administration or to the depression remains a matter of debate.

Among opponents of concentration there was increasing dissatisfaction with the operation of the Sherman Act. Considerable evidence showed that competition had been eliminated by particular business practices, and that these practices had not been held to be in violation of the Sherman Act. Further, the Supreme Court held in 1911 that combinations that were not unreasonable would be allowed to stand. Monopoly again became a political issue, and in 1914 the Clayton Act and the Federal Trade Commission Act were passed. The Clayton Act forbade price discrimination, exclusive and tying contracts, intercorporate stock holdings, and interlocking directorates where the result was to "substantially lessen competition or tend to create a monopoly." The Federal Trade

Commission Act declared that unfair methods of competition in commerce were unlawful, and created the Federal Trade Commission.

The second period of merger activity began in the 1920's and ended with the stock market crash of 1929. This wave of mergers was marked by (1) an extension of the holding-company concept to the public utility field; (2) the formation of combinations among medium-size manufacturing firms; and (3) the emergence of many different patterns of combination: vertical, horizontal, and conglomerate. As in the earlier period, the merger movement was greatly helped by an apparently insatiable public demand for corporate securities and by the prospect of quick profits from promotional and speculative activities.

By 1929 the structure of the American economy had changed dramatically from what it had been before the Civil War. Mass production and giant corporate enterprises dominated many manufacturing industries. Railroads had been consolidated into large systems, and public utility holding-company empires had emerged. In addition, financial institutions played a major role in shaping the structure and conduct of enterprises. Clearly, the United States economy had become one in which the big corporation was an outstanding characteristic. Only 20 per cent of the labor force was engaged in agriculture. More than 90 per cent of manufacturing was conducted by corporations, and virtually all of the activity in the public utility, transportation, and banking sectors was done by corporations. A pioneering study by Adolf Berle and Gardiner Means showed that in 1929 the two hundred largest corporations controlled 48 per cent of the assets of all non-financial corporations.

The holding company, which had figured prominently in the merger movement at the turn of the century achieved particular importance during the second merger period. The holding-company concept deserves special attention because it demonstrates how the corporate form could be manipulated to facilitate concentration. From the standpoint of management, the intriguing feature of the holding company was that it permitted a centralized management to control the operations of many diverse corporations by virtue of the ownership of the voting stock of those corporations. Further, it became possible through the process of pyramiding to control large blocks of assets with a relatively small investment, so that significant economic power could be exercised and handsome returns earned on a relatively small financial commitment by the parent holding company. This can be best illustrated by the public utility holding companies developed in the 1920's. In 1929, for example, it was possible to control the entire holdings of the Associated Gas and Electric Company, amounting to over $1 billion, through an investment which represented 1/20 of 1 per cent of the total capitalization of the system. The holding company proved that it was no longer necessary to dissolve or even absorb the businesses acquired. All that was necessary was to obtain enough stock to control their activities. As an added bonus, the holding company made it possible to expand control without facing diminishing returns in terms of managerial competence.

After a period of relative inactivity in the 1920's, government control of business increased considerably in the New Deal era. The Roosevelt administration sought to achieve far-reaching social and economic reforms through the introduction of government controls and increased government involvement in the economy. In the anti-trust field, the New Deal at first experimented with the encouragement of voluntary cartelization through the National Recovery Administration in the hope that this would help stop the deflationary spiral and provide employment. Subsequently, the administration reversed its policy and gave increasing support to the anti-trust activities of the Department of Justice and to the Federal Trade Commission. The New Deal also expanded federal commission regulation significantly with the creation of the Federal Communications Commission, the Securities and Exchange Commission, and the Civil Aeronautics Board. The powers and authority of the Federal Power Commission and the Interstate Commerce Commission were considerably expanded. The Federal Communications Commission was given jurisdiction over broadcasting and common-carrier communications; the Civil Aeronautics Board was given jurisdiction over the rate structures and rate levels of the airline industry; the Federal Power Commission was given increased jurisdiction over interstate electricity and natural gas sales; and the Interstate Commerce Commission was given jurisdiction over the motor carrier and water carrier industries. The Securities and Exchange Commission sought to provide greater information to the investor, to curb financial machinations, and to dissolve the public utility holding-company empires which had proved so vulnerable in the depression.

More than any other administration, the New Deal cast doubt on the implicit assumption that the conduct of the corporation was somehow synonymous with the promotion of the public interest. On the contrary, it showed that the corporate form was subject to manipulation and might abuse all sectors of the economy in the absence of adequate safeguards. The New Deal sought to impose such safeguards and thereby establish a greater compatibility between consumer requirements in the market, the structure of industry, and the promotion of the general welfare.

The third merger movement came in the years following World War II. It appears to be divided into two rather distinct phases. The first phase covered the years from 1944 to about 1948; the second phase began in 1954, and the upsurge in merger activity which began at that time still continues. The current merger movement, like the movement of the 1920's, involves segments of the distribution industries as well as manufacturing. A unique feature of the current phase has been the rapid increase in the number of conglomerate combinations. These include not only traditional conglomerate expansion by established firms but also a "new generation" of conglomerates based upon aggressive expansion through stock and debt financing in which promoters seek to acquire firms with a potential for improved earnings so that these acquisitions can be used to support further acquisitions. There also appears to be a resurgence of interest in the holding-company form concomitant with conglomerate expansion.

Public policy in the postwar years has had a number of distinctive features. First, the judicial reception accorded the decisions of the administrative agencies and the anti-trust efforts of the Department of Justice has become markedly more favorable as compared with previous decades. The commissions and the Justice Department can now be reasonably certain of a sympathetic ear from the judiciary on matters pertaining to regulation and the maintenance of competition. Second, an aggressive anti-trust policy appears to have been accepted by both Republican and Democratic administrations. Indeed, it is difficult to envision any future administration that will not concede that an active anti-trust program plays a major role in public policy toward business. While the budgets of the Department of Justice and the Federal Trade Commission continue to be woefully inadequate, the results during this period with only limited efforts should be sufficient to encourage further support. The Celler-Kefauver Anti-Merger Act of 1950, amending Section 7 of the Clayton Act, deserves special attention. This Act corrected a long-time deficiency by making it illegal to acquire either the stock or the assets of a competing corporation with a view toward lessening competition or creating a monopoly. Undoubtedly this legislation has been significant in curbing horizontal mergers during the last twenty years.

Third, there has been a marked decrease in the extension of direct economic regulation to new industries. With the exception of the independent producers of natural gas and satellite communications, it would be difficult to discern a major new industry that has been brought under regulation during the postwar years. This trend has been complemented by a growing criticism of the adequacy of conventional regulatory practices. It appears certain that a major restructuring of regulation will be forthcoming, in which commission planning and the purposeful employment of price and earnings controls will be substituted for case-by-case adversary proceedings.

What then can be said about aggregate concentration and industry concentration in the American economy? As noted earlier, the first wave of mergers (1897–1903) substantially increased all forms of concentration. It is also reasonable to assume that the second wave (1920–1929) increased such concentration. The pattern of concentration in the years since World War II is a little more difficult to categorize. In so far as aggregate or overall concentration is concerned, it would appear that the top one hundred and top two hundred largest manufacturing corporations have increased their share of total manufacturing assets during this period. By 1967 the one hundred largest corporations held 47.6 per cent, and the two hundred largest corporations held 58.7 per cent, of the assets of all manufacturing corporations. In fact, by 1967 the one hundred largest manufacturing corporations held about the same share of assets held by the top two hundred largest in 1948. This increase in concentration came about largely through mergers and acquisitions—primarily mergers of the conglomerate variety. Of all large manufacturing mergers during the period 1948–1967, only 20 per cent of the assets acquired involved mergers with direct competitors; the remaining 80 per cent involved vertical or conglomerate mergers. The Celler-Kefauver Act was clearly a deterrent to horizontal mergers. Overall concentration is only one indicator of the economic power located in the largest corporations. The existence of joint ventures, in which several giant corporations participate in jointly owned subsidiaries, tends to magnify aggregate concentration by producing a partial coupling of otherwise separate enterprises. Similarly, corporate interlocking directorates and connections with commercial banks tend to diminish competitive action and reinforce the impact of overall concentration.

In contrast, concentration in particular industries does not appear to have increased in the postwar period. Some industries are highly concentrated while other industries are characterized by low concentration. The intriguing fact is that industry concentration at the four-firm level (that is, the percentage of value of goods shipped accounted for by the top four firms) has remained remarkably stable between 1947 and 1966. Eight-firm concentration ratios have shown a somewhat more discernible trend toward increasing concentration.

If there is a relationship between concentration, corporate size, and greater efficiency, it is still something of an enigma. Viewpoints remain polarized, with the adherents of big business arguing that size is a requisite for the enjoyment of economies of scale as well as large research and development programs and a high level of innovation. On the other hand, there are those who argue for more competition as the greatest spur to efficiency and innovation. Simplistic answers to this set of problems are meaningless, and much more research remains to be done. For the present it is sufficient to note that there is reasonable doubt about the correlation between size and superior performance; the burden of proof therefore rests with the adherents of bigness. It should also be noted that while aggregate concentration is increasing, the relative standing of the giant corporations among the top two hundred firms is by no means assured. Shifts in position are quite common.

The Corporation in the 1970's

While the problems associated with size and concentration will undoubtedly continue to beset public policy, it is clear that both the corporation and government will be faced with a much broader set of challenges in the 1970's. During the thirties the corporation faced the depression and the rapid rise of the industrial unions. In the 1940's World War II and the readjustment to peace were major problems; and in the fifties and sixties the firm was confronted with the demands of the Cold War while also enjoying the longest period of sustained prosperity in modern times. Yet by the end of the sixties a new series of problems was beginning to emerge that could not be ignored. These problems will certainly make major demands on the corporation in the years to come, and it is appropriate to evaluate the corporation's role, together with its strengths and weaknesses, in terms of its potential response to such challenges.

Early in the 1970's the United States will become the world's first trillion-dollar economy. As part of this accomplishment, real national income can be expected to grow at an average annual rate of 4 per cent, and overall productivity will continue to gain at its historical average annual rate of 3 per cent. The nation's corporations will play a significant part in achieving these growth rates through their production, marketing, and investment policies and practices. Expenditures for new plant and equipment will reflect a steady increase of automation and new labor-saving devices. Improved communications, transport, and the computer-scientific revolution will open up new production and marketing possibilities which can only be vaguely perceived at present, providing a plethora of new products and services for the consumer. Corporations can also be expected to continue to expand the international dimensions of their operations. By 1969, one hundred of the five hundred largest companies had at least 25 per cent of their assets, earnings, or production overseas, and another two hundred were not far behind. It seems reasonable that this trend will continue.

In this setting there will of course be major economic problems facing corporate decision-makers. A continuation of world-wide price inflation, rather than a major recession, is a reasonable prospect, with price levels increasing at average rates of 2 to 3 per cent, and perhaps 4 per cent per year. Monetary and fiscal policies that place a high premium on full employment, together with the cost-push inflationary pressures associated with labor's demands for pay increases, guaranteed employment, and greater fringe benefits, will underwrite this trend. Also, the corporation will have to face a shift in the mix of expenditures with a retrenchment of military spending in the coming years. The result is certain to influence the relative growth rates of particular industries and the structure of research and development expenditures. These problems are not insurmountable, however, and the firm can make a contribution through the further refinement of internal efficiencies together with improved strategies for making the corporation more responsive to change and diverse markets.

There is not much argument that it is a legitimate role of the corporation to contribute to a high level of employment and economic growth through the pursuit of innovation and greater efficiency. Under these circumstances, the pertinent question for public policy becomes one of selecting a set of policies that will maximize performance objectives. But there is another side to corporate responsibility which is more controversial and certain to take on added importance in the 1970's. This is the interrelationship between the rapidly changing social environment on the one hand and appropriate corporate involvement on the other. Here the demarcation between public and private policies is far from clear, and the state of the argument rests solidly on value judgments and preconceptions.

A national realignment of objectives and values is currently under way in the face of rapidly mounting social pressures. The demand for institutional and social change stems from the decay of the cities, mounting resentment by the poor and the minorities, the threatened collapse of municipal facilities under the pressure of overcrowding and inadequate finance, and the destruction of environmental values. Pressure groups will seek to attain a particular advantage, and as these groups are located in increasingly influential urban areas, politicians are certain to be responsive. The result will be that the distribution of income will take on added importance, while at the same time there will be a shift away from quantitative measures of welfare toward greater emphasis on the "quality of living."

The problem for business, and especially for the giant corporation, will be to redefine its relationship to such a society. Two general courses of action appear to be open at this time. One is for business to continue its traditional posture as a profit-making enterprise, and participate in social issues only when they are consistent with the criterion of profit maximization. For example, the employment of minorities and the conservation of mineral and timber resources may enhance rather than reduce profits in certain cases. The firm would leave to government the decision to react to social tensions and to impose assessments to cover social costs. The second course of action is to have the corporation assume a greater share of the social burden as a member of society. Business would provide programs for urban development and job training, would take the initiative to control environmental pollution, and would try to come to terms with militant youth who do not care to become stereotyped "organization men" in order to succeed.

If the corporation is to assume the latter role in the coming decade, the criterion of profit maximization as a guide for management decision-making will have to be significantly relaxed. Instead, the corporation will be transformed into a major vehicle for social change, and it could come to act more and more as an agent for government. Corporate expenditures would become a primary means for diverting private incomes into public benefits. Paradoxically, the giant corporation acting in this capacity would take on many of the qualities—albeit at a more sophisticated level—of the first corporations to be chartered by legislatures in the late eighteenth century.

Whether the business firm will move in such a direction is debatable. For the small, highly competitive firm, the second option is largely irrelevant. For the giant firm seeking to express its corporate conscience, or simply seeking to justify noneconomic endeavors in terms of the need to create a setting more conducive to its long-run prosperity, the choice becomes more relevant. One of the factors in favor of the second option will be the emergence of a new generation of managers in the 1970's. They will be highly educated and very much at home in the world of ideas and conceptual debate over the objectives of business, society, and government. Aided by advanced quantitative techniques and the capacity to consider a wider range of variables, traditional profit criteria may become less important in the eyes of these managers, and extra-market values may take on new meaning. In this setting, what is now irrational may become rational in terms of the goals of the corporation. Further, the current trend for top management to assume responsibility for long-term planning, while decentralizing operating decisions, would expand the firm's horizon and strengthen the probability of its assuming a larger societal role.

Regardless of the route the corporation chooses, socio-economic problems will bulk large in the coming decade. Many of these problems will transcend the capabilities or the willingness of an individual company to act. Offshore oil leakages at Santa Barbara, California, in 1969; foundering oil tankers such as the *Torrey Canyon*; detergent pollution of lakes; the Northeast power failure in 1965; and even the growing gap between wealthy and poor nations illustrate just a few of these problems. A massive response by all levels of government in these areas could put the government administrator and scientist in an adversary position *vis à vis* the businessman. This would enhance the possibility that the technologist will replace the businessman as a policy-maker in these fields.

A confrontation between government and business is likely to develop along other lines as well in the 1970's. The growing importance of consumerism will pit government against business in the battle to curb product and service misrepresentation, and to establish safety standards. This will undoubtedly result in new concepts of regulation and intervention, supplementing the traditional policies of anti-trust and public utility regulation.

Yet the American corporation is a remarkably practical and adaptable institution, and it will undoubtedly display a unique capacity to respond while on the firing line in the coming decade. It could confound its critics by creating a fresh approach to the solution of many of these problems within the context of a market system. Whatever the outcome, the articles in this collection should give the reader a meaningful insight into the nature, organization, accomplishments, and problems of the corporation. Perhaps they will also encourage greater discussion of the future role of the corporation and the alternatives for public policy.

Part 1

THE CORPORATION AND MODERN INDUSTRIAL SOCIETY

CONTEMPORARY CAPITALISM, with its capacity for sustained economic growth and full employment, is a far cry from the industrial system studied by Karl Marx in the nineteenth century. A major factor in transforming advanced industrialized nations has been the emergence of the modern corporation. In the first article in this section, Adolf A. Berle examines the characteristics of modern capitalism and interprets the corporation's contribution to this change. Berle's discussion deserves attention because of its insight, and because it is representative of the work of those scholars who studied capitalism as a dynamic process and were able to supply a perspective that is not easily found in economic literature.

The corporation, however, is not an unmixed blessing. In the second article in this section, Andrew Hacker provides an overview of the criticisms that have been directed at the conduct and performance of corporations. He gives particular attention to the adverse effects of corporate power on resource allocation, the organization of technology and education, consumer wants, and individual values and aspirations. These criticisms must be considered as an offset to the advances attributed to the corporation. In addition, they constitute an impressive challenge to the adequacy of the competitive market and to public policies in the fields of anti-trust and regulation.

Recently, increasing attention has been given to a new dimension of corporate involvement in society, notably the emergence of a military-industrial complex. Continued massive defense expenditures have created a community of interest between the nation's largest industrial corporations and the military establishment. Richard F. Kaufman focuses attention on defense procurement and analyzes the resultant relationships between the military and its suppliers. The reader may wish to assess Kaufman's arguments in terms of the proposition that only giant corporations have resources adequate for the type of commitment necessary to supply national defense needs.

The issues raised by Berle, Hacker, and Kaufman are especially relevant at this time when there are mounting pressures for a reassessment of national objectives and priorities. While current waves of dissent and protest may be ephemeral, there appears to be a more permanent realignment of national values at work. It is interesting to speculate about the role the corporation should play in this process.

Marx Was Wrong and So Is Khrushchev

by Adolf A. Berle, Jr.

"YOUR GRANDCHILDREN will live under socialism," says Khrushchev to us. "We will bury you [capitalists]," he predicted to an American visitor in Moscow. Both comments capsule a major ingredient of Communist propaganda the world over: capitalism is doomed. It is self-destructive. Fate and history make communism the inevitably victorious system. Clever men had best get on the bandwagon now.

The line is not new. Westward-bound empire builders from Eurasia have always used it. Attila, Genghis Khan, Tamerlane, all urged their opponents to collapse gracefully because fate had written them off. But they did not base their claim on economics, or attempt a reasoned argument, as do present-day Communists.

But, in Moscow, doubts are arising. The American system, classified by Marxians as monopoly-capitalist and therefore due for death, gives surprisingly few signs of dying, or even of illness. Subtly, the Communist line is emphasizing a quite different note: "We can overtake and out-produce you; we can do everything you can faster and better."

One outspoken Soviet economist, Eugene Varga, ten years ago risked his career by predicting that the American system would not

From the *New York Times Magazine,* November 1, 1959, copyright © 1959 by The New York Times Company.

then destroy itself by a post-war economic crisis. After a period of disgrace, he was restored to favor. True, Karl Marx had asserted nearly a century earlier that capitalist industrial societies would create the conditions for their own self-destruction. But something had happened to delay the calculation, and careful Communist analysts knew it.

What had happened, certainly in the American case, was an evolution within the capitalist frame, knocking out the basis of Marx's prophecy and, incidentally, of the current Communist propaganda line. Briefly, the United States, without revolution, changed from the nineteenth-century "property system" to a social system. It did this in a way no Communist could have forecast, and it created what is, in essence, a different system; so different that one French scholar, Jacques Maritain, insists that it is a new and fluid system, still in the making, "which renders both capitalism and socialism things of the past."

Another scholar, Father Bruckberger, has recently written a book to prove it. It may not be an accident that both are French; the clearest estimates of America have come from France—witness Alexis de Tocqueville in the nineteenth century and André Siegfried in the twentieth.

This American system has not yet received a distinctive name. It has been called "people's capitalism." A new book about to come out, by Dr. Paul Harbrecht, calls it "para-proprietal society" (a society beyond property). When Khrushchev and his associates talk about capitalism, they describe a system which perhaps did exist a century ago. But in America it stopped existing somewhere between 1920 and 1930. It is important both for the Soviet Union and for America to know this. Kremlin Communists are fighting a ghost, and their more sophisticated analysts know it. Americans are just coming to realize that they are operators of a system more advanced and, in its way, more revolutionary than the Marxian.

Predictions of a short life for capitalist society, as it functioned about 1900, had, I think, a reasonable basis at the time. Marx thought private ownership of factories, plants and industry inevitably would cause the rich to grow richer as their profits accumulated. Meanwhile the workers and the poor would stay at subsistence level. The small owner class, he insisted, would own and operate the government, the courts and all social organization.

These would be used to defend the growing accumulations of this class. As the poor stayed poor (or grew poorer) markets for manufactured goods would not increase as fast as production—the masses would not have the buying power.

So, markets would have to be extended by military conquest and every capitalist state must become a built-in "imperialism," always seizing more territory to increase markets for its owner class. There would be recurrent crises of growing severity, as production outran markets and the going got harder. Eventually an insuperable crisis would blow up the whole system. Then the Communist dictatorship of the proletariat representing the masses would take over. So ran the argument.

If we had looked at Europe in 1870—or at America from 1890 to 1900—circumstances would have lent color to the idea. At that time, individual owners of private capitalist enterprise were in fact accumulating, high, wide and handsome. In America we were having the "age of the moguls"—proprietor-tycoons piling up fabulous fortunes from the profits of railroads and mines, steel, copper and oil. In England, Charles Dickens had described the plight of the masses in "Bleak House" and "Oliver Twist." In the United States, Upton Sinclair and his friends were telling a similar story, American-style.

Marx was right in one respect: it could not (and in fact, did not) last. But he was completely wrong in his guess as to how it would change.

In the United States three new elements (among other less powerful factors) emerged and changed both the direction and structure of affairs, though none of them involved or contemplated blowing up the system.

The first development was the American corporation. This operated surprisingly. In one generation it replaced the individual or family-owners. In a second period, it displaced the tycoons and moguls, substituting professional management. It did not behave at all like a personal fortune-builder.

The second was the rise of American labor unions. These refused to try to seize or take over government. Instead, they insisted only on representing workmen.

The third, and probably the most important, was the position of the American democratic government. This simply declined to be owned and operated by and in the interest of the tycoon (or any other) class. It intervened from time to time to steer the economic system toward social goals. None of these possibilities had figured in Marx's calculation, and Russian commentators today find difficulty in explaining them.

First, the corporations. These organizations became, and now are, the titular "owners" of American industry. But corporations are not individuals or families and do not behave like them. As productive organizations they can and do pile up huge aggregations of property. But simultaneously they must distribute much of their profit to a continuously growing proportion of the population of the United States. Corporations whose stock is listed on the New York Stock Exchange carry on at least three-fourths of all American industry; the 500 largest of them probably carry on about two-thirds of it. Were these 500 families, the results might have justified Marx's predictions and produced the foreseen catastrophe.

Actually, according to the New York Stock Exchange, they have about 12,500,000 direct stockholders. Even more important, a large and growing amount of their stock is held by institutions— notably pension trusts, mutual funds and, increasingly, life insurance companies. These in turn distribute the industrial profits. Probably 50,000,000 Americans who do not even know they derive income from stocks receive a share of these profits through the holdings of institutions. This number will grow. Their proportionate take of industrial profits will also grow—both factors are expanding just now with considerable rapidity.

Nor are the managers and groups controlling corporations owners. They are almost always salaried officials. They are becoming a kind of nonstatist civil service. The corporate system at present is thus in effect operating to "socialize" American industry but without intervention of the political state. No Marxist could ever have thought up that possibility.

Then there is the phenomenon of the American labor movement. For practical purposes, organized labor became a substantial economic factor after World War I. It gained full recognition through the Wagner Act. It has now become a vast, permanent and powerful element in the American economic system.

But it refused to behave like its European ancestors. It did not wish to own and manage the plants. In fact, it has steadily declined to enter management. Instead, it aimed only to represent the workers and to get for them, through wages, pensions and fringe benefits, the largest practicable share of national income.

In the past thirty years it has succeeded in steadily raising the "real" wage of workers about 3 per cent annually, or 30 per cent in each decade—though workers do not receive this only in cash but also in shorter working hours, vacations and more leisure. The net result has been that American labor now has the highest standard of living in the world. The workman himself lives, thinks and feels not as an oppressed proletarian seeking to be saved by revolution but as a member of the middle class to whose children any position is possible. It is, in fact, increasingly hard to find a "proletariat" in the United States except in a few isolated areas.

Still less has the labor movement followed European patterns in forming a political party or seeking to assume government; still less to overturn the existing system. It does get into politics very effectively to defend its own interests, dealing more or less impartially with both political parties. But it declines to become a Socialist party itself and shows no desire whatever to attempt creation of a "labor" government.

Finally, and certainly most important, the American Government most obstinately refused to be merely an expression of the "ownership class." According to Marx, such refusal could not happen—but it did. Surprisingly to European thought, many of the "ownership" group were outspoken in opposing that conception of government. President Theodore Roosevelt intervened violently against one ownership sector in the Mogul Age when he forced regulation of railroads and set a conservative party to control "malefactors of great wealth."

President Woodrow Wilson moved effectively against the financial ownership class, proclaiming the doctrines of the "New Freedom" and compelling passage of the Federal Reserve Act of 1913. With even more effect, he sponsored income and inheritance tax legislation about the same time.

In 1933, President Franklin Roosevelt and the New Deal undertook the larger task of moving the whole system toward a socially directed commonwealth. Social Security legislation was one great instrument. Systematic direction of a larger share of national income toward farmers and agriculture was another. Development of public works and state-directed production when unemployment threatens was a third. Use of the credit system to assure housing, electricity and land reclamation was a fourth. And there were many more.

Thus, in mid-century, Americans are operating a so-called "capitalist system" in which all the elements dominant in the nineteenth century have changed. What is left of the old system is its form of organization and, in general, its separation from the political government.

That organization has achieved a per capita level of production beyond older dreams—so much so that equaling it is the present expressed dream of the Soviet Union and of Communist China. In terms of distribution it has done better than Communist systems because it had more to distribute. And its methods of distribution have been on the whole less arbitrary and infinitely less oppressive. The results have been more satisfactory to 175,000,-000 Americans than those of Socialist distribution to the 210,000,-000 citizens of the Soviet Union.

This American system is miles from being perfect. All kinds of things turn up in it that should not be there. All kinds of inequities have to be dealt with. Our methods for keeping production and distribution in balance are still unsympathetic and crude; better means still need to be worked out. Steering an adequate amount of the national income into necessary noncommercial activities, notably education and the arts, remains a problem.

But, by comparative standards, our system is far out ahead. As a single example, during forty years of the Soviet system, Russia at all times has had more political prisoners in concentration camps behind barbed wire than the United States has ever had unemployed men—though Khrushchev is credited with having reduced the number materially in the past few years.

The vitality and rapid evolution of the American system—and it has not stopped growing and has not stopped evolving—has worried the Russian theoreticians. At the Twentieth Communist Congress in Moscow, a then favorite Communist doctrinaire, Dmitri Shepilov (later Foreign Minister), was put up as a principal speaker to explain true doctrine to the comrades. He did not ignore the fact that the United States and its system had evolved and was going great guns, but he had to prove nevertheless that "capitalism is doomed."

Taking account of the newer studies of the American system, he singled out for attention (along with John Foster Dulles) the work of Prof. J. Kenneth Galbraith of Harvard ("American Capitalism: The Concept of Countervailing Power") and a current book of mine. He made no attempt to meet the modern American facts. "It can't happen," he proclaimed. Socially directed capitalism, freed from the vices Marx had observed, must be like hot ice: it couldn't exist.

Sophisticated Communist scholars know better. A more serious explanation was attempted this summer, again by Eugene Varga, ablest of the Soviet economists. In the official "Problems of Peace and Socialism" last August, he published an article. He renewed the statement that "under capitalism crises of overproduction are inevitable," but he said we were now in a system of "state monopoly capitalism" and this system made it easier for "monopolies" to weather these crises.

Specifically, the state moved to support the "monopolies" (he means the big corporations) through Government orders, chiefly military, and thus assure a minimum of production even during crises. Further, we slowly inflated the currency, reducing real wages without direct wage cuts.

The fact that the corporations are not monopolies and neither control, nor are controlled by, the state, he ignored, and he omitted the fact that they now distribute profits as well as wages to a huge sector of the United States. Nor had he discovered that the real wage of the American workman steadily rises.

Still less, of course, had he noted that "Government orders" include nonmilitary items such as huge road systems, municipal improvements, housing, power, scientific development and other activities whose amount exceeds military expenditures. (If the armament burden were lifted tomorrow, that same machinery could be used with general approval from the American public to increase production and markets alike.) But he continues hopefully to assert that "the cyclic movement inherent in the capitalist mode of production will, we believe, resume its normal course with a world economic crisis occurring every six years or so."

Well, his reasoning does not take account of facts. It ignores the structural change in the property system achieved during the past fifty years, and the astonishing capacity of the American system to make new adaptations.

Its crises (there will be some) can be handled on a humane basis. They will be infinitely less dangerous than the recurrent bloody crises inescapable in the political monopoly built into the Soviet dictatorship. The American system continues to evolve successfully, and is keeping right on.

A Country Called
Corporate America

by Andrew Hacker

PROBLEMS LIKE poverty, civil rights and juvenile delinquency may have been "discovered" only in the past few years, but such can hardly be said about the issue of bigness in American business. On and off, for the last three-quarters of a century, the question has been raised whether the nation's large corporations have reached the point where they can cut a swath through society without having to account for the consequences of their actions.

Allusions to "the trusts," "robber barons" and even "Wall Street" may have an archaic ring. Nevertheless, the frequency and magnitude of recent corporate mergers, the high level of profits despite the persistence of poverty and the latest furor over safety in the country's leading industry are bringing renewed life to a debate that has as much importance for 1966 as it did for 1896, 1912 and 1932.

Our large corporations are very large indeed. General Motors, for example, employs more than 600,000 people, a figure exceeding the combined payrolls of the state Governments of New York, California, Illinois, Pennsylvania, Texas and Ohio. The annual sales of Standard Oil of New Jersey are over $10 billion, more than the total tax collections of Wisconsin, Connecticut and Massachusetts, in addition to the six states just mentioned. In fact, our 50 largest companies have almost three times as many people working for them as our 50 states, and their combined sales are over five times greater than the taxes the states collect.

Yet here, as elsewhere, statistics can be made to tell several stories. For example, is big business getting bigger? Between 1957 and 1965, nonagricultural employment in the United States rose by about 10 per cent. But during that same period the number of persons employed by the nation's largest industrial companies went up by 15 per cent. Measured in this way, the big corporations seem to be taking three steps for every two taken by the economy as a whole.

At the same time it must be acknowledged that corporate America is by no means the fastest-growing sector in the country. Government employment, especially at the local level, is increasing at a higher rate; from 1957 to 1965 the public payroll, excluding the military, rose by 25 per cent. Even higher was the percentage increase in service industries. Enterprises like boatyards, car washes and carry-out restaurants—many of them small and locally based—have come to constitute the most vital area of economic growth.

Moreover, the advent of automated processes in large-scale production has actually cut down corporate employment in several dominant industries. At the outset of 1965, for instance, such companies as General Electric and Gulf Oil and United States Steel actually had *fewer* people working for them than they had eight years earlier. While these firms are not yet typical, they may be harbingers of things to come—the apparent ability of corporations to increase their sales, production and profits with a decreasing work force.

If corporate size has a variety of yardsticks, corporate power is beyond precise measurement. It is not an overstatement to say that we know too much about the economics of big business and not nearly enough about the social impact of these institutions. Professional economists tend to focus on the freedom of large firms to set or manage prices, with the result that attention is deflected from the broader but less tangible role played by corporations in the society as a whole.

By the same token it is all too easy to expose egregious defects in consumer products or advertising or packaging. Congressional hearings make good forums for periodic charges of "irresponsibility," whether the target of the year happens to be automobiles or pharmaceuticals or cigarettes. It is true that the buyer is often stung—and sometimes laid to rest—by the products of even the most prestigeful of corporations. But the quality of merchandise, like the ability to fix prices, is only a secondary aspect of corporate power.

What calls for a good deal more thought and discussion is the general and pervasive influence of the large corporation entity in and on the society. For the decisions made in the names of these huge companies guide and govern, directly or indirectly, all of our lives.

The large corporations shape the material contours of the nation's life. While original ideas for new products may come from a variety of sources, it is the big companies that have the resources to bring these goods to the public. The argument that the consumer has "free will," deciding what he will and will not buy, can be taken just so far. (Too much can be made of the poor old Edsel.) For in actual fact we *do* buy much or even most of what the large corporations put on the shelves or in the showrooms for us.

To be sure, companies are not unsophisticated and have a fair idea of what the consumer will be willing to purchase. But the general rule, with fewer exceptions than we would like to think, is that if they make it we will buy it. Thus we air-condition our bedrooms, watch color television in our living rooms, brush our teeth electrically in the bathroom and cook at eye-level in the kitchen. It is time for frankness on this score: the American consumer is not notable for his imagination and does not know what he "wants." Thus he waits for corporate America to develop new products and, on hearing of them, discovers a long-felt "need" he never knew he had.

And more than any other single force in society, the large corporations govern the character and quality of the nation's labor market. The most visible example of this process has been the decision of companies to introduce computers into the world of work, bringing in train an unmistakable message to those who must earn a living. Millions of Americans are told, in so many words, what skills they will have to possess if they are to fill the jobs that will be available. A company has the freedom to decide *how* it will produce its goods and services, whether its product happens to be power mowers or life insurance or air transportation. And having made this decision, it establishes its recruiting patterns accordingly. Individuals, in short, must tailor themselves to the job if they want to work at all. Most of us and all of our children will find ourselves adjusting to new styles of work whether we want to or not.

The impact of corporate organization and technology on the American educational system deserves far closer attention than it has been given. Whether we are talking of a vocational high school in Los Angeles or an engineering college in Milwaukee or a law school in New Haven, the shape of the curriculum is most largely determined by the job needs of our corporate enterprises. The message goes out that certain kinds of people having certain kinds of knowledge are needed. All American education, in a significant sense, is vocational. Liberal-arts students may enjoy a period of insulation but they are well aware that they will eventually have to find niches for themselves in offices or laboratories.

While many college graduates go into non-corporate or non-business employment, the fact remains that much of their educational tune is still being determined by corporate overtures. Even the liberal-arts college in which I teach has recently voted to establish within its precincts a department of "computer science." It is abundantly clear that while I.B.M. and Sperry Rand did not command Cornell to set up such a department, the university cannot afford to be insensitive to the changing character of the job market.

Our large firms both have and exercise the power to decide where they will build their new factories and offices. And these decisions, in their turn, determine which regions of the country will prosper and which will stagnate. The new face of the South is, in largest measure, the result of corporate choices to open new facilities in what was hitherto a blighted area. Not only has this brought new money to the region, but new kinds of jobs and new styles of work have served to transform the Southern mentality. The transition to the 20th century has been most rapid in the communities where national corporations have settled. You cannot remain an unrepentant Confederate and expect to get on in Du Pont.

By the same token, the regions which have not prospered in postwar years have been those where corporations have opted not to situate. Too much can be made of the New England "ghost towns." Actually corporations have "pulled out" of very few places; more critical has been their failure to establish or expand facilities in selected parts of the country. Thus patterns of migration—from the countryside to the city and from the city to the suburb—are reflections of corporation decisions on plant and office location. If men adjust to machines, they also move their bodies to where the jobs are.

Related to this have been the corporate decisions to rear their headquarters in the center of our largest cities, especially the East Side of New York. Leaving aside the architectural transformation and the esthetic investment with which we will have to live for many years, the very existence of these prestige-palaces has had the effect of drawing hundreds of thousands of people into metropolitan areas not equipped to handle them. Thus not only the traffic snarls and the commuter crush, but also the burgeoning of suburbs for the young-marrieds of management and the thin-walled apartments for others in their twenties, fifties and sixties.

Much—perhaps too much—has been made of ours being an age of "organization men." Yet there is more than a germ of truth in this depiction of the new white-collar class which is rapidly becoming the largest segment of the American population. The great corporations created this type of individual, and the habits and style of life of corporate employment continue to play a key role in setting values and aspirations for the population as a whole. Working for a large organization has a subtle but no less inevitable effect on a person's character. It calls for the virtues of adaptability, sociability, and that certain caution necessary when one knows one is forever being judged.

The types of success represented by the man who has become a senior engineer at Western Electric or a branch manager for Metropolitan Life are now models for millions. Not only does the prestige of the corporation rub off on the employe, but he seems to be affixed to an escalator that can only move in an upward direction. Too much has been made of the alleged "repudiation" of business and the corporate life by the current generation of college students. This may be the case at Swarthmore, Oberlin and in certain Ivied circles. But in actual fact, the great majority of undergraduates, who are after all at places like Penn State and Purdue, would like nothing better than a good berth in Ford or Texaco. Indeed, they are even now priming themselves to become the sort of person that those companies will want them to be.

The pervasive influence of the large corporations, in these and other areas, derives less from how many people they employ and far more from their possession of great wealth. Our largest firms are very well-off indeed, and they have a good deal of spare cash to spend as and where they like. These companies make profits almost automatically every year, and they find it necessary to give only a fraction of those earnings back to their stockholders in the form of dividends.

(If the largest companies are "competitive" it is only really in the sense that we all are: all of us have to keep working at our jobs if we are to survive as viable members of the society. Quite clearly the biggest corporations stand no risk of going out of business. Of the firms ranking among the top 40 a dozen years ago all but two are still in preeminent positions. And the pair that slipped —Douglas Aircraft and Wilson meatpacking—continue to remain in the top 100.)

Thus the big firms have had the money to create millions of new white-collar jobs. Department heads in the large companies ask for and are assigned additional assistants, coordinators, planners and programmers who fill up new acres of office space every year. What is ironic, considering that this is the business world, is that attempts are hardly ever made to discover whether these desk-occupiers actually enhance the profitability or productivity of the company. But everyone keeps busy enough: attending meetings and conferences, flying around the country, and writing and reading and amending memoranda.

White-collar featherbedding is endemic in the large corporation, and the spacious amenities accompanying such employment make work an altogether pleasant experience. The travel and the transfers and the credit-card way of life turn work into half-play and bring with them membership in a cosmopolitan world. That a large proportion of these employes are not necessary was illustrated about 10 years ago when the Chrysler Corporation had its back to the wall and was forced to take the unprecedented step of firing one-third of its white-collar force. Yet the wholesale departure of these clerks and executives, as it turned out, had no effect on the company's production and sales. Nevertheless, Chrysler was not one to show that an empire could function half-clothed, and it hired back the office workers it did not need just as soon as the cash was again available.

If all this sounds a bit Alice-in-Wonderland, it would be well to ponder on what the consequences would be were all of our major corporations to cut their white-collar staffs to only those who were actually needed. Could the nation bear the resulting unemployment, especially involving so many people who have been conditioned to believe that they possess special talents and qualities of character?

Corporate wealth, then, is spent as a corporation wishes. If General Motors wants to tear down the Savoy-Plaza and erect a corporate headquarters for itself at Fifth Avenue and 59th Street, it will go ahead and do so. Quite obviously an office building could, at a quarter of the cost, have been located on Eleventh Avenue and 17th Street. But why should cost be the prime consideration? After all, the stockholders have been paid their dividends, new production facilities have been put into operation, and there is still plenty of money left over. Nor is such a superfluity of spare cash limited to the very largest concerns. Ford, who is generally thought of as General Motors' poor sister, was sufficiently well-heeled to drop a quarter of a billion dollars on its Edsel and still not miss a dividend.

If our large corporations are using their power to reshape American society, indeed to reconstruct the American personality, the general public's thinking about such concentrated influence still remains ambiguous.

There persists, for example, the ideology of anti-trust and the fond place in American hearts still occupied by small business. Thus politicians can count on striking a resonant chord when they call for more vigorous prosecutions under the Sherman Law and for greater appropriations for the Small Business Administration. Most Americans, from time to time, do agree that our largest companies are too big and should somehow or other be broken up into smaller units. But just how strong or enduring this sentiment is is hard to say. No one really expects that Mobil Oil or Bethlehem Steel can or will be "busted" into 10 or a dozen entirely new and independent companies. Thus, if the ideology that bigness equals badness lingers on, there is no serious impetus to translate that outlook into action.

Part of the problem is that if Americans are suspicious of bigness, they are not really clear about just what it is about large corporations that troubles them. Despite the periodic exposures of defective brake cylinders or profiteering on polio vaccine, the big story is not really one of callous exploitation or crass irresponsibility. Given the American system of values, it is difficult to mount a thoroughgoing critique of capitalism or to be "anti-business" in an unequivocal way. The result is that our commentaries in this area are piecemeal and sporadic in character. We have the vocabularies for criticizing both "big government" and "big labor" but the image of the large corporation is a hazy one, and despite its everyday presence in our midst our reaction to its very existence is uncertain.

Take the question of who owns our big enterprises. In terms of legal title the owners are the stockholders, and management is accountable to that amorphous group. But it is well known that in most cases a company's shares are so widely dispersed that the managers of a corporation can run the firm pretty well as they please. Yet even assuming that the executives are acting with the tacit consent of their company's theoretical owners, it is worth inquiring just who these stockholders are.

Interestingly, a rising proportion of the stockholders are not people at all but rather investing institutions. Among these non-people are pension funds, insurance companies, brokerage houses, foundations and universities. Thus some of the most significant "voters" at the annual meetings of the big companies are the Rockefeller Foundation, Prudential Life and Princeton University. And these institutions, out of habit and prudence, automatically ratify management decisions.

It is instructive that the corporations' own public-relations departments have just about given up trying to persuade us that these stockholder gatherings are just another version of the local town meeting. The last report I saw that did this was filled with photographs showing average-citizen stockholders rising to question the board of directors on all manner of company policies. "A sizable number of shareholders participated in the lively discussion periods," the reader is told. "Many more spoke individually with directors and other executives about the affairs of the company." However, in small type in the back of the report is an accounting of the five votes that were actually taken at the meeting. In no case did the management receive less than 96 per cent of the ballots (i.e., shares) that were cast.

From these observations at least one answer is possible: yes, there is a "power élite" presiding over corporate America. Yet the problem with this term is that the "élite" in question consists not so much of identifiable personalities—how many of the presidents of our 20 largest corporations can any of us name?—but rather of the chairs in the top offices.

The typical corporation head stays at his desk for only about seven years. The power he exercises is less discretionary than we would like to believe, and the range of decisions that can be called uniquely his own is severely limited. (It is only in the small companies on the way up, such as the Romney days at American Motors, that the top men impress their personalities on the enterprise.) John Kenneth Galbraith once noted that when a corporation president retires and his successor is named, the price of the company's stock, presumably a barometer of informed opinion, does not experience a perceptible change.

Unfortunately it is far easier to think in terms of actual individuals than of impersonal institutions. Therefore it must be underlined that the so-called "élite" consists not of Frederic Donner and Frederick Kappel and Fred Borch but rather of *whatever* person happens to be sitting in the top seat at General Motors and A.T.&T. and General Electric. We are reaching the point where corporate power is a force in its own right, for all intents and purposes independent of the men who in its name make the decisions.

The modern corporation is not and cannot be expected to be a "responsible" institution in our society. For all the self-congratulatory handouts depicting the large firm as a "good citizen," the fact remains that a business enterprise exists purely and simply to make more profits—a large proportion of which it proceeds to pour back into itself. (True, the big companies do not seek to "maximize" their profits: their toleration of make-work and high living is enough evidence for this.)

But corporations, like all businesses whether large or small, are in the primary business of making money; indeed, they do not even exist to produce certain goods or services that may prove useful or necessary to society. If Eli Lilly or Searle and the other drug companies discovered that they could chalk up larger profits by getting out of vaccines and manufacturing frozen orange juice instead, they would have no qualms or hesitation about taking such a step.

A corporation, then, cannot be expected to shoulder the aristocratic mantle. No one should be surprised that in the areas of civil rights and civil liberties our large companies have failed to take any significant initiative. The men who preside over them are not philosopher-kings, and no expectation should be held out that they may become so. At best they can be counted on to give some well-publicized dollars to local community chests and university scholarships. But after those checks are written (and the handing-over of them has been photographed) it is time to get back to business.

And this is as it should be. Corporate power is great—in fact, far more impressive than corporation executives are willing to admit—and were large corporations to become "social-minded," their impact would be a very mixed blessing. For then the rest of us would have to let corporate management define just what constitutes "good citizenship," and we would have to accept such benefactions without an excuse for comment or criticism.

Therefore, when corporations, in the course of doing their business, create social dislocations there is no point in chiding or exhorting them to more enlightened ways. It would be wrong, of course, to lay the blame for all of our social ills at the doorsteps of the large firms. If the drug companies manufacture cheap and effective birth control pills it is a trifle presumptuous to take them to task for whatever promiscuity occurs as a consequence.

Nevertheless, the American corporation, in the course of creating and marketing new merchandise, presents us with temptations —ranging from fast cars to color television—to which we sooner or later succumb. There is nothing intrinsically wrong with color television. It is, rather, that the money we spend for a new set is money that can no longer be put aside for the college education of our children. (Thus, no one should be surprised when, 15 years from now, there is a demand for full Federal scholarships for college students. Not the least reason for such a demand will be that we were buying color TV back in 1966.)

Specific questions can be framed easily enough. It is the answers that are far from clear. We have unemployment: how far is it because corporations have not been willing or able to create enough jobs for the sorts of people who need them? We have a civil rights problem: how far is it because corporations have been reluctant to hire and train Negroes as they have whites? We have a shortage of nurses: how far is it because corporations outbid and undercut the hospitals by offering girls secretarial jobs at higher pay for less work? We have whole waves of unwanted and unneeded immigrants pouring into our large cities: how far is it because corporations have decided to locate in Ventura County in California rather than Woodruff County in Arkansas?

Questions like these may suggest differing answers but they do add up to the fact that a good measure of laissez-faire continues to exist in our corporate economy. For all their ritual protestations over Government intervention and regulation, our large companies are still remarkably free: free to make and sell what they want, free to hire the people they want for the jobs they have created, free to locate where they choose, free to dispose of their earnings as they like—and free to compel the society to provide the raw materials, human and otherwise, necessary for their ongoing needs.

The task of picking up the pieces left by the wayside belongs to Government. This is the ancient and implicit contract of a society committed to freedom of enterprise. But whether the agencies of Government have the resources or the public support to smooth out the dislocations that have been caused to our economy and society is not at all clear. Negro unemployment, the pollution of the Great Lakes, the architectural massacre of Park Avenue and the wasteland of television seem to be beyond the power and imagination of a Government that has traditionally understood its secondary and complementary role.

Corporate America, with its double-edged benefactions and its unplanned disruptions, is in fact creating new problems at a rate faster than our Governmental bureaus can possibly cope with them. Given that the articulate segments of the American public seem at times to show more confidence in United States Steel than in the United States Senate, the prognosis must be that the effective majority today prefers a mild but apparently bearable chaos to the prospect of serious Government allocation and planning.

The American commitment to private property means, at least for the foreseeable future, that we will be living with the large corporation. On the whole, Americans seem vaguely contented with this development, unanticipated as it may have been. In light of this stolidity, the order of the day—to reverse Karl Marx's dictum—is to understand our world rather than change it; to identify, with as much clarity and precision as is possible, the extent to which a hundred or so giant firms are shaping the contours of our contemporary and future society. Only if we engage in such an enterprise will we be able to make any kind of considered judgment concerning the kind of nation in which we wish to live and the sort of people we want to be.

As Eisenhower Was Saying…"We Must Guard Against Unwarranted Influence by the Military-Industrial Complex"*

by Richard F. Kaufman

EIGHT YEARS have gone by since President Eisenhower opened the door on the military-industrial skeleton in the closet. Yet only recently has research started to hang some real meat on his bony, provocative phrase, "military-industrial complex." What is emerging is a real Frankenstein's monster. Not only is there considerable evidence that excessive military spending has contributed to a misallocation of national resources, but the conclusion seems inescapable that society has already suffered irreparable harm from the pressures and distortions thus created.

* Farewell radio and television address to the American people. January 17, 1961.

Military and military-related spending accounts for about 45 per cent of all Federal expenditures. In fiscal 1968, the total Federal outlays were $178.9-billion. The Defense Department alone spent $77.4-billion, and such related programs as military assistance to foreign countries, atomic energy and the Selective Service System raised the figure to $80.5-billion. The $4-billion program of the National Aeronautics and Space Administration and other activities intertwined with the military carry the real level of defense spending considerably higher.

To place the defense bill in perspective we should note that 1968 appropriations were less than $500-million for food stamps, school lunches and the special milk program combined. For all federally assisted housing programs, including Model Cities, they were about $2-billion. The poverty program received less than $2-billion. Federal aid to education was allotted about $5.2 billion. The funds spent on these programs and all those categorized as health, education, welfare, housing, agriculture, conservation, labor, commerce, foreign aid, law enforcement, etc.—amounted to about $82.5 billion, if the space and veterans' programs are not included, and less than $70-billion if the interest on the national debt is not considered.

The largest single item in the military budget—it accounted for $44-billion in 1968—is procurement, which includes purchasing, renting or leasing supplies and services (and all the machinery for drawing up and administering the contracts under which those purchases and rentals are made). Procurement, in other words, means Government contracts; it is mother's milk to the military-industrial complex.

The Pentagon annually signs agreements with about 22,000 prime contractors; in addition, more than 100,000 subcontractors are involved in defense production. Defense-oriented industry as a whole employs about 4 million men. However, although a large number of contractors do some military business, the largest share of procurement funds is concentrated among a relative handful of major contractors. Last year the 100 largest defense suppliers obtained $26.2-billion in military contracts, 67.4 per cent of the money spent through contracts of $10,000 or more.

Similarly, the Atomic Energy Commission's contract awards tend to be concentrated in a select group of major corporations.

Of approximately $1.6-billion awarded in contracts last year, all but $104-million went to 36 contractors. As for NASA, procurement plays a larger role in its activities than in those of any other Federal agency. More than 90 per cent of its funds are awarded in contracts to industry and educational institutions. Of the $4.1-billion worth of procurement last year, 92 per cent of the direct awards to business went to NASA's 100 largest contractors.

In terms of property holdings, the result of almost two centuries of military procurement is a worldwide and practically incalculable empire. An almost arbitrary and greatly underestimated value—$202.5-billion—was placed on military real and personal property at the end of fiscal year 1968. Weapons were valued at $100-billion. Supplies and plant equipment accounted for $55.6-billion. Most of the remainder was in real estate. The Pentagon says the 29 million acres it controls—an area almost the size of New York State—are worth $38.7-billion. (The official Defense Department totals do not include 9.7 million acres, valued at $9-billion, under the control of the Army Civil Works Division or additional property valued at $4.7-billion.) The arbitrariness of those figures is seen in the fact that they represent *acquisition* costs. Some of the military real estate was acquired more than a century ago, and much of it is in major cities and metropolitan areas. The actual value of the real estate must be many times its acquisition cost.

But the important fact about procurement is not the extent of the Pentagon's property holdings; it is that defense contracting has involved the military with many of the largest industrial corporations in America. Some companies do almost all their business with the Government. Into this category fall a number of the large aerospace concerns—such giants as General Dynamics, Lockheed Aircraft and United Aircraft. For such other companies as General Electric, A.T.&T. and General Motors, Government work amounts to only a small percentage of the total business. But the tendency is for a company to enlarge its share of defense work over the years, at least in dollar value. And whether defense contracts represent 5 per cent or 50 per cent of a corporation's annual sales, they become a solid part of the business, an advantage to maintain or improve upon. A company may even work harder to increase its military sales than it does to build commercial sales because military work is more profitable, less competitive, more susceptible to control through lobbying in Washington. The industrial giants with assets of more than $1-billion have swarmed around the Pentagon to get their share of the sweets with no less enthusiasm than their smaller brethren.

The enormous attraction of military and military-related contracts for the upper tiers of industry has deepened in the last few years as military procurement has increased sharply. For example, G.E.'s prime-contract awards have gone up from $783-million in 1958 to $1.5-billion in 1968; General Motors went from $281-million in 1958 to $630-million in 1968. While much of this increase can be traced to the Vietnam war boom and many contractors would suffer a loss of business if the war ended, there was steady growth in the defense industry during the fifties and early sixties (in 1964 and 1965, before the Vietnam build-up, there was a decline in prime-contract awards). In the five years from 1958 to 1963—five years of peace—the value of G.E.'s prime contracts increased $217-million and General Motors' rose $163-million. The same trend can be shown for many of the large corporations in the aerospace and other industries.

What seems to be happening is that defense production is gradually spreading throughout industry, although the great bulk of the funds is still spent among relatively few companies. Still, as the defense budget increases the procurement dollars go further. The geographical concentration of defense production in the industrialized, high-income states also suggests that military contracts have come less and less to be restricted to an isolated sector of the economy specializing in guns and ammunition. Military business has become solidly entrenched in industrial America.

Considering the high degree of mismanagement and inefficiency in defense production and the tendency for contractors to want more sales and therefore to support the military in its yearly demands for a larger budget, this is not a healthy situation. The inefficiency of defense production, particularly in the aerospace industry, can hardly be disputed. Richard A. Stubbing, a defense analyst at the Bureau of the Budget, in a study of the performance of complex weapon systems, concluded: "The low over-all performance of electronics in major weapon systems developed and produced in the last decade should give pause to even the most outspoken advocates of military-hardware programs." He found that in 13 aircraft and missile programs produced since 1955 at a total cost of $40-billion, fewer than 40 per cent of the electronic components performed acceptably; two programs were canceled at a cost to the Government of $2-billion, and two programs costing $10-billion were phased out after three years because of low reliability.

And the defense industry is inefficient as well as unreliable. Albert Shapero, professor of management at the University of Texas, has accused aerospace contractors of habitually over-staffing, over-analyzing and over-managing. A. E. Fitzgerald, a Deputy Assistant Secretary of the Air Force, in testimony before the Joint Economic Subcommittee on Economy in Government, described poor work habits and poor discipline in contractors' plants. In the same hearing, a retired Air Force officer, Col. A. W. Buesking, a former director of management systems control in the office of the Assistant Secretary of Defense, summarized a study he had conducted by saying that control systems essential to prevent excessive costs simply did not exist.

In a sense, industry is being seduced into bad habits of production and political allegiance with the lure of easy money. And industry is not the only sector being taken in. Consider conscription (3.6 million men in uniform), the Pentagon's civilian bureaucracy (1.3 million), the work force in defense-oriented industry (4 million), the domestic brain drain created by the growth in military technology, the heavy emphasis on military research and development as a percentage (50 per cent) of all American research, the diversion of universities to serve the military and defense industry. These indicators reveal a steady infiltration of American values by those of the military establishment: production for nonproductive use, compulsory service to the state, preparation for war. In the process, the economy continues to lose many of the attributes of the marketplace. In the defense industry, for all practical purposes, there is no marketplace.

The general rule for Government procurement is that purchases shall be made through written competitive bids obtained by advertising for the items needed. In World War II the competitive-bid requirements were suspended. After the war the Armed Services Procurement Act was passed, restating the general rule but setting out 17 exceptions—circumstances under which negotiation would be authorized instead of competition. The exceptions, which are still in use, are very broad and very vague. If the item is determined to be critical or complex or if delivery is urgent or if few supplies exist and competition is impractical or if emergency conditions exist or if security considerations preclude advertising, the Pentagon can negotiate for what it wants.

When President Truman signed this law in 1948 he saw the possibilities for abuse and wrote to the heads of the armed services and the National Advisory Committee for Aeronautics. "This bill," he said, "grants unprecedented freedom from specific procurement restrictions during peacetime. . . . There is danger that the natural desire for flexibility and speed in procurement will lead to excessive placement of contracts by negotiation and undue reliance upon large concerns, and this must not occur." Unfortunately, Truman's apprehensions were well justified. Last year about 90 per cent of the Pentagon's and 98 per cent of NASA's contract awards were negotiated under the "exceptions."

What this means is that there is no longer any objective criterion for measuring the fairness of contract awards. Perhaps more important, control over the costs, quality and time of production, insofar as they resulted from competition, are also lost. Negotiation involves informal discussion between the Pentagon and its contractors over the price and other terms of the contract. It permits subjective decision-making on such important questions as which firms to do business with and what price to accept. The Pentagon can negotiate with a single contractor, a "sole source," or it can ask two or three to submit proposals. If one later complains that he had promised to provide a weapon at a lower price than the contractor who obtained the award, the Pentagon can respond by asserting that the price was not the major factor, that the Government simply had more faith in the contractor who won. This, in effect, is how the Army responded to the Maremont Corporation's recent challenge of a contract award to General Motors for the M-16 rifle. The Pentagon, because of its almost unbounded freedom to award contracts, can favor some companies. And over long periods, this practice can lead to a dependence by the Government on the technical competency of the suppliers on whom it has come to rely. For example, the Newport News Shipbuilding Company has a virtual monopoly on the construction of large aircraft carriers.

Typically, the Pentagon will invite a few of the large contractors to submit proposals for a contract to perform the research and development on a new weapon system. The one who wins occupies a strategic position. The know-how he gains in his research work gives him an advantage over his rivals for the larger and more profitable part of the program, the production. This is what is meant when it is said that the Government is "locked in" with a contractor. Because the contractor knows he will obtain a lock-in if he can do the initial research work, there is a tendency to stretch a few facts during the negotiations.

Contractor performance is measured by three factors: the total cost to the Government of the weapon system, the way in which it functions and the time of delivery. During the contract negotiations over these factors the phenomenon known as the "buy-in" may occur. The contractor, in order to "buy in" to the program, offers more than he can deliver. He may promise to do a job at a lower cost than he knows will be incurred or to meet or exceed performance specifications that he knows are unattainable or to deliver the finished product long before he has reason to believe it will be ready.

Technically, the contractor can be penalized for his failure to fulfill promises made during the negotiations, but the Government rarely insists on full performance. The contractor knows this, of course, and he also knows the "get-well stratagem. That is, he can reasonably expect, on practically all major weapon contracts, that should he get into difficulty with regard to any of the contract conditions, the Government will extricate him—get him well.

The contractor can get well in a variety of ways. If his costs run higher than his estimates, the Pentagon can agree to pay them. (Cost increases can be hidden through contract-change notices. On a typical, complex weapon system, the changes from original specifications will number in the thousands; some originate with the Pentagon, some are authorized at the request of the contractor. The opportunities for burying real or phony cost increases are obvious, so much so that in defense circles contract-change notices are sometimes referred to as "contract nourish-ment.") The Government can also accept a weapon that performs poorly or justify a late delivery. If for some reason it is impos-sible for the Pentagon to accept a weapon, there is still a way to keep the contractor well. The Pentagon can cancel a weapon program for the "convenience" of the Government. A company whose contract is canceled for default stands to lose a great deal of money, but cancellation for convenience reduces or eliminates the loss; the Government makes reimbursement for costs incurred. An example of this occurred recently in connection with the F-111B, the Navy's fighter-bomber version of the TFX.

Gordon W. Rule, a civilian procurement official who had re-sponsibility for the F-111B, said in testimony before the House Subcommittee on Military Operations that General Dynamics was in default on its contract because the planes were too heavy to meet the height or range requirements. Rule proposed in a memo-randum to Deputy Secretary of Defense Paul H. Nitze that the contract be terminated for default. At the same time, Assistant Secretary of the Air Force Robert H. Charles and Roger Lewis, the General Dynamics chairman, proposed that the Navy reim-burse the company for all costs and impose no penalty. Nitze's compromise was to make reimbursement of $216.5-million, mostly to General Dynamics, and to impose a small penalty.

In a memo written last year Rule made this comment on the attitude of defense contractors: "No matter how poor the qual-ity, how late the product and how high the cost, they know noth-ing will happen to them."

There are many other ways to succeed in the defense busi-ness without really trying. The Pentagon generously provides capital to its contractors; more than $13-billion worth of Govern-ment-owned property, including land, buildings and equipment, is in contractors' hands. In addition, the Pentagon will reimburse a supplier during the life of his contract for as much as 90 per cent of the costs he reports. These are called "progress" pay-ments, but are unrelated to progress in the sense of contract objectives achieved; they correspond only to the costs incurred. The progress payments are interest-free loans that provide the contractor with working capital in addition to fixed capital. They minimize his investment in the defense business and free his assets for commercial work or for obtaining new defense work.

Investigations by the General Accounting Office have revealed that the Government's money and property have been used by contractors for their own purposes. The most recent incident involved Thiokol Chemical Corporation, Aerojet-General (a subsidiary of General Tire & Rubber Company) and Hercules, Inc. From 1964 through 1967 they received a total of $22.4-million to be used for work on the Air Force Minuteman missile program. The Government accountants found that the three contractors misused more than $18-million of this money, spending it for research unrelated and inapplicable to Minuteman or any other defense program.

The defense industry is perhaps the most heavily subsidized in the nation's history. Thanks to Pentagon procurement policies, large contractors find their defense business to be their most lucrative. Although no comprehensive study of such profits has been made, the known facts indicate that profits on defense contracts are higher than those on related nondefense business, that they are higher for the defense industry than for manufacturing as a whole and that the differential has been increasing. In a study that compared the five-year period from 1959 through 1963 with the last six months of 1966, the General Accounting Office found a 26 per cent increase in the average profit rates negotiated. Admiral Hyman G. Rickover has testified that suppliers of propulsion turbines are insisting on profits of 20 to 25 per cent, compared with 10 per cent a few years ago, and that profits on shipbuilding contracts have doubled in two years.

The figures cited by Rickover relate to profits as a percentage of costs, a measure that often understates the true profit level. The more accurate measure is return on investment. An example of the difference was demonstrated in a 1962 tax-court case, North American Aviation v. Renegotiation Board. The contracts provided for 8 per cent profits as a percentage of costs; the tax court found that the company had realized profits of 612 per cent and 802 per cent on its investment in two succeeding years. The reason for the huge return on investment was the Defense Department policy of supplying both fixed and working capital to many of the larger contractors. In some cases the amount of

Government-owned property exceeds the contractor's investment, which is sometimes minimal. It is no wonder that contractors prefer to talk about profits as a percentage of costs.

Murray Weidenbaum, recently appointed Assistant Secretary of the Navy, found in a study that between 1962 and 1965 a sample of large defense contractors earned 17.5 per cent net profit (measured as a return on investment), while companies of similar size doing business in the commercial market earned 10.6 per cent.

The Pentagon has attempted to answer the critics of high defense profits by citing the findings of the Logistics Management Institute, a think tank that has done a study showing declining defense profits. The trouble with the institute's study is that it used unverified, unaudited data obtained on a voluntary basis from a sample of defense contractors. Those who did not want to participate simply did not return the questionnaires; in fact, 42 per cent of those contacted provided no data. There is no way of knowing whether the group of contractors who refused to participate in the study included the ones making the highest profits.

There is almost no risk in defense contracting except that borne by the Government. If a major prime contractor has ever suffered a substantial loss on a defense contract, the Pentagon has failed to disclose his name, although it has been requested to do so by members of Congress. On the other hand, the disputed Cheyenne helicopter and C-5A cargo plane projects could conceivably result in large losses for Lockheed, the contractor in both cases. Lockheed asserts that it might still make a profit on the C-5A (which is being produced in a Government-owned plant), and denies that it is at fault in the cancellation of production on the Cheyenne helicopter (on which research work has been resumed). Past experience suggests that one should await the final decision, which may be two years in coming, before making flat statements about profit and loss.

In fairness, it ought to be pointed out that Secretary of Defense Melvin R. Laird has talked about a new get-tough policy with contractors. New procurement techniques that would, for instance, require contractors to meet specific cost benchmarks have been announced; increased prototype development is planned; greater public disclosure of cost overruns and performance or scheduling problems have been promised; the production of the Cheyenne helicopter and the Air Force's Manned Orbiting Laboratory program have been canceled. Whether any of these measures will produce real savings has yet to be determined. The Pentagon is famous for its paper reforms.

The defense industry, in addition to providing high profits at low risk, offers fringe benefits for everyone. One of the important advantages for those in procurement, on either side of the bargaining table, is the opportunity for career advancement. There is a steady march of military and civilian personnel back and forth between the Pentagon and the defense industry. It is not considered unusual for someone like Maj. Gen. Nelson M. Lynde Jr. to retire from the Army after being directly involved in the procurement of the M-16 rifle and go to work five months later for Colt Industries, originally the "sole source" of the M-16; nor is it a matter for comment when Lieut. Gen. Austin Davis retires from the Air Force after playing an important role in procurement for the Minuteman missile program and becomes vice president of North American Rockwell, one of the Minuteman's prime contractors.

This is not to say that the interchange of personnel between the Pentagon and the defense industry is harmful or that it ought to be prohibited. There is a problem in finding qualified people, and one would not want to deprive either the Pentagon or contractors of a source of trained manpower. While it would not be fair to condemn the practice and everyone engaged in it out of hand, there is a serious conflict-of-interest problem.

The conflict-of-interest laws apply primarily to military personnel and are easily evaded. Therefore, the solution to the problem does not seem to lie in expanding the legal restrictions. What might help is the public disclosure of the names of high-ranking Pentagon officials who have moved on to jobs in the defense industry and those who have made the reverse trip. The Subcommittee on Economy in Government has recommended that such a list be compiled. It would facilitate scrutiny of the interchange problem by revealing obvious conflicts of interest that should be investigated.

Individuals in the field of procurement naturally have an interest in the continued growth and importance of their field. The same could be said of people in many other fields. What is disturbing here is the opportunity that many officials have to influence procurement policy while in the Pentagon and then benefit from their actions or those of their former associates when they join the defense industry or, possibly, one of the 16 Federal-contract research centers supported by the Pentagon.

The 16 centers, including the Rand Corporation and the Institute for Defense Analysis, receive at least 85 per cent—and in some cases as much as 99 per cent—of their income from the Pentagon. With contracts totaling more than $300-million a year, they form a kind of halfway house between the military establishment and the defense industry, serving the interests of both.

Last year, Senator J. W. Fulbright, the chairman of the Senate Foreign Relations Committee, obtained from the Pentagon a list of the top officials of the research centers and their prior Government affiliations. Seven center presidents and five vice presidents —including Maxwell D. Taylor, former chairman of the Joint Chiefs of Staff—had once held high posts in the Defense Department. Taylor's salary as president of the Institute for Defense Analysis was reported as $49,200; he also, of course, received retirement pay as a general. The highest-paid research-center officer was the president of the Aerospace Corporation, an Air Force creation, who received $90,000 a year.

In hearings last fall before the Subcommittee on Economy in Government, Senator William Proxmire looked briefly at the Logistics Management Institute, a Pentagon-created research center that worked exclusively for the Defense Department until recently, when it obtained permission to devote 10 per cent of its time to other assignments. Senator Proxmire learned that, of the institute's 18 professional staff members, six came directly from defense contractors, six were formerly employed by research centers or consultant firms whose work was heavily defense oriented and one was a retired Air Force Reserve officer.

More recently, Proxmire asked the Pentagon for a list of the retired regular military officers holding the ranks of Army colonel, Navy captain or higher employed by the 100 largest defense contractors. As of February, 1969, 2,072 retired regular military officers were employed by the 95 top contractors who responded to the inquiry, an average of 22 in each company. The 10 companies employing the largest number had 1,065 on their payrolls, an average of 106, triple the average number they employed in 1959.

Proxmire, in a March 24 speech, commented, "What we have here is almost a classic example of how the military-industrial complex works." His point was that there is a growing community of interests between the military and the large contractors and that it militates against the public interest. Former high-ranking military men have a special entrée to the Pentagon; they have friendships with those still there and may even negotiate contracts or be involved in developing plans and specifications with officers with whom they served, whom they promoted or vice versa. "In addition," Proxmire said, "there is the subtle or unconscious temptation to the officer still on active duty. After all, he can see that over 2,000 of his fellow officers work for the big companies. How hard a bargain does he drive with them when he is one or two years away from retirement?"

The interchange of personnel, according to testimony by Admiral Rickover, has helped spread a business-oriented philosophy in the Defense Department. One might equally well observe that a military-oriented philosophy has been spread in the defense industry. Several kinds of institutional arrangements in addition to the interchange of personnel help bind military power to industrial wealth. Representatives of industry, in such groups as the Aerospace Industries Association, and of the military, in such organizations as the Air Force Association, agree on the basic issues: a large military budget, a high cost base in defense production, no losses, high profits and Congressional and public compliance.

Though ostensibly preoccupied with national security and maintaining a strong defense against potential foreign aggressors, these institutions interpret domestic criticism of military spending as a problem of the highest priority. Witness a meeting of the Industry Advisory Council and representatives of the Defense Department in October, 1968. (The Industry Advisory Council is one of a dozen or more business-advisory groups which meet regularly with officials in the Pentagon to discuss matters ranging from foreign policy to the latest proposed changes in armed services procurement regulations. The Industry Advisory Council until recently was called the Defense Industry Advisory Council. Dropping the word "Defense" from its name suggests its concern over public relations. The council's membership at the time of the October meeting included the presidents or board chairmen of Boeing, G.E., Brown and Root, Western Electric, DuPont, Lockheed, Newport News Shipbuilding, Northrop, General Dynamics, Olin Mathieson, Tenneco, Litton and Ford.)

The immediate outcome of the October meeting was an outline of major problems facing the Pentagon and industry. The outline and a memorandum from Assistant Secretary of Defense Thomas Morris were circulated to officials on the assistant-secretary level of the Defense Department and each of the armed services. The subject was: "Fundamental Problem Areas: Key areas worthy of joint exploration by D.O.D. and industry in calendar year 1969."

Four major problem areas were listed. The first was how to "maintain public and Congressional confidence in the integrity and effectiveness of defense procurement and contractor performance." Others were how to obtain full compliance with procurement policies by both Pentagon and industry officials; how to maintain a healthy defense-industrial base, and how to increase the effectiveness of the major-weapon-system acquisition process.

The memo, in discussing how to shore up lagging public and Congressional confidence in the defense procurement process, listed some more specific, "detailed problems," including these: uniform-accounting-standards legislation; excess-profits hearings; the Truth-in-Negotiations Act; General Accounting Office investigations and audits; investigations of such specific programs as the TFX and the M-14 rifle and statutory profit limitations. In other words, the chief worries of the industry and Pentagon representatives in 1969 are legislation that would tighten controls on procurement and defense profits, the investigation of specific weapons programs and investigations and audits by Government accountants.

The danger of the military-industrial complex lies in its scale. Reasonable men will tolerate a war machine as a necessary evil. It is the size of the machine and its claim on national resources and individual lives that is at issue. What is alarming is the growth of the complex.

The great leap of the military budget in the last few years, from about $50-billion to $80-billion, and its earlier growth, beginning with the Korean war, have helped to bring about serious stresses in the economy. Although no one factor can be identified as the sole cause of inflation, it is no accident that the three most recent price surges accompanied sharp increases in military spending, between 1950 and 1953 (the Korean war period), between 1955 and 1957 and since the build-up in Vietnam began. Defense expenditures have contributed substantially to these inflationary trends. The consequent reduced value of savings and fixed-income assets during each of these periods is an indirect cost of defense; the 10 per cent tax surcharge made necessary by the Vietnam build-up is a much more direct one.

More ominous than the economic consequences of a bloated defense budget are expanding and sometimes furtive military activities in such areas as foreign affairs, social-science research, domestic riot control and chemical and biological warfare. In hearings last year on Pentagon-sponsored foreign-affairs research, Senator Fulbright quoted from a 1967 report of the Defense Science Board (a scientific counterpart to the business-advisory groups): "The D.O.D. mission now embraces problems and responsibilities which have not previously been assigned to a military establishment. It has been properly stated that the D.O.D. must now wage not only warfare but 'peacefare' as well. Pacification assistance and the battle of ideas are major segments of the D.O.D. responsibility. The social and behavioral sciences constitute the unique resource for support of these new requirements. . . ."

Fulbright's reminder that the military's responsibility is "to prosecute war or to provide military forces which are capable of defending against an external attack" might have sounded like naïveté to the Pentagon, but his point is important. Social-science research conducted in foreign countries by foreigners should, if it is to be supported at all, be supported by the State Department, not the Pentagon. Research into socio-cultural patterns or the social organization of groups or processes of change should not be a military responsibility. Yet the Pentagon does support foreign research all over the world, awarding contracts to G.E. to make projections of "future world environments" and to Mc-Donnell-Douglas to do a study entitled "Pax Americana," later retitled "Projected World Patterns, 1985."

The Army's new domestic "war room" in the basement of the Pentagon is also of doubtful legitimacy. This "operations center" is supposed to help dispatch and coordinate troops for urban riots (maybe that's "pacification assistance"). Even assuming the need for this kind of activity, one can raise the same question that disturbs Senator Fulbright with regard to social-science research: Is this a proper military responsibility?

The most recent example of the Pentagon's "independent thinking," brought to light by the efforts of Congressmen Richard D. McCarthy and Cornelius Gallagher, is the controversial Army plan to transport about 27,000 tons of obsolete poison gas across the country by train to New Jersey to be loaded onto old hulks, towed out to sea and sunk. Both the State Department and the Interior Department have a direct interest in this project, yet the Army did not bother to coordinate its plans with them until long after the plans were formulated.

Such incidents as the construction of the domestic war room and the independent decision to ship poison gas across the country symbolize the drift of power in the executive branch to the Pentagon and show the extent to which military authority has exceeded its traditional limits. Swollen by overgenerous appropriations, the defense budget has become the source of frightening political as well as economic power. Practically freed of the fiscal limitations that restrain other agencies, the Pentagon seems to be able to exercise its will in almost any area it chooses, foreign or domestic, from negotiating a new lease for bases and promising military assistance to Spain (as it was recently alleged to have done) to launching programs of social reform.

The nature of the problem was simply stated recently at a hearing of the House Subcommittee on Military Operations. Testifying was Phillip S. Hughes, deputy director of the Bureau of the Budget. Representative William Moorhead had charged that the bureau was unable to scrutinize Defense Department expenditures to the same extent that it reviews nondefense spending. The budget requests of Government agencies, except the Defense Department, are subjected to an independent analysis and review, which is then submitted to the Budget Director. The director makes his recommendations to the President, subject to challenge by the Cabinet. officer concerned. But the Defense Department is treated differently. In the Pentagon, Moorhead said, Budget Bureau analysts must work alongside their Defense counterparts, not independently. The results of this joint review are submitted to the Secretary of Defense, who sends it to the President, subject to challenge by the Budget Director. The result is that the burden of persuading the President to change the budget he receives is shifted from the agency head to the Budget Director in the case of the defense item, but only there. (The Nixon Administration's Budget Director, Robert P. Mayo, testified recently that the defense budget would be transmitted to the President in the future just as other departmental requests are.)

"The most relevant consideration," Hughes testified, "is, in blunt terms, sheer power—where the muscle is—and this is a very power-conscious town, and the Secretary of Defense, and the defense establishment are a very different group to deal with, whether the Congress is dealing with them or whether the Budget Bureau is dealing with them. . . ."

The military-industrial complex has become a massive, tangled system, half inside, half outside the Government. Like the Gordian knot, it is too intricate to be unraveled. But like the dinosaur, its weakness lies in its great size. If its intricacy rebuffs us, its grossness is vulnerable; it can be reduced by substantially cutting the defense budget.

This is the only viable immediate solution, for innovations in contractual procedures, regulatory statutes such as the Truth-in-Negotiations Act and such watchdog agencies as the General Accounting Office have not been able to cope effectively with the major excesses in military procurement. The Bureau of the Budget has been in a subordinate position, notwithstanding its recent success in challenging the Manned Orbiting Laboratory funds and its claims to more power over the defense budget. The deck is stacked against those who would sit down across the table from the military-industrial complex.

The only way to change the game is to cut the budget.

Part 2

MANAGEMENT AND
THE CORPORATION

THE TOP executive in the large corporation today is certainly a different breed from the titan of industry who held power at the turn of the century. Not only has the executive prototype changed, but management's responsibilities have grown in complexity and have assumed a more sophisticated perspective. For example, contemporary management must be capable of long-term planning in order to meet the requirements of national and regional markets. This necessitates decisions regarding market research, product lines, pricing, and location of plants and facilities. At the same time, management is confronted with powerful labor unions and complex interactions with all levels of government. From within the corporation, management is faced with a continuing series of challenges in the form of new techniques and decision-making processes. Operations research, decision theory, and advanced information-retrieval systems give the top executive more sophisticated tools; but they demand from him greater competence and flexibility.

What can be said about the men who must fill these positions? The three articles in this section provide an interesting insight into the personality, background, and career problems of the executive. Andrew Hacker examines the values and background of the management hierarchy, as well as the requisites for success. He points to the demand that the corporation makes in terms of dedication and commitment. In the next article, Clarence B. Randall examines the problems of the top executive as seen through the eyes of a former board chairman. Randall points to the danger that the chief executive of the corporation may be cut off from direct contact with the work around him as corporate responsibilities circumscribe his opportunity to be creative.

Finally, the chief executive is becoming more and more vulnerable to a special type of pressure—that associated with corporate mergers. What does the merger do to the executive who has struggled to reach the top in the setting described by Hacker and in the isolation described by Randall, when the independence of his firm disappears through acquisition and merger? Isadore Barmash's short report on this subject will be of interest.

The Making of a (Corporation) President

by Andrew Hacker

AMONG THE MANY offices filled at inauguration ceremonies during the opening weeks of this year, the half-dozen most important were probably those assumed by Ronald Reagan, Lester Maddox, Lurleen Wallace, Otto Miller, Gordon Metcalf and Haakon Ingolf Romnes.

While the first three obviously need no introduction or identification, it is also safe to suppose that the last three require a good deal of both. Virtually nothing is known about the men who just took over as presiding officers of Standard Oil of California, Sears, Roebuck and the American Telephone and Telegraph Corporation. Yet Messrs. Miller, Metcalf and Romnes sit at the apexes of corporate edifices that employ over a million people, with five times the combined payrolls of California, Georgia and Alabama, the states governed by Reagan, Maddox and Mrs. Wallace, respectively. Their companies sell goods and services to the annual tune of $20-billion, whereas together the three states collect only $4-billion in taxes each year.

Though these men are representative of America's industrial and financial leadership, the curiosity is that the holders of such pervasive power and influence should remain anonymous—even invisible to the public eye. This is not due to any conspiracy of silence; on the contrary, most companies have public relations departments working overtime to publicize the performance and personalities of their top men. Nevertheless, these efforts are largely in vain. The American preference is for glamour or controversy, characteristics not usually associated with corporation executives. Still, sooner or later we will have to face up to the fact that a Frederic Donner of General Motors is a more potent figure than a John Lindsay, that a David Rockefeller at Chase Manhattan Plaza has a greater ultimate impact on our lives than does his brother in Albany.

The top men in the top companies are symbolic of a new breed of American. Their distinction lies in having passed the stringent series of tests set by our society to determine who will rise to its heights and who will be left behind. Every modern organization has such multiple hurdles, and the route to the top for an archbishop, a four-star general or a university chancellor has a great deal in common with that traveled by a corporation president. Career success nowadays is based more on talent than on birth or background, and what is especially rewarded is an ability and a willingness to devote those talents to goals decided upon not by oneself but by others.

The future corporation president can emerge from anywhere in the generous bosom of the American middle class. All that companies ask, in their initial recruitment of potential executives, is that a young man possess a college diploma. It doesn't matter where you went to school, and in most cases no one cares who your father was or what he did for a living. Among the top executives of today there are actually more products of the Big 10 than of the Ivy League, and in the corporate circles of the future it is clear that graduates of Purdue will far outnumber those from Princeton.

The president of Boeing Aircraft was born in Lolo, Mont. (population 235) and went on to Montana State University. Itasca, Tex., Walton, Ky., Hattiesburg, Miss., and Shelby, Neb., produced local boys who ultimately made it to the top ranks of Gulf Oil, North American Aviation, Texaco and the Ford Motor Company. Very few went to private preparatory schools and hardly more than three or four out of 100 are listed in the metropolitan Social Registers.

In a way, this is altogether plausible, for the majority of companies now do most of their promoting from within, and they draw on the pool of management talent that is subsequently discovered among the college graduates they originally recruited for specialized jobs. Thus, a large corporation will hire as many as 1,000 graduates each year, and the assumption is that out of this legion of engineers and scientists and accountants will eventually emerge enough individuals with executive potentialities.

It is worth noting, therefore, that only a minor fraction of the men who make it to the top have liberal arts degrees. This preference for the practical persists despite the pronouncements of sundry corporate chairmen that business needs more people with backgrounds in the human disciplines. History and philosophy majors should be warned against taking such assurances too seriously, however. The story is told of the head of a large chemical company who sang the praises of liberal learning in the course of receiving an honorary degree at a Midwestern university, while at that very moment a recruiter from his own company was in the school's placement office with requests for seven chemical engineers, three electrical engineers, two mathematicians and an accountant.

The open-eyed young man, first taken on as a technician of one sort or another, soon discovers what is wanted if he is to distinguish himself from his classmates. This is the comprehension and conviction that he is, above all else, working in and for a business. "It's remarkable how many of the young fellows we take in go along for years without realizing that their real job is to make money for the company," one executive remarked.

The up-and-comer, however, soon learns to think first and foremost in business terms: the specialized skills he was taught at college are only useful if they can be applied to augmenting the firm's earnings. At a certain point he may have to compromise with professional standards in making or promoting a profitable but less-than-quality product. How he reacts to this challenge will be noted by his superiors.

By the time he is in his early 30's, the man-on-the-way-up will have left his old friends behind at their account books and drafting boards. He is now a manager, of either a large department or perhaps a branch plant. The best indication of his early success is that he now has as his subordinates men older than himself; not only has he passed his peers but he has bypassed people who were once ahead of him. "Anyone can head a department staffed with a lot of youngsters or working stiffs," admitted one executive. "The big step is the one that takes you over people like yourself."

The 10 years between the ages of 35 and 45 are the critical ones. It is here that a junior executive can stop at $20,000—a title on the door but no carpet on the floor—or go on to $100,000. What is required now is the top-management look. This is usually achieved by emulating the appearance and outlook of one's immediate and remote superiors. It is generally an air of taciturn toughmindedness, an impression of deliberate decisiveness. Those who best manage such a transformation do so not self-consciously but as a responsive adaptation to unwritten codes and customs. However, the change should not take place too suddenly; the trick is to show all the sound sense of middle age without sacrificing one's boyish vitality.

The executive personality, let it be said, can probably be mastered more easily by the boy from Itasca than by the graduate of Groton. The corporate graces are, on the whole, those represented by the middle-class life of Detroit or Chicago. In contrast to his European counterparts, the American executive does not have to know wines and is actually a step ahead if he prefers his steak without *sauce Béarnaise*. In this, our top men undoubtedly have more in common with Soviet managers than they do with those of France or Britain.

One of the specific lessons to be learned is to be moderate and open-minded in one's politics and to avoid ideological dogmatism of any sort. The potential president will register as a Republican but will refrain from taking positions that are too off-base or far-out. The man who comes out foursquare for Barry Goldwater will probably find himself spending the rest of his career in the Denver office. In fact, it is best to opt out of politics altogether.

A social scientist who has done a good deal of consulting for executive-development programs, often living with these young men for a week or more, has remarked: "It's not that they're afraid to have opinions on touchy subjects like Vietnam or civil rights. They simply don't have any views at all and they don't want to have any. One reason for this may be that they know that politics change and they don't want to be caught out having been on the wrong side."

But what is needed most in these years is ambition, drive and a willingness to make company business the center of your life. The real difficulty is that this test comes at just the wrong time. Your children are in high school and faced with all the problems of adolescence; your wife is beginning to feel the passing of the years and starts to wonder just where she stands in your diffused affections. This is just the period when the attaché-caseful of work must be brought home every night—except those nights you are off traveling to a trade association meeting in San Francisco, to a Congressional hearing in Washington, to merger negotiations in Chicago or simply to see what has gone wrong at the subassembly plant in Shreveport.

No one can assert with complete confidence that the 14-hour day is absolutely necessary for high-quality executive performance. Walter Bagehot once observed that businessmen work much too hard for their own good; the result is that they make a lot of money in the morning and then, instead of stopping when they're ahead, proceed to lose half of it in the afternoon. However, if the sheep are to be separated from the goats, certain rituals must be enforced and observed. In the academic world it is the writing of a Ph.D. thesis that no one will ever read; with psychoanalysts it is four years of medical schooling. For the rising executive it is being on company time all the time. One corporation chairman calls frequent Sunday morning meetings just to see which of his vice presidents grumble over intrusions into what more mortal men might consider to be the private hours of life.

Quite obviously, not everyone is willing to consent to such a regimen, and not a few who had once set their sights on the top suite now get off the A-train. One such deserter was Tom Rath, the man in Sloan Wilson's gray flannel suit, who had reached the $20,000 level and was on deck for better things. But as he pondered over the state of his stomach and the perils of absentee-husbandhood he decided to climb no further. The reaction of his boss sums up the view from the top: "Somebody has to do the big jobs. This world was built by men like me. To really do a job, you have to live it body and soul. You people who just give half your mind to your work are riding on our backs!" It is here, indeed, that there is a parting of the ways between the organization men and the company men.

During this period, also, a presidential contender will have to become something of a philosopher. The theoretical underpinnings of American business have actually not changed much since the days of Adam Smith, although there is a curious materialist overlay that has a lot in common with a brand of thinking that had better not be mentioned here. Thus, the need to affirm that the economy is the central institution of the society, that business profit is the prime mover in the nation's life.

"Our economy, our standard of living, our society result from the success of business in making profits," said the president of the Aluminum Corporation of America in a recent full-page advertisement. "Wages, payments for goods and services, taxes and contributions—all stemming from profits—are what makes the world go 'round."

Other, more spiritual, philosophers have been pondering for centuries just what it is that turns our globe on its axis. The on-the-rise executive will display no such perplexity.

He will, moreover, come to believe that whatever it is his company produces is absolutely necessary for the well-being of the American citizen-consumer. He must take the view—and this attitude cannot be faked—that the six-sided frozen French-fried potato is an asset to the nation's dinner table; that automobile exhaust is not really responsible for air pollution; that his firm is doing all it can to give jobs to Negroes and school drop-outs. For only if such sentiments are uttered with a ring of inner conviction will you be adjudged a true company man who can be relied upon in all crises and circumstances.

As a candidate approaches 45, and if no mishaps have occurred, he will be a $75,000 vice president and waiting for the final move upward. His competition will have been narrowed down to three or four brother vice presidents, all about his age and all aspiring to the executive vice presidency that is the grooming position for the top job in the company. The problem is that everyone in the final heat has pretty much the same qualities and abilities: energy and ambition, the right look and outlook, judgment and decisiveness and dedication.

At this point the incumbent president and chairman will make the decision—sometimes easy, sometimes agonizing—as to who will be their heir apparent. And it is not possible for an outsider to generalize about how they go about making up their minds. There are occasions when the choice has actually been settled on many years in advance. Thus, an observer at Standard Oil of California said of Otto Miller, the recently elected chairman: "You could see 20 years ago that the right hand of God was on Otto's shoulder." But such predestination is rare in the career service of corporate America.

Just what constitutes "executive ability," especially at the higher reaches, is a difficult question to answer. Companies themselves have expensive management "development" programs, and not a few corporations send the more promising of their men to special courses at such places as Harvard and M.I.T., where it is hoped that some insights on business leadership will be obtained. Indeed, the whole puzzle of what-makes-an-effective-executive has become a minor industry in itself, producing endless shelves of self-help books and hint-filled articles in business magazines. (One such piece even went so far as to portray the successful "executive face." The chin was very important.)

All this scurrying after definitions and definitiveness suggests that you know executive ability when you see it but that it is not something you can describe without a specific example to point to.

What *can* be said is that the ascent of a corporation vice president is frequently aided by a specific "record" he has acquired, most usually by taking on a very tough assignment and doing well at it. For example, he may have raised the sales of one line of the company's products from a quite average showing to new and unexpected heights. He may have introduced a new set of procedures and made them work despite the forecasts of doom and disaster from more cautious quarters. In short, a man's ability is best known by his tangible accomplishments; he is tabbed as "the man who. . . ." Gordon Metcalf's promotion to the top job at Sears Roebuck was in large measure due to his identification with the fabulously successful Midwest division of the company.

Another—less predictable—consideration has to do with the

fact that every executive tends to be earmarked as having some "strength" in a particular field. Thus, a man's fate can be shaped by whether the special area of interest he developed many years ago turns out to be a critical one for the corporation at the time when the penultimate promotions are made.

A director who serves on several boards put it this way: "Immediately after World War II, the need was to get civilian production rolling again as fast and as efficiently as possible. So, the big emphasis was on production and the men from the manufacturing end were put in the top slot. After a few years it became a buyers' market, so the stress was on sales and you found a lot of salesmen heading companies." This principle was well illustrated at General Motors, where Charles E. Wilson ("Engine Charlie") was succeeded by Harlow Curtice ("Sales-Curve Curtice").

Interestingly, the men picked as presidents in the last few years have come up largely on the financial side of the business. The current presidents at Chrysler, General Telephone and Electronics, Caterpillar Tractor, Consolidated Edison and International Business Machines all held the position of company controller at an earlier stage in their careers. Their elevation may be symbolic of the current importance of budgetary controls, internal economies, interest rates and minimizing the tax bites.

There appears, then, to be a semi-deterministic Law of Strategic Talents, accelerating the rise of individuals who have skills that unexpectedly take on central significance. Nevertheless, it would be a mistake to counsel an ambitious young man, now entering college, on how to equip himself for the semifinals of 1995. Any advice that he prepare himself for computerized investment programming or psychoanalytic labor relations could well be an act of misguidance. For just when he is ready for the final round the company may discover that consumer resistance has returned and the top job will be given to an old-fashioned sales type who has the unscientific knack of making people want to take out their checkbooks. There are, as the sages keep telling us, some things that just can't be planned. Had Robert McNamara been born 10 years earlier he would probably still be processing payroll vouchers at Ford instead of having been whizzed up to its presidency.

The final step to the top takes place in a man's early or middle 50's, and he can expect to serve as the company's president for four to five years and then another three or four as its chairman. (In most companies the chairman is now the No. 1 man, with the president as his heir presumptive. But there are still some firms which follow the older pattern of the president as chief executive officer while the chairmanship is a semihonorary post for an ex-president. In a few corporations the two jobs are separate and each has its own line of succession.)

During his tenure his annual salary will be between $200,000 and $300,000, with stock options that permit building up a personal fortune of a few million dollars. He will visit the White House, attend meetings of the prestigious Business Council at Hot Springs and receive a handful of honorary degrees. While his picture will not be in every office, his name will be treated with great respect in the corporate corridors. (This is in marked contrast to at least one other corner of American life. Walk onto any campus and ask any random group of professors what they think of their university's president. The ensuing comments, readily made even to visitors, would be considered high treason in a corporation.)

It is also worth noting, if only in passing, that most corporation executives do not become *multi*millionaires. When Charles E. Wilson stepped down after many years in the higher echelons of General Motors, he had amassed only $3.5-million. Robert McNamara left the Ford presidency for the Pentagon with only $1-million. And lesser executives, and those in smaller companies, retire with even smaller estates.

This is not to shed a tear for today's impecunious tycoons but simply to point out that the progeny of our executive élite will not be a new leisure class. A recent Wall Street Journal study of presidential sons showed that virtually all of these young men were hard at work, with most of them in business (but only a fraction in their fathers' firms).

The vice president who loses out may well be given as consolation prize an executive vice presidency, and in all likelihood he will remain in that position until his retirement. He may scout around for the presidency of a smaller company, but the chances are increasingly against this.

Yet, there are not a few large corporations where the No. 2 spot is as far as any career man can go. In a significant number of corporations family succession still operates. There is a Ford still in charge at Ford, a Douglas at Douglas, a Grace at Grace and a Zellerbach at Crown Zellerbach. This is surprising because the stock ownership in these firms is now widely diffused and the founding families no longer have a majority vote. Nevertheless, a tendency persists to reserve the top position for a scion of the original founder.

In recent years, Lammot du Pont Copeland, Samuel Johnson and Robert Sarnoff were all elevated to the No. 1 jobs at the Wilmington, Racine and Radio City enterprises which have long been their families' preserves. Another noteworthy case is Armco Steel, which was presided over by its founder, George Verity, for 30 years and which, on his retirement, came under the management of salaried executives. However, just a few months ago the company chose George's grandson, Calvin, as its new president, even though the Verity clan owns only one-tenth of 1 per cent of Armco's stock.

The only explanation is that some American corporations, like some American voters, are attracted by the monarchical principle: tradition, continuity and memories of past glories. The consequence is that red-blooded executives must content themselves with second-rung jobs, and not a few make a judicious move to another company when they hear that Junior is homeward bound from the Harvard Business School. The prospect for the career man is becoming brighter, though, in some firms where royalty once reigned. At I.B.M. it seems that the Watson succession is coming to an end, and there is every indication that the next chief at Ford will not be a Ford.

The typical corporation president will have had almost 30 years of service with the company prior to his final elevation, and the great majority of firms seems content with the promotion-from-within principle. Accusations of in-breeding, conformity and complacency do not seem to bother them, for most large businesses can point to a record of expanding sales and earnings over the past decades. "Something has to be terribly wrong if you have to go outside," one bank director explained. "A company will have at least a half-dozen decent men in the top ranks and to admit that there isn't a single able candidate among them is a pretty sad commentary on the whole outfit."

Even if there is the feeling that a company's management has grown soft, the preferred recipe for shaking it up is to promote a vigorous younger executive over the heads of senior men who have been waiting in line. "Bringing in an outsider is bad for morale," another director indicated. "He will arouse resentments and suspicions, and good people who are coming along further down the line may get the idea that their own prospects for advancement are limited." In fact, if an outsider is chosen as president he will probably insist on bringing in his own circle of executives with him, if only to insure that the new broom he sets in motion will not bump into sloth or sabotage from aggrieved old-timers.

There are rare occasions when a giant firm will run into financial trouble and undergo the humiliating experience of having a new chief executive forced on it, in the expectation that a transfusion of new blood and ideas will set things to rights. A recent example of such a beleaguered leviathan was Trans World Airlines which, owing to the erratic superintendency of Howard Hughes, was virtually taken into custody by a consortium consisting of two insurance companies and 15 banks. Their terms for renewing a series of loans was T.W.A.'s acceptance of a new president, Charles Tillinghast from the Bendix Corporation. The moral of this story has not been lost on other companies, and it helps to explain the general preference for remaining financially independent.

All things considered, the American corporation has become a self-selecting, self-contained civil service. The men at the top of corporate America undergo far less criticism than the average Senator or Governor, in part because they don't have to face popular elections and in part because the ideology of private property insulates them from public scrutiny.

It may well be that the time has come to alter outdated assumptions about the presumed "private" character of our major corporations. By any reasonable measure Haakon Romnes' A.T.&T. is as important an institution in American society as the state of Alabama, and the presiding officer of that company clearly deserves as much attention as Mrs. Lurleen Wallace. The difficulty, when all is said and done, is that corporation executives are not

very interesting people. And not the least reason for their bland-
ness is the sort of individuals they have to become in order to get
where they do.

The more one watches the men being chosen for the top jobs,
the more one is impressed with a certain air of reserve, indeed
caution, they possess about themselves and the world in which
they travel. However, it would be wrong to call them conservatives, for once again the conventional language of ideology does
not apply here. Many of the decisions they make, whether so in-
tended or not, have revolutionary consequences for all of society.
The technological and marketing transformations they have ef-
fected have served to give a new shape to postwar America, and
the plans they are making for the nineteen-seventies may alter the
face of the nation beyond recognition.

If an appreciable proportion of executives abandoned Goldwater, it was in the belief that he simply did not understand the
new world of corporate business. Even the ideology-bound National Association of Manufacturers is looked upon as out-of-date
and ill-equipped to serve as a spokesman. "They're just a bunch
of top-drawer guys in their ivory tower, stewing in their own juice
and issuing feudal and futile pronouncements," one executive
remarked recently.

Both Henry Ford 2d and David Rockefeller have come out for
establishing trade ties with Communist China; after all, there is
money to be made by having branch banks in Shanghai and clog-
ging the streets of Canton with Mustangs. To be sure, not all corporation chiefs are as secure as Ford and Rockefeller, but most
tend to share their view that the world is best regarded as a
marketplace rather than as a political arena.

Over a century ago, Alexis de Tocqueville observed that "a man
who raises himself by degrees of wealth and power, contracts, in
the course of this protracted labor, habits of prudence and restraint he cannot afterwards shake off. A man cannot gradually
enlarge his mind as he does his house."

This judgment on the bootstrap entrepreneurs of the Jack-
sonian age has not a little relevance to the career servants of our
own time. The men who preside over American corporations are
chiefly of unpretentious origins, and they have got ahead by passing the tests and following the rules in a race where there is room

at the finish line for only a few. At no time in these trials are they expected to display humane learning, any more than a philosophy professor is asked to show a profit for his department.

"We chief executives are just employes like the others these days," one of them said. And the job of an employe is to protect the interests of his employer, even if that employer is an abstract association of assets called a corporation. Most corporation presidents nowadays would not even belabor the theory that what is good for General Electric or General Dynamics is good for the country. Their job, for which they are paid, is to look out for the good of their company.

There are, of course, important exceptions. But it is interesting to note that displays of new and different qualities of personality usually appear after an executive has departed from the corporate precincts. That Robert McNamara and Charles E. Wilson were willing and able to become public figures deserves recognition, especially in light of the popular criticism that Secretaries of Defense have to undergo. Charles Percy and George Romney are two examples of executives who have left corporate havens for the political rough-and-tumble. However, the fact remains that apart from these four it is hard to think of many corporation presidents who have demonstrated abilities that proved applicable to other sectors of our national life.

This should not be construed as criticism. Most of these men have invested their energies and emotions in a particular line of endeavor. To expect that our corporations will somehow produce an aristocratic echelon is, in fact, to misunderstand important conditions that have accompanied recent changes in the structure of American life.

There is not much point, then, in musing about how nice it would be if our corporate managers underwent more instruction in moral philosophy or modern sociology. The simple fact is that they are busy men, on the way up during most of their formative years, and the exigencies of the climb compel them to think of themselves rather than for themselves. This is an inevitable consequence of opening careers to the talented, of breaking down the barriers that once prevented men of inauspicious backgrounds from rising to the top. These men are, more than anything else, products of an open and a democratic society.

Yet it may well be that these men are less important than the oversized machines at whose controls they temporarily sit. It may be that a Ronald Reagon's impress on the State of California will be greater than the imprint that a Gordon Metcalf can leave on a Sears, Roebuck. "Organization replaces individual authority and no individual is powerful enough to do much damage," John Kenneth Galbraith has written. "Were it otherwise, the stock market would pay close attention to retirements, deaths and replacements in the executive ranks of large corporations. In fact, it ignores such details in tacit recognition that the organization is independent of any individual." If this is so, then the personality is subordinate to the position and we should study the chair rather than the men who sit in it.

Obviously, there is something a bit terrifying about a self-running machine, especially one of great power and influence. Nevertheless, this condition is becoming increasingly evident throughout our entire society. Not only corporations but universities and medical centers, foundations and research institutes, government agencies and the military establishment are recruiting and shaping individuals to serve their needs and eventually fill their top positions. The making of a corporation president is more than a success story. Its greater significance is as part of the natural history of our times, wherein men perceive the personalities that are wanted of them and then pattern their lives to meet those specifications.

Business, Too, Has Its Ivory Towers

by Clarence B. Randall

IN THE OLD whaling days a man did not get to be master of the ship unless he was by all odds the best sailor aboard. When the going was rough, the crew expected to see him standing on deck in the storm, handling the ship himself. He knew every star in the heavens, and when the gale struck he did not need to ask from which direction the wind was blowing. He felt it directly in his face.

The counterpart of this is not true in American industry today, and this may be what is wrong with it. The men at the top of our great corporations, those who direct the vast enterprises that mean so much both to our economy and to our social welfare, so live their lives that they no longer take the wind directly in their faces.

Responsibility breeds isolation. As a man's authority increases, so do the barriers that cut him off from direct contact with the world about him. This may not be his nature, nor his wish, but the manner of life he feels compelled to follow causes him steadily to withdraw into the shelter of his own intimate circle. After he reaches the very top, he is seldom seen in public, and seldom heard. He becomes a myth. An aura of mystery surrounds him

From the *New York Times Magazine,* July 8, 1962, copyright © 1962 by The New York Times Company.

which is unwholesome both for the man and for his company. The consequence is that when the great storm comes, as it does sooner or later to every large corporation, and he is driven out into the turbulence of public opinion, he may not be ready to go on deck. He may still be the best sailor on the ship, but something vital, something essential to leadership, has gone out of his life.

Why is this so?

First of all, it stems in part from the changes in his daily routine which necessity seems to force upon him. Take, for example, the simple matter of transportation to and from his office in a large city like New York or Chicago. As a youngster, he lived in a suburb, and rode the commuting trains. Every morning, as he waited on the station platform for the 8:04, he rubbed elbows with a motley group of friends and neighbors and scrambled with them for a seat when the train came in.

For the most part, they had no idea what his job was, and cared less. They pulled no punches when they talked to him. He and his chance companion of the day read their papers together and argued about the headlines. Public opinion flowed around him.

Later on, as he rose in the business hierarchy, when occasionally his name was mentioned on the business page, the commuters took notice. If he had made a speech, and was quoted, there was an immediate reaction next morning. As he walked down the aisle in the train he was greeted with a genial mixture of cheers and boos. Every word he had spoken was scrubbed in his presence and he learned at first hand just what people thought of him.

This built up until it brought his first restrictive change. On the rear end of his daily train there was a special car, chartered by the year for the exclusive use of a snug little well-heeled group. With a gracious gesture of condescension they finally invited him to join the club because of his surging prominence. He was complimented, sensed that here were men who might be helpful to him, and accepted. Thus, overnight, he cut to a mere handful the number of individuals with whom he exchanged views each day, and sharply reduced his personal exposure to divergent opinions. The scrubbing was nearly over.

When he became chief officer of his corporation, even this had to go—not because he wanted it to, but because he sincerely believed that circumstances compelled it. He lost control over his engagements. His schedule became so complex and the end of his day so unpredictable that a limousine and chauffeur became indispensable. His associates urged it upon him to conserve his time and effort and, somewhat against his better judgment, he acquiesced. Thereafter, he made those morning and evening trips alone on the back seat. He talked with no one but the chauffeur, and gone forever was the boisterous elbow-rubbing with friends who might hold contrary opinions.

In due course, this was followed by the purchase of an executive plane. Once more his associates, acting with the most earnest good faith, convinced him that his time and effort were too valuable to the corporation to be wasted by the delays of commercial transportation. But the result intensified his withdrawal.

Now, wherever he traveled, he spent the entire period closeted with his staff and, upon arrival, plunged with them into a waiting limousine. Gone were the chance encounters. No more taunts from the taxi driver about how bad things were, no more chatter with the man ahead of him in line at the gate, no more locked-in sessions with a seat mate on the plane who forced him to listen whether he wanted to or not. He was never to be anonymous again. Never really one of the people. Just always the big shot, whether he wanted to be or not.

And with this there were other changes. As a young man he had been proud to play a vigorous part in everything that went on in his suburban community. While his children were in grade school, he was active in the parent-teacher association, and later he served a term or two on the park board. People liked him for what he was, not who he was.

Conscious of an obligation to the city, he carried his part of the load there as well. When the Red Cross campaign came along he served as chairman for his industry, and he never missed a luncheon of his college alumni. Gregarious by nature, he thrived on the give-and-take of everyday debate. But when he became chairman of the board all this had to stop. The curtain came down. He seldom saw anyone except those who showed him deference, and almost never those who talked back.

Trivial as it sounds, the change in his luncheon habits was significant, too. As a cub, he used to dash across the street to the nearest restaurant for a quick bite at noon, and sit down with the first acquaintance whose eye he caught. The talk was lively for the next forty-five minutes. Later, when he advanced to where he could join his first club, he still mixed with the crowd. He made straight for the long "members" table in the middle of the dining room, and differed violently at times with the fellow across from him. But when he became chairman, he gave all this up.

Had you asked him why, he probably would have confessed that his name had become so well-known that he felt conspicuous in such surroundings. Besides, every moment had to count. He could get more done by lunching quietly in his own private dining room with his banker or his lawyer or, at the most, with five or six associates. If he did leave the office at noon, he joined a small group of close friends in a private dining room at a very exclusive club—a club within a club.

About the same time, his recreations became marked by the same withdrawal. When he was first married, Saturday had been a big day. Early in the morning he hustled out of the house with his golf bag, dashed over to the public links and drew a number. He did not care with whom he played, so long as he played.

Not so as chairman. His golf dates now are rare, are always arranged in advance by his secretary, and the foursome is invariably selected from not over six possibilities. If duck shooting is his sport, he will be found at a small private club where no uncouth voice is heard; if it is fishing, the lodge will be remote, and the waters privately stocked and patrolled; if it is yachting, only a very few carefully chosen guests will ever see his boat.

None of this has come about because high office has made him snobbish, or prestige-conscious. It stems naturally from the responsibility he bears, and the honest desire of those about him to protect him. Nevertheless, it is wrong.

As chief officer, he does almost nothing on his own. All day, every day, he is looked after by a highly competent staff. The routines of life that would compel him to be in touch with other people are lifted from him, thus accentuating his inwardness. Sometimes he even has a private elevator. Only the seniors in his organization get through to him. Lacking time to read the newspapers thoroughly, he comes to rely upon digests prepared for him by his public-relations staff and unconsciously he is likely to absorb their opinions, too.

In the meetings of his board of directors, it is difficult for him to develop genuine independent thinking from the members, no matter how hard he tries. Many of those present are company officers and it is doubtful that they will deliberately antagonize him. Others are what might be called professional directors. They are on many boards, and their opinions tend to become orthodox. Were he to propose a real outsider for board membership such as a university president, who could be counted upon to scrutinize sharply the social implications of corporate decisions, there would be a general lifting of eyebrows.

Such studied withdrawal from public view on the part of men bearing great responsibility needs most urgently to be re-examined. Though it may be effective for taut internal administration, it is breeding danger for all concerned—the man, the company and the American people.

There is obvious and direct prejudice to the corporation itself, for, as has been pointed out, in times of crisis such an officer is not ready to face sudden storms of public opinion. But that is not the basic problem; the real loss is to the country.

Here are men of unusual ability. They have reached their high position through the most rigorous competitive tests and possess proven qualities of leadership. Yet their talents are devoted almost exclusively to the advancement of self-interest, as distinguished from participation in solving the broad questions that currently challenge the United States. For the most part, such men are not sharing in our country's great decisions. Though superbly equipped for public leadership, they shun it, and the American people are compelled to turn to lesser men.

It is not their physical withdrawal, as such, that is significant, but that of which it is the symbol—namely, their intellectual divorcement from the tumult of outside thought. Preoccupied with the complex affairs of their own corporations, they cut themselves off from the sources of facts and ideas by which mass judgments are formed in our country. Their thinking on the great questions is borrowed and the opinions they hold are seldom tested by controversy.

The corrective which such men need is the sort of grilling a Congressman must take when he has to stand up in succession before each unit in his constituency and justify his every vote and conviction. Questions from the floor never come to the chairman of the board, save at the annual meeting, and then only on company business. The best thing that can happen, both for him and for the country, is a revolutionary readjustment in his life that will give him the wind in his face.

Happily, many of our industrial leaders, though themselves the victims of this withdrawal, are nevertheless deeply concerned at its implications and are earnestly seeking ways to reverse the trend. What, they ask, may be done about it?

The suggestions I have to offer stem from my own experience, but let me say frankly, before my friends do, that they are the creatures of my retirement. I behaved the other way myself when I was active in business.

First of all, the chief officer should make himself more readily available to the press. Not just the grand interview at the time of the annual meeting, but continuously. The myth is created by reporters, and only they can end it. In order that they may know him better, let him encourage them to drop in on short notice if they would like some special background briefing on a story that has been assigned to them. Let him dare to see them alone with no one else present.

Let him cultivate the editorial writers, too, and be willing to sit down with them at their own desks for a friendly give and take. Let him call up a columnist to talk about a paragraph that impressed him, and ask whether he would like to come around for lunch to pursue it further. All of this will be time-consuming, but it will make him think of something other than fourth-quarter earnings, and will open up to him a direct opportunity for putting his first-class mind to work on the problems of the nation.

Let him behave this way also toward the important figures in public life. Assuming, for example, that he holds strong views on the necessity for revision of depreciation allowances, the thing for him to do is to telephone the Secretary of the Treasury personally and ask if he may come down and see him. He will get in when a lobbyist would not. Or if he has convictions with respect to world trade, he should go and see his Senator. Let him leave his public-relations man at home, ignore his trade association's Washington man, and do the job strictly on his own. The Senator will have some tough decisions to make on the subject, and he will genuinely value an opportunity to get directly the views of a man of such broad experience. He is tired of lobbyists, and is flattered to talk with the man who makes the decisions. Mystery always fades before directness, and when the day comes that such a chairman is called before a Congressional committee, word will spread in advance that he is a regular fellow.

And let him seek out the colleges and universities. It is almost unheard-of for a chairman of the board to appear on campus, and when that incredible event does occur, immediate and favorable repercussions follow. The offhand talk given in chapel to the entire student body, done breezily, using any subject of the moment, spreads at once to every part of the country. Each student present will write home about him that night because of who he is. He needs no manuscript, for this can be done off the record.

Then, later that afternoon, when he goes over to the business school and sits down for a frank talk with the faculty and a group of students, he will have a rich experience that will teach him much about himself. Their questions will be searching, but honest —the sort his staff will never ask. He will leave with some of his favorite biases reduced by abrasion, but with some of his convictions strengthened for the reason that he has been compelled to make them acceptable to fine minds.

There are other antibiotics for this disease of isolation, and each chief officer must develop those best suited to his own situation, but the problem can no longer be ignored without serious prejudice to the future of industry in this country. The American people are impatient with us, and ready to become distrustful. *Noblesse oblige.* Those at the top must really lead, in public as well as in private, and not delegate to others the preservation of the corporate image. They must throw wide the curtains of their withdrawal and face the hot glare of publicity, no matter how unpleasant or unfair that may be. They must stand up in the marketplace and be counted—face to face with their critics.

Merger Expendables: Men

by Isadore Barmash

ERNEST HENDERSON 3D, the 44-year-old son of the late chairman of the Sheraton Corporation of America, is busily involved these days in setting up a string of convalescent care centers.

In January, less than a year after Sheraton was acquired by the International Telephone and Telegraph Corporation, Mr. Henderson resigned as Sheraton's president to devote himself to the new project.

Gene C. Brewer resigned for "personal reasons" last week as president of U.S. Plywood–Champion Papers, Inc., two years after the merger of the two companies. According to strong reports, the problem in this otherwise successful merger lay in the fact that it involved two concerns of equal size, leading to a smouldering dissension among the executives of the companies that had married.

J. Edgar Bennett is spending the next few weeks with his family in the resplendent sun of St. Croix in the Virgin Islands.

On March 3 Mr. Bennett announced his resignation as president of the Lorillard Corporation, about four months after the 208-year-old tobacco company had been bought by Loew's Theaters, Inc. Before taking off for the Caribbean, Mr. Bennett said his leaving stemmed from "a conflict of management philosophy."

These are three of the more recent examples of what has been called the "people crunch" effect of conglomerate and inter-industry mergers.

But the thrust of a merger on the top management of an acquired company is not always up or out. Or sideways, for that matter.

Louis Epstein, former president of the Colonial Corporation, an apparel complex acquired two years ago by the Kayser-Roth Corporation, is today president of Meller, Inc., a New York stock brokerage concern, and "doing better than ever."

Louis Putze, formerly the president of the Controls Company of America, moved up with each of two successive acquisitions of that company—first by the General Precision Equipment Company and then by the Singer Company.

Today Mr. Putze, as a deputy group vice president of Singer, is instrumental in the administration of several different divisions with estimated annual sales of $600-million, compared with merely running a $60-million concern such as Controls Company.

The great flap that has developed in recent weeks over the merger trend has raised pointed questions about their effects.

Richard W. McLaren, the new United States Assistant Attorney General in charge of the Justice Department's anti-trust division, was quoted on two occasions as having expressed concern about mergers' effects on people. Speaking in New York, he said that the "current tax-propelled merger mania" had produced "severe human and economic dislocations."

The actual effects on people, at least on top executives and some middle-management executives, are unexpected, based on the experiences of many who have been involved in business mergers and of professional merger specialists. For example:

¶There are few displacements of top executives in a conglomerate merger, mainly because management of the acquired concern has a skill and knowledge that the conglomerate owners do not have and must retain.

¶Conversely, often top executives are removed or reassigned in mergers that take place between two companies in the same industry. The reasons are policy conflicts after long experience in the same field and duplication of executive functions.

¶Not so many top executives are eased out in acquisitions of smaller or medium-sized companies, principally because such men in companies with sales up to $25-million a year are usually given employment contracts and the purchase price is contingent on their performance over the next three to five years. But there are not nearly so many contingency deals in take-overs of companies with sales of $30-million and higher.

¶Middle management often finds itself in a "delicate" position when its company is acquired. The psychological difficulty is simply that many of these people—regional sales managers, plant managers, divisional advertising directors and divisional or group controllers—have been attempting to earn promotions. But now their situations seem to have become frozen. "What should I do about any sudden loss of identity?" such persons are prone to ask themselves.

¶The biggest human difficulties come when a company with problems agrees in desperation to a merger or a take-over. The displacements of many executives in such concerns as the Curtis Publishing Company and Allis-Chalmers are good examples of what follows from the "new broom" effect of the new management.

One of the greatest professional and human hurdles facing a chief corporate executive frequently occurs when, after he has reached the age of, say, 55, his company is acquired by another. Is he flexible enough to continue under the new and different policies of the new owners? Is he sufficiently motivated after having ostensibly reached a comfortable economic state? Why should he remain, anyway?

William G. Hamilton, Jr., now a group vice president in charge of the metering and controls group of the Singer Company and president of its American Meter Company, made that decision. He decided he wanted to remain with Singer after having served as chairman of the General Precision Equipment Corporation, which was merged into Singer in 1968.

In an interview late last week, Mr. Hamilton said that a prime motivation for his decision was the fact that "they [Singer] felt that they needed our management and showed it by using our 'family' in making decisions." He added: "I have gone more than halfway to conform to working in a giant company—it's a state of mind. Did I have the flexibility to do so at the age of 60? Yes, I told myself, I did. And I'm really very happy now."

But some conglomerate chiefs seem to enjoy "shaking up" the acquired company just for the "sake of shaking them up," according to Howard Suslak, president of MacDonald & Co., New York financial and merger consultants.

"Is the chief of the acquiring company making personnel changes for the sake of change—or for good and valid reasons?" Mr. Suslak asked. "What is buying goodwill, if not also buying that management which has built the goodwill? And what's the point of buying a company and doing that? It would make more sense to start a company from scratch."

Mr. Epstein, former president of the Colonial Corporation, found that his duties were changed after it was acquired by Kayser-Roth. Mr. Epstein, a certified public accountant who had come to be instrumental in mergers and acquisitions as head of Colonial, found that there was no demand for him in that capacity at Kayser-Roth, which already had its own experts.

"So," he said, "in April, 1967, less than 18 months after the merger, I resigned from active association, although I'm still an adviser to Kayser-Roth, and bought a partnership in Meller, Inc., the brokerage house." Since then, Mr. Epstein said, he has been involved in arranging four mergers for other companies. At 53, he observed with a smile, "I have a new, exciting and interesting career."

If the "people crunch" of corporate take-overs seems inhuman at times, how much this trend will continue will depend greatly on the result of the big furor in Congress and in the Federal agencies over the corporate merger trend, according to Louis Perlmutter, executive vice president of Octagon Industries, corporate development specialists. In his view, the merger trend has slowed recently because of this Government scrutiny, as well as because of tight money and the erratic pattern of the stock market.

This, however, did not occur before perhaps the biggest merger in modern history, that of the Pennsylvania Railroad and the New York Central Railroad, with some interesting examples of the "people crunch."

Railroads have been the slowest major industry to participate in the merger trend, perhaps because of the reality of "Willard's Law." This alludes to a remark by Daniel Willard, former president of the Baltimore & Ohio Railroad. In the nineteen-thirties he commented, in effect, "The reason that there haven't been any railroad mergers is that no railroad president wants to merger himself out of a job."

What about the recently merged Penn Central Company?

In an interview less than two weeks ago, Stuart T. Saunders, Penn Central's chairman, said that David E. Smucker, executive vice president in charge of operations, has been appointed "to my staff to handle special studies of work for me." Robert G. Flannery, who "we are told by even our competitors is one of the best operating men in the industry," was named vice president of operations.

Replying to further reports from Wall Street of some "people problems" emanating from the railroad merger, specifically that the former New York Central's "forward" marketing department has become an "empty shell," Mr. Saunders said: "We had over 500 people in our marketing department when the two systems were merged—far more people than we needed. We've got over 300 now. And we still have too many."

How are Mr. Saunders, the former chairman of the Pennsylvania, and Alfred E. Perlman, who headed the New York Central and is now the Penn Central's president, getting along? Their relations are fine, but there are reports of some grit in the meshing process of their staff. After all, the Penn Central merger is a consolidation of two companies long in the same field. And that, as has been said, holds danger signals for the people involved.

Part 3

OWNERSHIP AND CONTROL OF THE MODERN CORPORATION

IN A SMALL business, the entrepreneurial function is often centered in one person who acts as both manager and owner of the firm. This person makes all the managerial decisions and receives all gains or losses associated with risk and uncertainty after expenses are met. In the giant corporation, the function is not so readily identified. A professional management, on the one hand, has a clear operational responsibility, while a changing mix of shareholders, on the other, maintains at least a minimal claim to ownership.

The Modern Corporation and Private Property, by Adolf A. Berle and Gardiner C. Means, has become the classic statement of the divorce of ownership and control in the large corporation. According to Berle and Means, economic power is concentrated in the management of the large corporation while ownership is diffused among numerous stockholders. There has always been considerable doubt about the effectiveness of shareholder control in the giant corporation. In fact, Thorstein Veblen referred to the shareholder as the "absentee pensioner" of the modern corporation. But Berle and Means's effort was a significant advance because it subjected a long history of decisions and a great deal of data to careful, meticulous scrutiny. Thirty-nine years after its publication, the book remains the foundation for all discussion in this area.

It is appropriate, therefore, that this section should begin with a careful and detailed review by Robert Lekachman of the revised edition of Berle and Means's work. Of particular interest is Lekachman's observation that the split between ownership and control focuses attention on the logic of private-profit maximization, the appropriate role for government *vis à vis* the giant corporation, the social responsibilities of management, and the almost sovereign economic power of the corporation.

In the second paper in this section, Michael D. Reagan looks closely at the American shareholder and what he owns. Reagan calls attention to the concentration of ownership and the special problems raised by executive stock-option programs.

The third article focuses attention on a unique annual occurrence in the United States—the annual shareholders' meeting. Many will be surprised to learn the amount of planning and attention that is given to such meetings. Indeed, the American shareholder is presented with a great deal of information about the company in which he has invested, as well as an opportunity to express his views. While it is possible to have reservations about shareholder control in the absolute sense, one need only look to the European experience to rank the American shareholder in a relatively more advantageous position.

Finally, the last paper in this section by David Dworsky addresses itself to a new voice raised at the annual shareholder meetings. Social protest appears to have found a new vehicle for attracting attention to itself. Whether this will be a particularly fruitful channel for social dissent remains doubtful.

The Corporation Gap

by Robert Lekachman

THE MODERN CORPORATION AND PRIVATE PROPERTY. By Adolf A. Berle and Gardiner C. Means. Revised Edition. 380 pp. New York: Harcourt, Brace & World. $9.75.

Two tests of a book's classic status in the social sciences are easily passed by "The Modern Corporation and Private Property": its major conclusions have been so generally accepted that their source has been mislaid, and though everybody has heard the title almost no one has recently read the book. In this reissue, separate prefaces by the two authors and a new statistical appendix by Mr. Means have been attached to the unchanged original text. The 36 years since original publication have certainly not diminished the social significance of the large corporation, any more than time has weakened the power of Berle's and Means's analysis of its operations. But the book's major influence has perhaps been in a direction unforeseen by its authors and its earliest readers.

The two authors came to three main conclusions about the American corporation: First, economic power was becoming increasingly concentrated as larger and larger percentages of business wealth fell into fewer and fewer corporate hands. Second, the ownership of these huge corporations was increasingly dispersed among a swelling army of stockholders. Third, the separation of ownership and control had gone very far and was likely to proceed still farther.

Berle, a Columbia Law School professor soon to be a member of Roosevelt's Brain Trust and then of his administration, and Means, a Harvard-trained economist, based their judgments upon an elegantly analyzed body of statistical information revealing the size and ownership characteristics of corporations, and an equally impressive interpretation of the case law applicable to modern business. Little by little, Berle demonstrated, the courts had nibbled at the powers of stockholders over corporations which legal myth if not legal fact entitled them to run in stockholder interests. The judges had simultaneously expanded the discretion of managers who owned little or no stock in the huge institutions over which they exercised something approaching plenary power.

On the whole these empirical findings have stood up well over the years, although economists still amuse themselves by debating whether corporate concentration has or has not increased. The authors were boldest when they came to evaluate the significance of their conclusions. The transformed corporation, by its very success, they declared, had "cleared the way for the claims of a group far wider than either the owners or the control. They have placed the community in a position to demand that the modern corporation serve not alone the owners or the control but all society." The issue was one of legitimacy.

Yet, even though Berle and Means were convinced that "the rise of the modern corporation has brought a concentration of economic power which can compete on equal terms with the modern state—economic power versus political power, each strong in its own field," they did not proceed to a program of nationalization or even extensive public control in the manner of liberal commentators like Stuart Chase, who hailed the book in The New Republic and Ernest Gruening (now the senior Senator from Alaska), who praised it in The Nation.

The authors' own somewhat vague and general preferences were for a voluntary reinterpretation of corporate goals by the corporate managers themselves. Their key statement contained an implicit appeal to executive statesmanship:

"When a convincing system of community obligations is worked out and is generally accepted, in that moment the passive property right of today must yield before the larger interests of society. Should the corporate leaders, for example, set forth a program comprising fair wages, security to employees, reasonable service to their public, and stabilization of businesses, all of which would divert a portion of their profits from the owners of passive property, and should the community generally accept such a scheme as a logical and human solution of industrial difficulties, the interests of passive property owners would have to give way. Courts would almost of necessity be forced to recognize the result. . . ."

How faithfully has business followed this prospectus? What impact have Berle and Means had upon academic economics? Although John Kenneth Galbraith has said of "The Modern Corporation and Private Property" that "with Keynes' 'General Theory of Employment, Interest and Money,' [it is] one of the two most important books of the 1930's," Berle and Means did not, as Keynes did, revolutionize economic theory—at least as the theorists practice its mysteries.

Although Berle and Means believed that the logic of profit maximization has been fundamentally altered by the tendencies they documented, most economists continue to believe that managers maximize profits very much as owners do. Corporate officials may aim directly at growth rather than profit and they may even appear to perform the political role of harmonizing the interest groups— labor unions, suppliers, stockholders, customers and the anti-trust division of the Department of Justice—that affect the corporation's environment. But the managers' conduct is or at least can be made to seem consistent with the pursuit of all the profits that can be squeezed out of the market.

For economists, Professor Ben Lewis's 1935 review in the Journal of Political Economy probably stated the case best. It was his judgment that the study "will be productive of more pronounced and sustained results in the field of law and public policy than in the realm of economic theory." One such substantial result was the Securities Exchange legislation whose detailed provisions and regulations rested very heavily indeed upon the analysis of the stockholder's situation in Book Three of "The Modern Corporation and Private Property." Public regulation of the stock exchanges is a large monument to any book.

The comparative freedom from major scandal that the securities industry has enjoyed since the 1930's owes much to the vigilance of the Securities and Exchange Commission. In turn the continuing dispersion of stock ownership, the emergence of "People's Capitalism," and the refurbished reputations of investment bankers and brokers all flow from a new public confidence created by the cleansing of the Augean stables of finance. Berle and Means identified a trend toward stock dispersion. The reforms they stimulated undoubtedly accelerated that trend.

It is time to return to the harder questions Berle and Means posed and, in part, answered. Should corporations as gargantuan as General Motors be allowed to operate without explicit federal supervision? Is Berle's and Means's favorite proposal of corporate self-redefinition feasible? Has it indeed occurred? Should corporations "as the dominant institution of the modern world," be responsible for eliminating poverty, rescuing the cities, restoring the countryside and placing social welfare on a paying basis? Where is the public consensus that might guide corporate executives in the performance of their new duties?

The mere statement of such questions should remind us what a very short distance has been traveled toward explicit and acceptable redefinition of the corporation's legitimate role. Here is one illustrative puzzle: this summer the steel industry did its very best to raise prices by five per cent, in the wake of a moderately expensive settlement with the steelworkers. Presidential wrath, reinforced by threats to take defense contracts away from the offenders, led to a compromise increase of about half the industry's original change.

Query: by what legal right does a President intervene in the pricing decisions made by private corporations? In fact President Johnson did not have a legal leg to stand upon. Nevertheless, the episode is symbolic of a change in public and even business opinion that dates from President Kennedy's successful showdown five years ago with the leaders of the same industry. The men who run the steel industry have come grudgingly to accept the power, if not the right, of Federal government to oversee steel-pricing policy. What steel does substantially influences other prices and the balance of payments. Therefore steel, in common with other large concentrated industries, is seen to be affected with a public interest.

Or consider another of the role conflicts in which large enterprises get entangled. The major life-insurance companies have committed $1 billion to urban slum investment, at interest rates said to average 1 per cent below the market. One per cent of $1 billion is $10 million annually. A tax of $10 million has been assessed upon the owners of the life-insurance companies without their consent. What entitles the life insurance executives to take such action?

The still inchoate doctrine of social responsibility upon which Berle and Means rested so much hope is possibly surfacing here. It is obvious, however, how far from general acceptance this doctrine is. Businessmen find it so uncomfortable that they are often constrained to conceal their good deeds under the cloak of normal greed. A Henry Ford explains his company's serious and costly attempt to recruit hard-core blacks from the Detroit slums with the argument that such action is a protection against a recurrence of last summer's Detroit riots. Now while it is undeniable that the fortunes of Ford and Detroit are connected, it is hard to believe that Ford's action alone will really protect Detroit (and Ford) against the possibility of future riots.

A different sort of redefinition of corporate goals appears more significant, and in it profit retains its traditional primacy. Many alert business leaders seem to have identified social welfare with a new and promising market. Litton and Philco among others have managed job camps. U.S. Gypsum seeks to boom sales of its products by dramatic demonstrations of instant rehabilitation of dilapidated slum structures. Innkeepers enter the nursing home industry, bolstered by medicare benefits to the elderly. Alert plumbing-equipment concerns restyle themselves for the growing anti-pollution market. Businessmen have discovered a new set of public markets.

An important factor in encouraging business commitment to these new ways of making money is the drastic change in old, New Deal ideological animosity between government and business. A sophisticated grasp by each party of the potential benefits of partnerships between business and government made possible the love affair between the Johnson Administration and many of the most prestigious members of the business establishment. Of the varieties of such cooperation there is no end. Major defense contractors like McDonnell Douglas and General Dynamics are almost subdivisions of the Pentagon. Supersonic transport is being developed partly by public and partly by private research and development. One current and fashionable tendency is legislation encouraging business housing and plant investment in the slums by intricate combinations of tax incentives, credit guarantees and direct subsidies.

The traditional logic of profit maximization is not seriously jarred by slum-investment programs that guarantee returns to private corporations of 12 to 14 per cent. Profit maximization may be a tougher beast, and social responsibility a more distant prospect, than Berle and Means believed.

Berle and Means made a final major contribution in their classic study. Their analysis struck a blow, possibly decisive, at the school which has sought early and late to break up large corporations and restore a regime of atomistic competition. For even in describing desirable corporate reforms, Berle and Means were affirming the legitimacy of the large corporation as very nearly a sovereign economic power.

Modern critics of the large corporation usually take for granted its inevitability. Galbraith's imaginative analysis of the techno-structure that manages the corporations really centers upon increasing its enlightenment and enlarging the government's capacity to supervise it in the interest of objectives the corporations neglect. The anti-trust movement has come on sad days because most Americans and even many economists judge large corporations to be useful, important, efficient and occasionally even benevolent. For better or for worse, Berle and Means played a large role in the evolution of the corporation's good contemporary reputation.

Somewhat paradoxically, then, the largest influence these two critics of corporate practices have had is their contribution to the legitimacy of the giant corporation. Even political liberals are inclined to accept the giant corporation as an inevitable fact. The more cheerful among them do their best to see the corporation as potentially a powerful engine of social as well as economic progress. The liberals of the 1930's interpreted "The Modern Corporation and Private Property" as a radical tract. As matters have turned out, this book has done as much to promote a healthy capitalism as Keynes's "The General Theory of Employment, Interest and Money."

What 17 Million Shareholders Share

by Michael D. Reagan

THE YEAR 1963 may go down in the annals of Wall Street as the Year of the Stock Split. The Columbia Broadcasting System, Chrysler Corporation and Radio Corporation of America announced splits entitling a holder of one existing share to receive two or three shares instead. The biggest was a two-for-one split by the American Telephone and Telegraph Company. And, in the largest corporate financing effort on record, A. T. & T. offered stockholders the rights to purchase $1,225,000,000 of new stock. Recently these rights set off an unprecedented trading scramble.

A. T. & T., with 2.25 million shareholders holding 244 million shares, epitomizes "people's capitalism," a term popularized by the New York Stock Exchange in recent years to suggest widespread participation of the general public in the ownership of American industry and, implicitly, popular participation in the operation of big businesses. "People's capitalism" conveys an image of economic togetherness, the little fellows and the big, the stockholders and the presidents and directors of corporations. But is the image accurate?

From the *New York Times Magazine,* February 23, 1964, copyright © 1964 by The New York Times Company.

First, some 15 billion shares of publicly held corporations are now in circulation. According to a recent report by Jean Crockett and Irwin Friend, of the Wharton School of the University of Pennsylvania, the value of stocks held by individuals is approximately $400 billion; another $100 billion is owned by domestic corporations.

The striking fact about stock distribution, on which rests the claim of a "people's capitalism," is the substantial increase in the number of shareholders that has occurred since 1952. In that year, there were 6.5 million stockholders—somewhat less than the estimated total for 1929, before the crash. By 1962 the New York Stock Exchange reported 17 million owners.

Part of this increase is attributable to employe-participation plans, part to the increased popularity of investment companies, which permit a purchaser to spread his risks while buying only one issue. Nearly a quarter of a million holders have been attracted by the widely publicized Monthly Investment Plan—the application of installment buying to stock ownership. But most of the increase must be credited to greater affluence (more families with savings to invest) and, apparently, to a belief that the market can only go up.

On the basis of the New York Exchange's studies the average shareholder bears little resemblance to the bloated cigar-smoking capitalist of the old cartoons. He—or, more likely, she, since 51 per cent of shareholders are women—is 48 years of age, has finished high school, has had some college training and has a family income of $8,600.

The average stockholder lives in a middle-sized city. If his home is a metropolis, however, it is more likely to be San Francisco than New York or Chicago (26.6 per cent of San Francisco's residents hold stock, as against 14.4 per cent in New York, and 13.8 per cent in Chicago). As for states, Connecticut has the highest proportion of shareholders—18.1 per cent—while Alaska, Hawaii, Mississippi and South Carolina have no more than 3 per cent.

Stockholders are to be found in every occupational category, but the percentages vary decidedly. Thus while 36 per cent of the nation's professional men and 32 per cent of its proprietors and managers own stock, only 6 per cent of service workers, 3 per cent of laborers and 1.4 per cent of farmers are shareholders. In between are clerical and sales workers—nearly 25 per cent—and housewives—15 per cent. Considering these occupational categories from another angle, the housewives make up the largest group among the country's stockholders: with 5.4 million of them, they account for about 33 per cent of the total. They are about equaled by the professionals and managers together, with clerical and sales workers next in line.

The relationship of the small stockholder to the corporation whose shares he owns is generally minimal: he signs an annual proxy approving the management-selected slate of directors, looks for the dividend checks in the mail, and, if they stop coming, sells the stock.

As Prof. Bayless Manning of the Yale Law School has said, "It is the corporation as an institution which is permanent and the shareholders who are transitory." The average stockholder is not a proprietor, but an investor or speculator. When hundreds of thousands of individuals share the "ownership" of a company, what each of them owns is really the stock certificate—a claim to dividends or capital appreciation—rather than the corporation. The exceptions are the small number of individuals who may own a substantial percentage of the shares of a particular corporation, enough to demand a representative on the board of directors. The Mellon family's position in Gulf Oil, the McCormick family and International Harvester, and the Watson family and I.B.M. are examples.

Even among small holders, however, there are some who use their ownership rights for purposes other than investment. Perhaps the best known are those champions of "corporate democracy," Lewis D. Gilbert and Wilma Soss, the latter the president of the Federation of Women Shareholders in American Business. These very individualistic individuals appear at hundreds of annual meetings a year—on the basis sometimes of hundreds of shares, sometimes a single share—to demand more accessible meetings, more information for the stockholders, limitations on executive compensation and stock options, and other asserted reforms based on the assumption that managements will shortchange the small shareholder unless closely watched and subjected to periodic criticism.

In the last five years, stockholding has also been taken up, on a single-share basis, by members of CORE and other race-relations groups, who then use their rights acquired by shareholding to urge integrated employment or integrated lunch counters. This has been done at annual meetings of some of the major variety-store chains.

Another minority group of small shareholders consists of trade-union members. Some are long-time employes proud to own a piece of the company to which they have devoted their lives. Some are union leaders. In the case of James B. Carey's electrical workers, the union owns shares of each company with which it bargains. In recent years, executive stock options have been a favorite target for Carey at annual meetings.

While these minority stockholders buy stock in order to voice criticisms, the vast majority of stockholders apparently cares little how the firm is run so long as it is financially successful. When some stockholders rose to demand the ousting of top officials at General Electric's meeting following the price-fixing scandal of 1961, they were roundly booed by the majority, which usually comes for the box lunch served after the polite speeches.

In our picture of the average stockholder, "average" refers to characteristics of the people who own shares, but *not* to the dollar value of their holdings. On this crucial matter, the New York Stock Exchange does not collect current figures, but a 1952 report prepared by the Brookings Institution for the Exchange suggested a very uneven distribution. It found that security holders who had more than 1,000 shares accounted for 58 per cent of the total shares, although they made up only 2.1 per cent of total shareholders.

Other sources confirm this pattern and do devastating damage to the picture of a "people's capitalism." For example, according to income tax records used in the Wharton School study of stock ownership, as of 1960 those families with incomes over $25,000—constituting only 1 per cent of all tax filers—owned 48 per cent of all the stock held by individuals.

(It is pertinent that, according to figures developed by the Conference on Economic Progress, more than 20 million families—

almost half the nation's total—had incomes of $6,000 or less in 1960. One would not expect the amount of stock held by families at this income level to be substantial, even when they are shareholders.)

The most striking estimate of the concentration of stock ownership is by Robert J. Lampman in a National Bureau of Economic Research study, "The Share of Top Wealth-Holders in National Wealth"; he reports that 80 per cent of all personally held stock in 1953 was in the hands of 1.6 per cent of the adult population. Because of this, and because stock prices have risen several times in recent years, these top wealth-holders accounted for 26 per cent of all personal wealth as of 1956. This figure was lower than it was in 1929, but noticeably higher than it was in 1949, when this group's share had reached a post-1929 low of 20.8 per cent.

Thus, while optimists may point to 17 million shareholders in the nation, pessimists will note that most of these shareholders hold very few shares. "People's capitalism" may mean a large number of stockholders, but it does not mean an equal sharing of industrial ownership.

Concentrated ownership has a direct effect upon participation in the elections of corporate boards and other matters, like mergers and executive stock option plans, which shareholders may vote on. Such elections, unlike Presidential elections, are not on the basis of one-man-one-vote; they operate on the principle of one-*share*-one-vote. One shareholder with many shares outweighs many shareholders with a few shares each.

Here a significant paradox emerges. Along with the idea of "people's capitalism" has gone the notion of "corporate democracy": That the more shareholders there are, the more democratic will become the control of large corporations. Bayless Manning has pointed out, however, that diffusion of ownership in fact produces a concentration of control—either in the hands of directing groups (a high proportion of whom are managing officers as well as directors) or stockholders having the largest single blocks of stock (even though far below a majority of shares) in a given corporation. (Not all corporations are like A. T. & T., in which no individual holds even half of 1 per cent of the shares.)

Why should this be so? The answer lies in the nature of the

corporate election. The board of directors nominates a single set of candidates for the shareholders to vote on. A few vote personally at the annual meeting; most vote by proxy. No organized alternative slate is presented.

In effect, the "choice" is to vote for the official slate or not at all, for neither the 2.25 million stockholders of A. T. & T. nor the 200,000 in each of many other corporations possess any mechanism for getting together to promote a write-in substitute. Corporate elections are not a vehicle for the effective participation of average stockholders in major corporate decisions.

What then are the consequences of a substantial increase in the number of persons holding equity shares? One effect may be psychological. Those who have a stake in a corporation—even to the extent of a single share—may feel an increased sense of involvement in the business system. The owning of shares may thus be a minor impulse toward political conservatism in economic matters.

Another effect may be to unstabilize the stock markets to some degree because amateurs are easily scared—and few of the 17 million consider themselves to be experts in market analysis. Wall Street columnists often distinguish between professional and small-stockholder reactions and rates of participation in the market. One tangible effect is to increase the sales of market analysis newsletters. The cynic might also suggest that the more popular the stock market becomes, the less need there will be for race tracks to satisfy the gambling urge.

The real consequence for the economic system of 17 million shareholders may be, as was suggested by Adolf A. Berle Jr. and Gardiner C. Means in their 1932 classic, "The Modern Corporation and Private Property," to divorce ownership from control in large, publicly-held corporations.

The logic of this position is that the function of the corporation changes from the delegated task of making a profit for the owners to self-perpetuation of the firm as an autonomous entity with responsibilities to employes, customers, suppliers, distributors—perhaps even the community at large—as well as to shareholders. So, too, corporations talk of themselves as "balancing the best interests" of these various claimant groups.

Thus the rise of the corporate-conscience doctrine, with its emphasis on good works rather than high profits—though the more down-to-earth proponents will point out that good profits are a prerequisite to expenditures on good works.

The Berle-Means theme, taken up by business spokesmen as well as by a host of social scientists and law-school writers, has come to dominate sophisticated thinking about the shareholder-corporation relationship in the 30 years since its first publication, and the evidence of "people's capitalism" does not dispute it. There is one development, however, that may require modification. This is the rapid growth of the executive stock-option plan since it was first made possible by changes in the tax regulations of 1950.

The executive stock option sets aside shares of stock, as of a given date and market price, for later purchase by selected executives. If the price rises, the option is exercised and a sizable no-risk profit may be secured. Previously, if the optioned stock was held by the executive for at least six months, the profit secured was taxable at the capital-gains rate, with a maximum of 25 per cent. The new 1964 tax legislation requires that such stock be held for three years before sale if it is to qualify for the capital gains privilege. The rationale for the option plan is that hired managers are in this way encouraged to take a proprietary, not just an employe, interest in the firm.

Almost all the larger firms now have such plans, and they do indeed create a profit interest for the executive. It was announced in December, for example, that Chrysler executives had recently obtained gains in the neighborhood of $4 million by the sale after six months of stock obtained through options. The option price was, in some cases, $20, while the sale price was $85.

The option plan certainly provides a strong personal incentive for large-corporation executives to increase profits. To this extent, it seems to undercut assertions about the loss of the profit motive that were derived from the Berle and Means thesis and may mean more emphasis on short-run profit, less on intangible restraints in the name of future goodwill.

On the other hand, the stock option does nothing to compel distribution of a larger proportion of profit to ordinary shareholders, nor does it affect the use of corporate profit for charitable, educational or quasi-political purposes. If anything, higher profits may simply provide that much more revenue which directors and officers can apply to whatever purposes they deem suitable, within the broad boundaries set, not by nonexistent stockholder control but by the rather permissive attitudes of the courts toward directorial decision-making. "Executives' capitalism" may be a more apt name for our corporate system than the overworked, largely unsupported slogan of "people's capitalism."

Annual Meeting: An All-Year Job

by Douglas W. Cray

A FEW WEEKS ago, an eager woman shareholder telephoned the Radio Corporation of America with some questions about the company's upcoming annual meeting.

Promptly transferred to stockholder records, she asked: "When's the annual meeting?"

"May 3, the first Tuesday in May," replied the person fielding the call.

"What time?" she asked.

"At 10:30 A.M.," she was told.

"Is lunch being served?" she persisted.

"No," answered R.C.A.'s man. "Along with other companies we haven't served lunches for several years now."

"Well, where is the meeting going to be?" asked the lady.

"Carnegie Hall," she was told.

"Who's singing?" she persisted.

"No one is scheduled for singing, ma'am," replied the patient R.C.A. man.

In tune and in time with his brethren throughout the land, he realized full well that the peak of the annual meeting season was at hand and that stockholders would indeed be heard from—by letter, by phone and, ultimately, in person.

Companies such as R.C.A. and others are mindful of stockholders all year long. Their planning of these annual get-togethers, with or without singing, is almost a full-time assignment for a number of corporate officers.

Stockholder performances, including singing, may be difficult to anticipate. But seasoned annual-meeting hands within the major American corporations have by now polished their skills to the point where little, if anything, is left to chance. They literally spend a full year preparing for annual meetings.

This weekend, for example, officers and directors of the Allied Chemical Corporation have an inch-thick, looseleaf booklet in their hands.

Compiled and edited by Allied's secretary, Richard F. Hansen, the booklet contains hundreds of questions and answers, the kind that might possibly arise at the company's annual meeting that will be held here tomorrow in the Salomon Auditorium on the ground floor of Nichols Hall, 100 Trinity Place.

Mr. Hansen explained last week that he began putting this cram-course booklet together shortly after the first of the year. Stockholders' letters are re-scanned. Penciled notations on proxy returns are carefully noted. Newspaper accounts of company meetings already held are closely read to pick up the thread or the theme of this year's crop of questions from stockholders.

Questions are prepared on the basis of all this data, along with material found in the annual publication of Lewis and John Gilbert, two of the most familiar figures on the stockholder meeting scene. Mr. Hansen turns to various department and division heads for the preparation of answers that are typed up and put into this one-shot booklet.

This year's Allied Chemical meeting is scheduled to consider nothing more, formally, than the election of directors. However, Mr. Hansen, in consultation with Allied's chairman and president, Chester M. Brown, also works up a theme for assorted exhibits that will then be on display inside the meeting room itself.

Shareholders tomorrow will get a look at, in Mr. Hansen's words, "what we're doing in the plant food business." A map has been prepared showing the company's distribution system of fertilizers. There will also be pictures of the company's new plant that is under construction south of Baton Rouge, La.

Allied's meeting normally draws 200 to 250 shareholders. R.C.A., on the other hand, has been preparing all year, and then some, for accommodating nearly 3,000 shareholders.

Last year, the company held its meeting in Chicago and linked it to a New York outpost by way of closed-circuit color television. The year before, it was held in Burbank, Calif., also hooked into New York by closed-circuit TV.

George E. Morris, assistant secretary of R.C.A., began planning for a return to New York after two years on the road almost as soon as last year's meeting ended. Mr. Morris works closely all year long with the corporate attorney's office and the public affairs division in preparation of each year's meeting.

As early as last June, he was out checking sites in the city. Once Carnegie was secured, he turned his attention to the preparation of a theme for the meeting, working closely with Kenneth W. Bilby, executive vice president for public affairs.

Leaving nothing to chance, R.C.A. constructed a scale model of the Carnegie Hall stage and tried out various backdrops, lighting and seating arrangements. By now, all is in readiness.

The agenda has been prepared. So have the remarks that will be made by David Sarnoff, chairman of the board; Elmer W. Engstrom, chairman of the executive committee; Robert W. Sarnoff, president, and other corporate officials.

By Thursday, R.C.A. will begin moving its gear and its props into Carnegie. A week from today, it will take over in earnest, checking lighting and instructing the N.B.C. pages who will be on hand in the intricacies of manning the fishpole microphones that will permit stockholders throughout the hall to be heard.

On Monday, May 2, the entire cast will assemble about 2:30 P.M. for a dress rehearsal. Since there will not be any closed-circuit TV this year, the rehearsal will not include a run-through on possible questions and answers.

But, like their Allied counterparts, R.C.A.'s officers and directors will also have at their fingertips an inch-thick booklet containing all the questions, and the answers, that Mr. Morris and others can imagine might come up.

In short, the year-long effort is aimed at one thing: being prepared.

Europeans Begin Meeting Season

by Richard E. Mooney

PARIS, APRIL 19—This is annual meeting season in Europe, as well as in the United States. But the European way is not the American way.

"Corporate democracy" is not democratic on either side of the ocean. Company rule is not one man, one vote. It is one share, one vote.

In Europe, stock ownership is still relatively limited. Control of even the largest companies tends to be closely held, often family held.

The special stockholders' meeting last week of Compagnie des Machines Bull—Continental Europe's largest computer manufacturer—provides some examples of the differences between the European and United States systems.

The differences are, in short, that in Europe stockholders— that is, the small stockholders—are told relatively less.

The Machines Bull meeting was called to vote on a plan that the Government had arranged to save the company through a large injection of new capital, Government-guaranteed loans and defense contracts and new management. The plan has never been popular at Machines Bull or in the group of banks and companies that the Government lined up to perform the rescue operation.

Five days before the meeting there was a major development that changed the outlook. A tentative agreement was signed on Thursday, April 9, by Machines Bull and the General Electric Company, under which G.E. would take part in Bull's operations.

A comparable development in a United States company's affairs on the eve of a stockholder vote would have required that all stockholders be told by a special mailing, according to American lawyers here. The general mass of Machines Bull stockholders was not told by the company until the meeting last Tuesday afternoon.

Tuesday's vote was on the original Machines Bull rescue plan arranged by the Government after the Government itself had refused to let the company accept an earlier G.E. offer. The vote was not on the new deal with G.E., but the deal had considerable bearing on the matter at hand.

As it turned out, the question period was more a demonstration period. Mr. Callies did not answer the questions one by one. Rather, when the prime mover in a committee of minority stockholders posed his questions after the demonstration had gone on for an hour or so, Mr. Callies responded to him. Then came the vote.

But the outcome was never really in doubt. The result was 20 to 1 in favor of the Government plan. The final deal with G.E. is still to come.

New Annual-Meeting Note: Social Protest

by David Dworsky

STOCKHOLDERS WERE rocked this spring by the winds of social protest as they made their way to annual meetings across the country.

The protests were not the familiar ones of skimpy dividends, low earnings and high executive sales, as articulated in recent years by a small but highly vocal group of professional stockholders, but of creeping Communism, involvement in the war in Vietnam and racial discrimination.

While only about five of the 1,500 corporations that held their annual meetings in March, April and May fell prey to pickets and demonstrators, they are among the country's most important and affluent companies.

They are the Chase Manhattan Bank, the General Motors Corporation, the Eastman Kodak Company, the Xerox Corporation and the R. J. Reynolds Tobacco Company.

Significantly, observers now feel that social objectors have discovered a heretofore untapped stage for dissent, and one to which they will return next year in large numbers.

A group in opposition to the Chase Manhattan Bank's lending policy in South Africa picketed its meeting, which was held on

March 28 in New York. Several of the 30 pickets carried signs which read: "Apartheid has a friend in Chase Manhattan," an intentional distortion of the bank's advertising slogan, which says "You Have a Friend at Chase Manhattan."

In rebuttal, David Rockefeller, president, told stockholders that "none of us at Chase Manhattan holds any brief for the South African Government's policy of separation of the races."

He explained that Chase Manhattan felt no obligation to endorse the political or economic policies of countries in which it conducts business.

When protests against similar involvement were raised by pickets at the annual meeting of General Motors in Detroit, Frederic G. Donner, chairman, retorted that G.M. runs its South African plant "in its usual nondiscriminatory manner within the laws of the country."

Angry Negro members of a militant organization known by its initials of FIGHT descended on sleepy Flemington, N. J., on April 25 to demand that the Eastman Kodak Company honor an alleged agreement to hire and train 600 unemployed Negroes.

Kodak claimed it had been made a party to the agreement in question by an assistant vice president who had exceeded his authority.

The Xerox Corporation, which like Eastman Kodak is based in Rochester, also encountered members of "Freedom, Integration, God, Honor—Today," at its annual meeting here on May 19, but with vastly dissimilar results.

A speaker who identified himself as the Rev. Herbert C. Shankle, vice president of FIGHT, read a telegram from his organization congratulating Xerox on its "willingness to shoulder community and social responsibility in tackling the hard core unemployment problem."

On April 12, in Jersey City, members of the Peter Fechter Brigade distributed to stockholders arriving for the meeting of the R. J. Reynolds Tobacco Company literature protesting the use in cigarettes of tobacco imported from Communist Yugoslavia.

The Brigade was described by a member as an anti-Communist group formed in 1962 to protest the death of Peter Fechter, a young German who was killed by East German guards while attempting to cross the Berlin Wall to the West.

Its literature further contended that "all Iron Curtain countries use profits derived from the sale of goods to the Free World to aid the Viet Cong, who are killing American boys every day."

Bowman Gray, chairman of R. J. Reynolds, asserted that the company bought less than one per cent of its tobacco from Yugoslavia, and that the practice was emulated by other cigarette producers and endorsed by the Johnson Administration.

What exactly do protests and demonstrations at stockholder meetings mean? Many observers feel nothing will be gained by those who are demonstrating, or by those against whom the demonstrations are directed.

To Sidney J. Weinberg Sr., an outspoken critic of unbusinesslike conduct at annual meetings, the protests and demonstrations mean little.

Mr. Weinberg, a partner in the investment banking firm of Goldman, Sachs & Co., said such disruptions are "isolated."

He asserted, however, that "I don't think the annual meeting is the proper forum for such protests to be raised."

Adolf A. Berle is equally opposed to the use of stockholder's meetings for organized protests, but feels they are not so easily dismissed.

"When you combine politics and business," he warned, "you are in dangerous waters. We ought not to mix drinks."

Mr. Berle, a professor at Columbia University's Graduate School of Business, and a writer on corporate affairs, anticipates an increase in such proceedings.

Joseph Livingston, author of "The American Stockholder," believes it is useless to demonstrate before small stockholders because they are powerless to influence the policies and decisions of the corporation.

"Only major shareowners have the power to change corporate policy," he said, "and I don't think they are going to be influenced by such demonstrations."

In a chapter of his book devoted to "Shareholder Inter-Communication," he writes that "The Securities and Exchange Commission will permit the management to omit proposals of a political or philosophical nature."

The book adds that "a resolution that the Greyhound Corporation do away with segregation in its buses in the South was excluded on the theory that a corporation is run for the profit of shareholders, not for social reform."

Lewis D. Gilbert, who attends about 150 stockholder meetings each year, said, "management should expect social protests and prepare for them."

He thinks many demonstrators stage their protests to gain publicity, and have little hope of accomplishing their goals.

He predicts that protests will continue "for as long as The New York Times writes about them."

Clearly then, these unprecedented intrusions were among the most important developments to emerge from the spring meeting season just ended.

What follows will be a summer, fall and winter of contemplation, and, perhaps, concern, for Lewis D. Gilbert, his brother John, Mrs. Wilma Soss, Mrs. Evelyn Y. Davis and other professional stockholders who clock considerable mileage on the annual meeting circuit.

It appears likely that the conduct of this group has so alienated the country's 22 million shareowners that clamps may be placed on their future activities.

This growing animosity was generated largely through the snarling reluctance of professional stockholders to surrender the floor to others, costumes that diverted attention from the proceedings and many questions of special interest that prolonged routine meetings into lengthy sessions.

At the annual meeting of the International Business Machines Corporation, the first hour was consumed by questions from two women stockholders.

Questions from two minority shareowners sent the meeting of the Hotel Corporation of America into extra innings. Hungry stockholders demanded the meeting be adjourned after three and a half hours of questions on the efficiency of the hotel chain's coat rooms, restaurants, air-conditioning systems, and cigarette girls.

Corporate managements once schemed and plotted to silence such persistent stockholders in the hope of diluting their impact on the meeting. But such tactics led to charges of railroading.

Management has now learned to avoid this accusation by trusting impatient stockholders to boo and hoot noisy minority stockholders into silent submission.

Attendance at annual meetings this year was down sharply from preceding years.

The Communications Satellite Corporation expected 1,500 shareowners at its meeting, but instead welcomed only about 600.

The Bethlehem Steel Corporation rented an auditorium in Wilmington, Del., with a seating capacity of 900. Only about 200 stockholders attended.

Officials of Eastern Air Lines confidently reserved the mammoth grand ballroom of the New York Hilton Hotel for its meeting, and then suffered the embarrassment of speaking to fewer than 300 stockholders.

The Eastern stockholders who did not attend missed one of the most interesting and informative sessions of the season.

The airline rounded up about a dozen of its most attractive ground hostesses and stewardesses to act as guides. A booth with a sunny Mexican motif was built and coffee and Danish was served beneath its veranda.

The remarks of Floyd Hall, president, were pertinent and detailed, and were followed by a series of intelligent questions from the floor. There were no professional stockholders present. The meeting lasted one hour.

In Cobo Hall in Detroit, questions from the minority stockholders forced the meeting of the General Motors Corporation past the four-hour mark.

Although G.M. has disbursed a steady stream of discouraging information about itself in recent months, few of its trouble-spots were probed by stockholders.

Had someone asked about its defense business, Mr. Donner was prepared to report that "our forecasts for the next three years indicate that defense sales will be substantially above the 1966 level" of $552-million.

But the question was not asked. Mr. Donner's reply would have been lost completely, had not one reporter retrieved an unwittingly discarded copy of the chairman's prepared answer sheet.

Many companies were determined to have their day in the annual meeting, two if possible.

Although its annual meeting was a week away, the United States Steel Corporation released its first-quarter earnings on the day on which the Bethlehem Steel Corporation held its meeting.

The Anaconda Company played the same game with its arch competitor, the Kennecott Copper Company.

The annual meeting season was not without its lighter moments.

Charles E. Eble, who is retiring as chairman of the Consolidated Edison Company of New York, Inc., was told by a stockholder that he planned to return in five years to see how well the company had progressed.

"You might have trouble finding me," Mr. Eble told the stockholder.

Evelyn Y. Davis attended many meetings this year, clad in what came to be regarded as her "uniform,"—a miniskirt and black sweatshirt bearing the proclamation: "I was born to raise hell.

She was told by the chairman of the Columbia Broadcasting System, Inc., that she would be more effective in hell."

When Mrs. Davis later attended the meeting of the Radio Corporation of America, its chairman, David Sarnoff, told her that "I'm glad to tell you this is heaven and I assume from your dress that you are an astronaut sent to us from heaven [where] we're supposed to be on very good behavior."

Part 4

DIMENSIONS OF SOCIAL RESPONSIBILITY

THE QUESTION of the social responsibilities of business has received increasing attention in the years since World War II. In large part the discussion has focused on the proper obligations or responsibilities of the business firm in the face of growing public concern over such problems as air and water pollution, the deterioration of the central city, and hard-core unemployment among Negroes and other minority groups.

The appropriate corporate response to these problems has divided businessmen, economists, and others into two camps. On the one hand there are those who believe that the firm must make a major commitment to the resolution of these problems as part of its general involvement in modern society. Adherents of this view argue that the corporation is uniquely qualified to meet these challenges within the context of a market economy. On the other hand there are those who believe with equal conviction that big business should not concern itself with extra-market objectives. They contend that the firm should confine itself to its principal line of endeavor—namely, supplying goods and services at a profit. In so doing, it will benefit society by assuring that resources are employed efficiently and allocated according to consumer wants. Diluting this effort in the pursuit of noneconomic and social ends will have adverse consequences in terms of the distribution of income, resource allocation, and the expansion of corporate power.

Whichever position is taken, two factors are evident.

First, the debate over social responsibilities relates only to the large corporation with sufficient wealth and latitude to assume such burdens. If a highly competitive firm were to voluntarily assume these extra-market costs, it would soon find that its profits had fallen below the norm for the industry, and survival would be questionable. Such a firm would only absorb relevant social costs if required to do so by direct government intervention.

Second, the scope and nature of social responsibilities, or more correctly, changing social values, extend far beyond either the traditional problems of conservation, poverty, and the employment of minorities, or the capability and willingness of the giant firm to respond. For example, the growing consumer movement has focused attention on the quality of the firm's output—particularly in terms of public health and safety, dependability, and misrepresentation. Similarly, the problem of massive geographic or regional pollution of the environment transcends individual firms and even individual industries. In these instances, the more relevant question becomes one of assessing the changing roles of private industry and government in the face of such challenges.

The articles in this section deal primarily with the broadened scope and multi-dimensional nature of social responsibilities. In the first article, Andrew Hacker presents a critique of the argument that business is obligated to assume its social responsibility. The second article raises the question of the social responsibilities of the firm when its output may adversely affect the public health. As part of this controversial essay, Elizabeth Drew describes the strategies of the cigarette firms in circumventing government regulation. The third essay turns to another dimension of social responsibility, notably the obligation to provide acceptable working conditions. Ben A. Franklin outlines the inadequacy of both business and government efforts to secure safe working conditions in the coal mines for more than a century. The fourth essay, again by Andrew Hacker, examines aspects of corporate gift-giving for the arts, and so forth, and thereby raises the question of the relationship between the corporation and improvements in the cultural level of the community. Finally, Adolf A. Berle raises the issue of the broad responsibility of the giant corporation (and the giant labor union) to use its discretionary power to establish price and wage policies that promote price stability, full employment, and economic growth. This dimension of corporate responsibility was a significant factor in the abortive efforts of the Johnson administration to establish wage-price guideposts; perhaps it is even more relevant during the current quest for measures to curb inflation.

In each of these cases, the reader will wish to assess the logic of business responsibility and the appropriate role of government.

Do Corporations Have a Social Duty?

by Andrew Hacker

ANSWERING CHARGES that his company was not doing as much as it might to alleviate racial tensions in Birmingham, Ala., Roger M. Blough of United States Steel recently asserted that "for a corporation to attempt to exert any kind of economic compulsion to achieve a particular end in the social area seems to me to be quite beyond what a corporation should do." Moreover, he added, it was doubtful whether his company possessed sufficient power to influence attitudes on so controversial a subject as segregation in a Deep South community.

There has always been a running debate over whether corporations have "social responsibilities." But until now the dialogue has tended to be casual, even academic. Today, large companies are caught on the firing line amid the civil-rights controversy, and it is apparent that the easy answers of the past will have to be re-examined.

Traditionally the question has been whether a firm's sole obligation is to maximize its profits or whether it should expend some of its resources on improving the general quality of life in society. In recent years the notion that corporations should promote community welfare has become increasingly fashionable. The emphasis in business schools, management magazines and numberless conferences has been that a successful balance sheet is not enough.

"The modern large industrial corporation," a Ford vice president recently remarked, "holds power in trust for the whole community." Few are the executives who have not made at least one speech voicing similar sentiments. Yet the question remains: What social responsibilities are our corporations prepared to assume, and what are the consequences of such an interpretation of the corporate role likely to be?

There is, to be sure, a certain hardheadedness behind the "good citizen" concept. The donation of corporation facilities, money and personnel to community endeavors is often looked upon as a prudent investment. If companies work at building up a reservoir of public goodwill, the theory goes, there is less likely to be popular support for candidates and policies favoring government regulation of business. The image of a corporation that is selflessly dedicated to public service will, it is hoped, persuade voters and politicians that the nation's enterprise is best controlled by private hands.

Moreover, the current generation of managers seems anxious to bestow a mantle of legitimacy on both themselves and the companies over which they preside. In earlier days such legitimacy was secured simply by being an economic success, by outlasting one's competitors. With the transition from entrepreneurial to managerial control, however, burgeoning profits are not enough and hence the search for alternative means of imparting a moral justification to corporate power.

Until now, most corporations have been content to define their social responsibilities in rather conventional ways. They make the expected gifts to universities, hospitals and recognized charities; executives are given time off to assist in community-chest drives, and company premises are made available for civic activities. On occasion some imagination is shown. One company undertakes to promote the fine arts, another has sponsored serious television dramas that are directed to a limited audience. But the point about all these exercises in civic and cultural virtue is that they are eminently uncontroversial. Everyone is in favor of helping liberal-arts colleges, cancer research and the Boy Scouts.

But now the nation's corporations are being confronted with

some issues that cannot be handled on neutral ground. It is one thing to have the company treasurer write out a check for Cornell's centennial drive; it is quite another to line up behind Martin Luther King in Birmingham. Before asking whether a company like U. S. Steel is evading its social responsibilities, it would be well to consider whether corporations ought to be shouldering noneconomic obligations at all.

To begin with, "corporation" is a shorthand way of referring to the handful of top executives who make company policy. When General Electric or General Motors takes a position it does not imply that either the employes or the stockholders have been consulted or would even necessarily approve. Top management is accountable chiefly to itself, for if the firm continues to be profitable there will be little or no outcry at the annual meetings. What is really being said is that corporations are far removed from being democratic institutions. Therefore, if companies are to exert an influence in the social or political arena they must be judged by aristocratic, not democratic, standards.

This was understood by Alexis de Tocqueville who, over 100 years ago, entitled one of the chapters of his "Democracy in America," "How an Aristocracy May Be Created by Manufacturers." The United States, he pointed out, did not have a hereditary ruling class, but he held out the possibility that businessmen would have the freedom of action and the presence of mind to promote the nation's welfare.

Furthermore, de Tocqueville saw that on many occasions such a business aristocracy would find itself running counter to majority opinion. For the general public does not always recognize its own best interest, and those who are able to detect society's higher good have the duty to use their power even against the democratic tide.

Yet in applying de Tocqueville's prescription to the modern corporation one central fact emerges: In all cases corporate management will necessarily decide for itself which policies promote the best interests of society. For if company executives succumbed to popular pressure and majority opinion, they would cease to be aristocrats. If an aristocracy has any value it lies in its being impervious to public demands of the moment; the corollary is that those with power will know how it should best be used. In this light it may be asked how corporations have interpreted some of their responsibilities in recent years.

One company not only has taken an official stand favoring "right to work" laws but has worked openly for their adoption in various states. In 1958, $30,000 of company money was spent on a California referendum campaign against compulsory unionism. While it is true that a weakening of the unions might bring economic gains for the corporation, it took the philosophical position that it was fighting for the rights of the minority who did not wish to be forced to bargain collectively. The company executives who took this position probably felt that they were promoting the moral interests of society, not just their own.

Several other corporations have devoted a good deal of energy to sponsoring programs aimed at awakening both their own employes and the general public to the danger of Communist subversion in this country. They have shown films, distributed pamphlets and conducted lectures stressing the extent of Soviet infiltration at home no less than abroad. Again, there is no doubting the sincerity of the executives who saw it as their social responsibility to dispel apathy and encourage vigilance.

Not a few corporations took it on themselves, without outside prompting, to discharge any employe who refused to cooperate with a legislative investigating committee. There were others that cancelled the contracts of television performers who had been "listed" as belonging to subversive organizations. The evidence is that those who made these decisions judged that they were performing a public service in removing from their payrolls individuals of doubtful loyalty.

The civil-rights field itself provides an example of a corporation making social policy. For almost a decade now, since well before the current protests began, one large firm has been hiring and promoting Negroes to supervisory positions in its Memphis and Louisville plants. While these plants are not in the Deep South, there was nevertheless strong opposition from white employes, who threatened serious trouble if Negroes were upgraded.

However, management made it plain that its policy would be adhered to no matter whose sensibilities were shaken. Any wildcat strikes over Negro promotions would result in suspension and subsequent dismissals. The company had decided what was right, regardless of employe or community opinion, and proceeded to use its power to enforce those ideas.

The obvious conclusion is that the men who manage our corporations have differing and highly personal conceptions of what constitutes social responsibility. Most seek to avoid controversial issues altogether, settling for the safe path of civic endeavor. Those who define their companies' responsibilities in broader terms are as likely as not to see no conflict between their personal preferences and the best interests of society. It is fruitless to protest that the policies of some corporations promote freedom and justice while those of others fail to safeguard basic values. If one company is to have the freedom to promote its racial ideas in Louisville and Memphis, then another must be allowed to pursue its economic theories in California and yet another its notions of civil liberties in Chicago.

What is ironic today is that the Americans who are calling on large corporations to exert their influence in Southern cities in the cause of civil rights are the very people who are uneasy about the presence of corporate power in our society.

The chief characteristic of such power, as the critics point out, is its degree of independence from public control. This being the case, there is no reason to expect that U. S. Steel or similarly located companies will take their opinions from outsiders when it comes to a highly charged question like civil rights. If corporations have power to exert in such areas they will exercise it as they see fit. The logical alternative is to suggest that any political intervention on the part of corporations has no place in a democracy. This position, at least, has the virtue of consistency.

The tendency is for corporation executives to assume a pose of modesty when estimating the influence of their companies in local affairs. Nevertheless, it is common practice for the dominant employer in any industrial community to be consulted, often deferred to, when important decisions are being made. There is a close liaison between branch plant managers, the state capitol and city hall, the latter two checking with the former before going ahead on key policies.

More important are the unstated assumptions surrounding a corporation's decision to locate its plants in a particular locality. The chief determinant is, of course, economic; and this is as it should be. A company will select a location because of cheap or nonunion labor, proximity to market and related factors. At the same time, however, there is a tacit agreement on the part of management to accept the prevailing customs of the community. In the case of U. S. Steel in Birmingham this meant abiding by the principle of segregation. To be sure, the corporation was adjusting to a way of life that existed before it arrived on the scene. Nevertheless, it is clear that U. S. Steel's willingness to cooperate with the folkways of Birmingham actually served to strengthen those social patterns.

For this reason the company's officials cannot protest that they have been mere bystanders amid the racial controversy. It is not the only company that has found itself committed, at least by implication, to one of the two contending sides in the civil-rights struggle. If a corporation decides to go along with the dominant ideology of a region, that does not mean it must defend that ideology. It can and should justify its position solely on economic grounds. Moreover, if corporation executives find themselves involved in politics, on however informal a basis, they ought at least to explain their involvement by pointing out that this promotes the best interests of the company that has hired them.

At all events, such informal arrangements are not uncommon. These are facts of industrial life, whether one is speaking of Birmingham, or Winston-Salem, N. C., or Youngstown, Ohio. Corporate management in such communities inevitably becomes part of the local power structure, and politics and economics cease being separate categories.

Yet there are limits to management's influence: Corporations can play a role in spurring urban renewal and school construction. But there are questions the public wants to decide for itself, and in these touchy areas elected politicians are forced to defer to popular opinion.

In the Deep South, the white community has strong feelings that the races should be kept separate, and there is little room for maneuvering by a "power structure" on this issue. Even the plea that race tensions will harm the region economically can have little impact when emotions transcend interests. Therefore, U. S. Steel's protest that its power in Birmingham did not extend beyond the plant gates has some validity to it, at least on a question as inflamed as race relations.

Even on those occasions when corporations are able to bring influence to bear in local politics there remains the question of whether they ought to do so. The phrase "corporate citizen" has a certain appeal but it assumes that the voice of a corporation and that of the ordinary voters may be listened to with equal deference by those who make policy. Democracy takes on a curious form when both corporations and citizens are regarded as equal participants in the political process. And once again it must be pointed out that if corporate intervention is sought and permitted on certain issues then this opens the door for further intrusions on questions where corporate executives hold less palatable views.

It may well be that corporations should drop all ideas about their supposed "social responsibilities," or at least confine their good works to community-chest drives, gifts to universities and playing fields for the Little League. Once companies begin to assume more grandiose and controversial obligations they will inevitably be judged by standards they are ill-equipped to meet.

Preserving civil rights and civil liberties, and promoting internal security and the general welfare, are the tasks of judges, politicians and the American people themselves. If corporations ought to be doing things they are not now doing—such as hiring Negroes on an equal basis with whites—then it is up to government to tell them so. The only responsibility of corporations is to make profits, thus contributing to a prosperous economic system.

While society is too complex for a rigid boundary to be drawn between the economic and the political spheres in everyday life, some line of demarcation ought to be acknowledged. Certainly the political rights of Americans ought not to depend on the occasional helping hand of our corporations. Such liberties are ends in themselves and not by-products of the productive process.

The Cigarette Companies Would Rather Fight Than Switch

by Elizabeth B. Drew

WASHINGTON

THE STAGE is now set for a major confrontation in Washington between the giant cigarette industry and a growing battalion of politicians, health organizations and Government agencies who are determined to crack down on cigarette advertising. Such show-downs are rare here—the last comparable one was over the safety of automobiles three years ago. Politicians are generally reluctant to take on an industry with extensive resources and political contacts; and important industries which do sense a political storm coming usually will quietly offer, most often behind the scenes, to adjust their ways and thereby defuse and finally dissipate the controversy.

The current fight is about whether the cigarette industry will be able to head off a proposed ruling by the Federal Communications Commission to ban cigarette advertising from the airwaves, and also a proposal by the Federal Trade Commission to require a very tough warning about the dangers of smoking in all cigarette ads. The cigarette companies are taking their case against the agencies to Congress, asking it to pass a law to prevent the regulatory agencies from acting. Such explicit protection for one particular industry is indeed unusual, but, faced with a similar F.T.C. proposal four years ago, the industry did succeed in winning from Congress a law granting it a special four-year reprieve. Now that the reprieve is about to expire, and with the two agencies ready to move in, the industry is asking for another one.

The industry's strategy was fairly ingenious the last time around. It was the cigarette companies themselves that proposed (while appearing to oppose) legislation which required the warning that now appears on all cigarette packages: "Caution: Cigarette Smoking May Be Hazardous to Your Health." To the cigarette manufacturers, this was a small enough price to pay for other sections of the bill. Those sections—which escaped the notice not only of much of the public, but also of the Congressional press galleries and even Congressmen, who were under the carefully cultivated impression that they were voting for a health measure—barred the F.T.C. from requiring a more alarming warning on cigarette packages and in all ads.

In addition, the bill prohibited state and local governments from taking actions of their own against cigarettes, as several were considering doing. The industry's inventive strategy was a great success and, as everyone figured, the package warning had almost no perceptible effect on the nation's smoking habits.

Those parts of the bill which forbid action by Federal agencies or state or local governments will expire on June 30. If the industry does not succeed in winning an extension from Congress, the F.C.C. will proceed to issue its rule barring all radio and television cigarette advertising, and the F.T.C. will proceed to require in all cigarette ads, "Warning: Cigarette Smoking Is Dangerous to Health and May Cause Death from Cancer and Other Diseases" —the words "is" and "death" and "cancer" are considered key. Also, a number of states are again considering action against cigarette advertising; interest is particularly high in New York, Massachusetts, Michigan and California. The agency rulings may take some time to be issued, and they will be challenged in the courts, but even so, if the industry fails in Congress, it is widely expected that cigarette advertising will be off the air by the end of next year. And cigarette-industry officials have stated that they would not bother to broadcast or print ads which had to carry a dire health warning.

One problem faced by the industry this time around is that the requirement for the health warning on the package does *not* expire: it is permanent law. Therefore, the camouflage which was so effective four years ago is no longer available. Yet some tobacco-state Congressmen talk of the need to extend the life of the health warning, in the apparent hope that no one will be the wiser. What the bills sponsored by the industry actually do, of course, is continue the ban on regulation of cigarette advertising.

Yet the antismoking forces are more numerous, more alert and better organized than they were four years ago, and they have no intention of letting the industry have its way again. They feel, moreover, that times have changed, as has public opinion about the dangers of smoking. Their strategy is a simple one: Unless, as is highly unlikely, Congress seems ready to enact legislation which is as tough on advertising as the regulations the agencies are planning, they will try to block any new legislation, thus freeing the agencies and state and local governments to act.

One measure of what is being fought over is financial: The cigarette companies now spend a phenomenal $245-million a year on television and radio advertising. They are the largest single product advertisers on television, accounting for about 8 per cent of TV advertising time. (The next largest is the automobile industry, which accounts for about one-third less time.) Americans now spend about *$9-billion* a year on cigarettes. Tobacco farming alone is a $1-billion-a-year industry, employing about 600,000 farm families in 10 states, but with particular impact on the economies of Kentucky, Tennesssee, Maryland, North Carolina, South Carolina, and Georgia. This gives the industry, among other things, a substantial and fairly senior bloc of Congressmen who are interested in their case. (Cigarette manufacturing, however, is heavily automated and has surprisingly few employes— only about 36,000.) No one, however, is urging the abolition of smoking, and opinions differ as to the economic effects of a substantial reduction of cigarette advertising. In any event, the antismoking advocates argue, there has been too much focus on the economics of the industry, and too little on the substantial economic losses from disease and death due to smoking.

The first round of the cigarette battle has now opened in the House Interstate and Foreign Commerce Committee, where hearings began April 15. Seeking an extension on the bar to Government action, the cigarette industry argues that it is being harassed on the basis of dubious statistical relationships between smoking and disease, and that the Government is embarking on unprecedented interference with all of industry's freedom to advertise. Southern Congressmen propounded the dangers of alcohol and cholesterol and asked why cigarettes are singled out. Some went so far as to suggest that the tobacco industry should be viewed as an antipoverty program; if cigarettes were regulated, one warned, Northern cities would fill up with "undesirable people." The antismoking forces contend that the danger in smoking is a settled issue, that cigarettes present a health hazard unparalleled by any other product on the market, and that therefore cigarette advertising is a special case. Former Surgeon General Dr. Luther Terry, testifying for the Interagency Council on Smoking and Health (an amalgam of Government and virtually every major national health organization except, oddly, the American Medical Association), said that more than 45,000 Americans would die prematurely by July 1 "from causes which we believe are connected with cigarette smoking."

The controversy has been developing ever since the "Report of the Surgeon General on Smoking and Health," issued in January, 1964, warned that "cigarette smoking is a health hazard of sufficient importance in the United States to warrant appropriate remedial action." The report was the work of a panel that had been set up in 1962 at the behest of various health organizations, such as the American Cancer Society, which sought an official view on the increasing evidence of a connection between smoking and disease. The panel consisted of 10 physicians, who were approved by both the health groups and the tobacco industry, in the delusive hope on the part of the Government that the report would be accepted all around. The report, issued under top security regulations on a day that the stock market was closed, unanimously concluded that cigarette smoking was a cause of lung cancer and was also related to chronic bronchitis, emphysema, cardiovascular diseases and cancer of the larynx.

The F.T.C. had been having that uncomfortable feeling that it should be doing something about cigarette advertising, and was awaiting the Surgeon's General's report. Acting with unaccustomed speed and courage, within a week of the report's issuance, the F.T.C. proposed its stiff warning on all cigarette packages and in all advertisements. The proposal was issued over objections from the Johnson White House, which interceded with the "independent" regulatory agency in an attempt to delay it. Despite the strong support of the Surgeon General for the warning label, President Johnson never saw fit to mention it in his health messages, or to support his health officials when the industry took the issue to Capitol Hill.

A question of such importance to the tobacco-growing states is of course likely to arouse a number of important Congressional Democrats. Moreover, carrying the case to Congress for the industry was, in the forefront, Earle C. Clements, formerly a Democratic Senator from Kentucky, and Senate majority whip when Lyndon Johnson was majority leader; Clements' daughter, Mrs. Bess Abell, was Mrs. Johnson's White House social secretary, a fact of which Clements was not reluctant to remind people. Clements was the representative of the Tobacco Institute, an association of the major tobacco companies. In the background, helping Clements formulate the strategy, line up Congressional witnesses and write their testimony, and also preparing the industry's appeal to the courts in case the Congressional gambit failed, was a group of industry lawyers and Washington attorneys, including Johnson confidant Abe Fortas, then of the law firm of Arnold, Fortas and Porter and now a Supreme Court Justice. Fortas, whose firm was (and is) counsel to the Philip Morris Company, participated in the designing of the industry's strategy and, according to Congressional sources, made phone calls to Capitol Hill during crucial periods.

The industry's tactics succeeded in Congress because they were very well devised, because the antismoking forces were outmanned and outmaneuvered, because so many people did not know what was going on, and because the tacticians were able to knit together a coalition of tobacco-state Congressmen, other Southerners who normally stand by their regional colleagues in case of trouble, and conservatives, including many Republicans, who normally object when the regulatory agencies regulate.

Despite the warning on the package, cigarette smoking, which had dropped only once, just after the issuance of the Surgeon General's report, continued to rise. The estimate was that about one million people gave up smoking each year, but this was more than offset by the number of people who took it up. Then, at the end of 1968, there was an absolute decrease in smoking. About 59.7-million American smokers (58 per cent of the adult male population and 37 per cent of the adult female population) had consumed 27.3-billion packs of cigarettes that year. To the satisfaction of the health groups, who have learned to take comfort from small things, this represented a decline in the number of smokers from the year before of six-tenths of 1 per cent.

While there is some debate as to whether this represents a trend, both the cigarette companies and the health groups feel that the tide is with the antismokers. For one thing, a minor provision of the 1965 law requiring the Department of Health, Education and Welfare to produce regular reports on the relationship between smoking and health turned out to be a sleeper.

The result was a steady output of progressively grimmer official reports on the consequences of smoking. In 1967 the Public Health Service reported that a review of the more than three years of evidence since the Surgeon General's report indicated that the report may have understated the case. "Cigarette smokers have substantially higher rates of death and disability than their non-smoking counterparts in the population," said the 1967 report. "This means that cigarette smokers tend to die at earlier ages and experience more days of disability than comparable non-smokers. A substantial portion of earlier deaths and excess disability would not have occurred if those affected had never smoked." The following year, the P.H.S. reported that "life expectancy among young men is reduced by an average of eight years in 'heavy' cigarette smokers, those who smoke over two packs a day, and average of four years in 'light' smokers, those who smoke less than one-half pack per day."

Then, drumfire against smoking came suddenly from another and highly surprising source; the F.C.C., in an unprecedented move, ruled in June, 1967, that under the "fairness doctrine," which requires broadcasters to provide both sides of controversial issues, stations must offset cigarette ads by providing free time for messages on the harmful effects of smoking. The idea that "advertising" must be countered with "the facts" was a novel and, needless to say, controversial concept. The F.C.C. reasoned that since "the repeated and continuous broadcasts of the advertisement may be a contributing factor to the adoption of a habit which may lead to untimely death," broadcasters were obliged "to devote a significant amount of time to informing [their] listeners of the other side of the matter—that however enjoyable smoking may be, it represents a habit which may cause or contribute to the earlier death of the user." "The simple fact," said the F.C.C., is "that the public interest means nothing if it does not include such a responsibility."

The cigarette industry and the broadcasters took the ruling to the courts, and having been overturned below, now have it before the Supreme Court, where they are expected ultimately to lose. In the meantime, the antismoking TV spots have been appearing. Some of the liveliest minds in advertising have worked on them, and both sides believe they have packed a significant punch against smoking.

This February the F.C.C. announced that unless Congress specifically barred it from acting, it would, upon expiration of the 1965 law next month, order all cigarette advertising off the airwaves. There are precedents in other countries: Cigarette advertising is banned from television in Great Britain, and either from radio or television or both in Czechoslovakia, Denmark, France, Italy, Norway, Sweden and Switzerland. Liquor is not advertised over the airwaves in the United States through a voluntary agreement on the part of broadcasters. Because of the unique dangers of cigarettes, the F.C.C. said, this was a special action it did not intend to extend to other product commercials.

As for the argument that this was an infringement of the First Amendment's guarantee of free speech, the F.C.C. noted a string of court rulings that, if product advertising came within the First Amendment, it was at least less rigorously protected by it than other forms of speech. "The issue," it said, "is thus whether the First Amendment protects the advertising of a product as to which there is a most substantial showing that it is the main cause of lung cancer, the most important cause of emphysema and chronic bronchitis, and so on. We do not believe so."

The smoking issue is an odd one, as controversies in Washington go. It does not devolve into liberal-conservative or partisan or even industry-consumer line-ups. It often appears to be something of a sport, moving normally docile agencies and politicians to unaccustomed activity. It goes on, and is continually stoked, by a surprisingly few but strategically placed people about town who have examined the evidence and become at least alarmed and sometimes outraged. This explains, for example, the uncharacteristic vigor on the part of the regulatory agencies. In the case of the F.T.C., one commissioner, Philip Elman, has felt quite strongly about the hazards of smoking and the power of cigarette advertising, and persuaded a sufficient number of his colleagues to share his view.

At the F.C.C., the impetus came from the general counsel, Henry Geller, and the commission chairman, Rosel Hyde. There was inevitable speculation that the generally conservative and lenient Hyde was motivated by the fact that he is a Mormon, a religion which prohibits smoking. "There is no substance to that whatsoever," says an aide to Hyde. "If he had abstained, the result would have been the same." All seven F.C.C. commissioners unanimously supported the fairness ruling, and there was only one dissent on the proposed advertising ban. Under questioning by Congressmen, Hyde appeared to waffle, saying that it would be acceptable to him if, instead of the F.C.C. ban, there were a Congressional requirement for a very strong warning in ads—an approach also favored by the Surgeon General William H. Stewart —since he felt this, too, would result in elimination of the ads. Nonetheless, the F.C.C. remains ready to act if the warning is not strong enough and its hands are not tied by Congress, and the strategy of key antismokers in Congress remains one of permitting the agencies to move.

Also important in the Government's antismoking efforts has been its National Clearinghouse for Smoking and Health, which on an annual budget of about $2-million—or less than 1/100 of what cigarette companies spend on advertising and kept at that level through the efforts of tobacco-state Congressmen on appropriations committees—has been sponsoring research on smoking, particularly on methods of enabling people to give it up or cut it back.

A key architect of the Congressional antismoking strategy is Michael Pertschuk, a bright, 36-year-old attorney who is general counsel of the Senate Commerce Committee. A former assistant to the now-retired Senator Maurine Neuberger, one of the earliest and strongest official opponent of smoking, Pertschuk is an excellent example of the importance of the Congressional staff man. He keeps in touch with all of the antismoking forces, and it is through his efforts and contacts as much as anything that the powerful Senate Commerce Committee has enacted a string of consumer legislation in the past few years, and that the committee's chairman, Senator Warren Magnuson of Washington, stirred from a long and rather torpid Senate career to become a consumer champion. ("Keep the big boys honest," was Magnuson's 1968 election slogan, and it worked.) Chairman of the committee's important Consumer Subcommittee is Senator Frank Moss of Utah, a Mormon and a strong opponent of smoking.

Another Senator who became exercised over the pervasive cigarette advertising was the late Robert F. Kennedy. He was one of the few Senators to stand by Mrs. Neuberger against the industry bill in 1965, and thereafter he and Magnuson spent some time, while brandishing the threat of punitive legislation, trying to negotiate an agreement with the cigarette industry. In a series of meetings with and letters to cigarette company and network executives, they attempted to persuade them to limit cigarette advertising to certain hours, those when children were least likely to be watching television, and to bar it from sponsorship of certain types of programs, in particular professional football. In the course of the discussions Kennedy and Magnuson learned that while Lorillard had cooperated by dropping its sponsorship of pro football games, Reynolds had signed up in its place. This was, to the Senators, a show of bad faith, and the negotiations broke down.

The cigarette industry had had a go at a "self-regulation code," announced in 1964. The companies, with the once-and-would-be New Jersey Governor, Robert Meyner, as their overseer, pledged to stop saying or implying that smoking was good for your health, stop advertising in college newspapers or comic books or on "primarily" children's programs. The code became something of a joke, but the industry still points to it as an example of its "affirmative steps to meet criticism of cigarette advertising."

A relative newcomer to the antismoking forces is John Banzhaf 3d, a 28-year-old attorney who issues press releases calling himself "the Nader of the cigarette industry." Nader he is not, for among other things Ralph Nader would never issue such a release, nor does Nader, as does Banzhaf, somehow antagonize his potential allies. Nonetheless, Banzhaf, working virtually alone, has had an important effect. It was he, then a recent graduate of Columbia Law School, who filed the complaint with the F.C.C. that led to the fairness-doctrine ruling and in turn the antismoking ads, and who has fought for the ruling, against the industry, through the courts. Now a part-time teacher at George Washington University Law School, Banzhaf—balding, serious and soft-spoken—has started two organizations to carry on his anticigarette fight. One, Action on Smoking and Health—ASH, of course—with a number of noted physicians as sponsors, raised about $100,000 to defend and enforce the F.C.C. decision. The second, Legislative Action on Smoking and Health (LASH), has raised funds to fight the Congressional battle this year. Operating out of his law school office—with an entire wall covered with articles about and photographs of himself—Banzhaf receives about $20,000 a year from ASH. Recently he and some student assistants went about Capitol Hill distributing LASHtrays, an ashtray topped with a plastic model of lungs; cigarette smoke is routed up one of the lungs, which thereupon turns black. The press was alerted and the move was well-publicized, but this is the sort of stunt Congressmen, even those friendly to the cause, tend not to appreciate.

The tobacco industry feels, as one company executive put it, that it has been "terribly harassed by the anti-groups." Such pressures, he said, "are unwarranted . . . the evidence is not substantiated." It has been a first principle of the tobacco companies to argue against the medical evidence and to speak of the cigarette "controversy," conceding nothing. This strategy has caused some divisions within the industry, and last year Hill and Knowlton, a substantial public-relations firm with offices in New York and Washington, declined to continue to work for its long-time client, the Tobacco Institute, because of the industry's insistence on fighting the evidence. The institute is, despite its stately name, a lobby organization set up in Washington in 1958 to represent the cigarette manufacturers. With a staff of 25 and offices on K Street and a budget which it declines to reveal contributed by member companies, the institute, with Clements at its head, was at the center of the 1965 battle. The industry has also set up the Council for Tobacco Research—U.S.A., which, according to a recent institute release, has devoted "millions" to research to find a "scientific understanding of the actual facts, *whatever these facts turn out to be.*" (Italics theirs.)

Among the major recipients of the industry's research funds has been the American Medical Association, to which the industry has pledged $18-million for a 10-year research project, perhaps explaining the A.M.A.'s refusal to join the other health groups in the antismoking campaign. Since 1954, the companies have, according to the Tobacco Institute, "committed in excess of $31-million" to the council. Nonetheless, the industry's entire research effort is considered to be piddling compared to what the companies spend on advertising. Moreover, the industry has a bit of an image problem in talking about its research: If it says that it is researching to find a "safer" cigarette, it is suggesting that which it is not willing to suggest. The burden of a recent Tobacco Research Council press release—widely advertised in newspapers by the Tobacco Institute under the caption "How much is known about smoking and health?"—was that there are other causes of cancer, that statistical associations beween smoking and lung cancer do not prove a causal relationship and that effective tests of the real relationship have yet to be devised.

In 1967 the institute signed a $500,000 contract with Rosser Reeves, an advertising legend for his "hard-sell" approach. The plan of Tiderock, Inc., Reeves's company, was described in The Gallagher Report, an advertising newsletter: "Campaign to reach from grass roots to top men in Government. . . . Presidents [of cigarette companies] place hope in Rosser. Salesmen like Reeves able to sell cigarettes to infants." According to the December, 1967, issue of The Tobacco Reporter, a trade journal, the industry planned "a major saturation public-relations campaign to reestablish the smoking and health controversy." One of the ideas, the magazine said, was to "put the industry strongly on record that it feels smoking is an adult habit and opposes smoking by young people. . . . Some suggest that a campaign along these lines might help show the industry's sincerity in wanting to treat the problem responsibly. Others, however, feel such an effort might backfire." Still another idea within the industry was that "some feel the tobacco industry should go all the way, including attacking personally antitobacco spokesmen who make comments that the industry believes to be erroneous."

The Reeves campaign came a cropper after it was revealed that the industry had planted an article debunking the evidence of the dangers of smoking in True Magazine, and then had distributed more than one million copies of the article and taken newspaper ads promoting the article and printing excerpts, without revealing the sponsor of the ad. The bill for the advertising was found to have been paid by Tiderock, which was in turn compensated by the tobacco companies. The F.T.C. investigated and reported that these "are not the acts of an industry either confident of its facts or solicitous of its reputation."

The cigarette companies are now presenting their case both through their own public-relations men and through the institute. The institute's public relations are handled by William Kloepfer, a former newspaperman who has held a number of public-relations jobs, most recently with the drug industry. A tall, deep-voiced chain-smoker, Kloepfer explained: "We are going to do a little more in the way of public communication than there has been in the past. The content is not going to be cigarette promotion. That's not our bag. I think it can be characterized as an effort to promote objectivity in this controversy."

The institute's major activities thus far have been the widespread advertising of a Council for Tobacco Research pamphlet, which it describes as a "white paper," entitled: "The Cigarette Controversy: Eight Questions and Answers." Says Kloepfer: "The issuance of it has nothing to do with the Congressional hearings that are coming up, believe me. It is a document that we have worked on for a very long time. It has been very thoroughly examined by people in the industry and scientists who are involved in smoking and health research." He declined to give the names of the scientists. "Just people here and there," he said. The gist of the "white paper" is that the causal relationship has not been proved, particularly *how* it works: "Too many factors are involved. And until their roles and their relationships are understood, no one can be sure about the role of smoking."

The House Interstate and Foreign Commerce Committee, to which the industry chose to take its case first in this year's battle, has always been sympathetic toward the tobacco business. (When it decided to hold hearings on the industry's bills, the committee did not inform a member who is its leading opponent of the industry, Representative John Moss of California—a distant relative of Senator Moss, and not a Mormon. This is reminiscent of industry tactics in 1965, when company spokesmen persuaded House leaders to call the cigarette-labeling bill up on the House floor while the plane returning Moss from Europe was circling Dulles Airport.)

Both the industry and the antismokers consider the House committee and perhaps also the House floor as the most favorable terrain for the cigarette companies. A former senior member of the House committee, Horace Kornegay of North Carolina, now works for the Tobacco Institute as Clements' second-in-command. (Among other things, this means that through House and Senate rules extending special privileges to former members, Clements and Kornegay have access to the floors of each chamber during maneuvers over the smoking bills.)

Both sides also agree that the Senate will be more hostile. The antismoking Senate strategists are planning on delaying tactics to kill off the industry bill and, if all else fails, Senator Moss has threatened to lead a filibuster on the Senate floor. "I think there's a growing sentiment in the Senate," he says, "that, at least, tobacco is indeed injurious." Moss claims some 40 to 45 Senate allies on the issue. In order to shut off a Moss filibuster, Southerners would have to vote for the "gag" rule they despise and there would be the widely publicized spectacle of an industry organizing the Senate against one of its members defending, as he would undoubtedly put it, the women and children of this country.

There are other reasons why the industry will have more trouble this time. A great deal has happened since 1965. Ralph Nader, for one, has happened, and a number of politicians have learned that defending the consumer is good politics. A number of Senators are annoyed and embarrassed that they were had the last time around. Clements is ailing, and some of his most important Congressional allies four years ago have died or retired, and his Administration contacts are not nearly so impressive.

Some White House aides hint that President Nixon will take a firm stand on the side of the health forces, pointing out that the President is not a smoker. (Neither was Johnson.) Asked at a Feb. 6 press conference what he thought about the just-announced F.C.C. proposal to ban TV and radio advertising, the President commented that "as a nonsmoker, it wouldn't pose any problems to me." Characteristically, he said he would have an announcement on it later, but as of this writing his position, if any, has not been made known.

All that the industry will concede is that, as Kloepfer put it, "the greatest difference since 1965 is the multiplicity of hearsay. There may be a different climate popularly, but there won't be when it comes to a careful adjudication of the facts." Or, as one cigarette company executive suggests, "perhaps this is no more than a political platform where people can grab headlines and make points at home. What are the motivations of the Mosses and the Hydes? Is it because they are Mormons? I think it's a fraud."

By this time four years ago, the industry had designed its position in detail and made elaborate arrangements to sell it to Congress, and to some observers it is now dangerously, from its own point of view, underprepared and overconfident. It has done far less than it had before to contact Congressmen and smooth the way. There is a feeling among the industry's Washington strategists that they've done it before and they can do it again. Their attitude is similar to that of the automobile companies in 1966; they could not believe until it was almost too late that Congress would move against a great American industry.

Robert Wald, a longtime Washington attorney for one of the cigarette companies, believes that the industry's strategy to date has been shortsighted. "It is inevitable that TV advertising is going to end, one way or another," he says. "The industry should have been working out an orderly withdrawal with the Congressional staffs and the agencies. Warren Magnuson and Bob Kennedy offered them the chance. Instead, the sentiment is to fight this down to the wire and it could end up in a mess, with the industry the likely loser.

"Right now, they're getting hammered by the antismoking ads, which are better than their own, and by the antismoking people who are increasingly effective. Most of the industry's own advertising is pretty silly.

"What this industry needs is a period of stability, which it probably won't have until the advertising brouhaha is settled." This is the sort of astute advice, offered more in sorrow than anger, which the industry does not yet show signs of accepting.

As in most battles worthy of the name, both sides are bluffing a bit: The cigarette companies are not in quite as much political trouble as the antismoking advocates are putting about, and at least some of the industry already senses that it can't win it all. But although the industry will try to present a united stance before Congress, there are mixed views within it about both the style and substance of its defense. American and Lorillard have withdrawn from the Tobacco Institute.

The issue does not summon the masses on either side. There is a good possibility that if the industry offered to compromise—for example, to forgo advertising until after 10 P.M.—the antismoking Congressmen might accept, in exchange continuing the preemption on action by the Federal agencies and state and local governments. "One summer day," says one informed observer, "someone from the industry is going to wander into Magnuson's and other Senators' offices and offer a deal. My bet would be that if it's at all reasonable, they'll accept." The question is whether the industry will have waited too long, and in making the fight will have stiffened the spines of its opponents. What no one here except the official industry spokesmen professes to foresee is that Congress will once again permit itself to be portrayed as doing the bidding of the cigarette companies.

Moreover, despite the industry's apparent intransigence in Washington, there is a good deal of evidence that the higher executives are quietly making for the exits. Diversification in the cigarette industry has been proceeding at an increased rate. Lorillard has merged with Loew's, a hotel and movie theater chain (because of "the present uncertainties with respect to the future of the tobacco industry," said Lorillard chairman Manuel Yellen at the time), and Philip Morris, American, Reynolds and Liggett & Meyers have all moved into substantial noncigarette businesses.

Reynolds and American (whose slogan once was "tobacco is our middle name") are dropping the word "tobacco" from their company titles.

An increasing number of Congressmen are urging that the Department of Agriculture cease supporting and promoting tobacco and instead plan for an orderly transfer to other crops. At this time, the department spends $1.8-million a year to support the price of tobacco, $28-million a year to subsidize its export and $240,000 a year to advertise and promote the sale of cigarettes abroad; $30-million a year worth of tobacco is sent overseas to developing countries through the "Food for Peace" program.

There are persistent rumors, which the networks will not confirm, that plans are being drawn up on the basis of no cigarette ads in the near future. The loss, one network representative claims, could easily be compensated for with other advertisers. C.B.S., as a matter of public posture, did not join with the other two networks and the National Association of Broadcasters in fighting to the Supreme Court alongside the cigarette industry to overturn the F.C.C.'s fairness-doctrine ruling. The Straus broadcasting group in New York has already imposed limits on cigarette advertising, and recently The Washington Post Company announced that after June 1 it would no longer accept contracts for cigarette advertising on its two television and its AM and FM radio stations. Another indication that a trend might be under way came a little more than a week ago when Westinghouse Broadcasting stopped cigarette ads.

Despite the cigarette industry's warning that what is at stake is the freedom to advertise in general, the advertising industry is keeping its distance. "As a matter of public prudence," warned a recent editorial in Advertising Age, "the advertising business must recognize that there are an increasing number of people who do not approve of the way tobacco advertisers and media have responded to the Surgeon General's findings. . . . We would like to see the tobacco companies and the media enter the forthcoming Congressional debate with a real program of self-regulation, appropriate to the complex issues which arise from cigarette advertising. Considering the bad precedents which have already arisen from this issue, the rest of the advertising business cannot be expected to support unyielding resistance indefinitely."

The antismokers would not only like to have cigarette advertising dropped from television, and a tough warning in all ads, but also a continuation of the antismoking ads as a public service. This is undoubtedly more than they can win.

There are, too, mixed opinions as to what effect a ban on TV advertising would have on cigarette use; in Great Britain such a ban has not been reflected in a decrease in smoking. This may be why, despite the strong front in Washington and the complaints of harassment in the executive suites, the cigarette industry is not altogether in tears. Asked what he felt would be the effect of a ban on broadcast advertising, one company executive replied, "I would save a lot of money."

The Scandal of Death and Injury in the Mines

by Ben A. Franklin

"Of the 54 men in the mine, only two who happened to be in some crevices near the mouth of the shaft escaped with life. Nearly all the internal works of the mine were blown to atoms. Such was the force of the explosion that a basket then descending, containing three men, was blown nearly 100 feet into the air. Two fell out and were crushed to death, and a third remained in, and, with the basket, was thrown some 70 to 80 feet from the shaft, breaking both his legs and arms."

THESE SENTENCES matter-of-factly describing the pulverization of a shift of coal miners, including the three men grotesquely orbited out of the mine shaft as if launched from a missile silo, are from the first detailed record of an American mine disaster. Antiquity probably explains the nursery rhyme quality—*"two fell down and broke their crowns. . . ."* For this earliest remembered mine catastrophe, in the Black Heath pit near Richmond, Va., occurred March 18, 1839.

A primitive time, no doubt. The nation was then so new that Martin Van Buren, warming his feet at the coal-burning grates in the White House, was the first President to have been born a

United States citizen. The daguerreotype was introduced here that year by Samuel F. B. Morse, while awaiting the issuance of a patent on his telegraph. Half the coal-producing states were not yet in the Union.

The coal mines, on the threshold of fueling a manufacturing explosion that was to make this country an unmatched industrial power, produced barely one million tons in 1839, less than 1/500 of the output today. In the absence of all but the crudest technology, men relying on the death flutterings of caged canaries to warn them of imminent suffocation obviously would die in the mines. Some mines employed suicidal specialists known as "cannoneers," whose mission was to crawl along the tunnel floors under a wet canvas before a shift, igniting "puffs" of mine gas near the roof with an upraised candle. Dead miners were not even counted. Their enormous casualty rate was not archived until less than 100 years ago.

A glimpse into this dim crevice of American industrial history is necessary to put into perspective the myths and realities of the men who work in the mines today. For the real story of coal is not its multiplying inanimate statistics—tons and carloadings and days lost in strikes. It is the agony of those men—a tale as old as Black Heath and one that is so full of extravagantly evil personalities and atrocious acts that Charles Dickens would have loved to tell it. For behind and beneath the mountains of the Appalachian coalfield, miners have remained since Black Heath the most systematically exploited and expendable class of citizens (with the possible exception of the American Indian and the Negro) in this country.

The story at last may have an un-Dickensian ending. For now, coal miners can see light at the end of the tunnel. In this 1969 spring, 130 years after the Black Heath disaster, the mining industry may finally agree to pay the modest cost of keeping its work force alive, of abandoning the embedded idea that men are cheaper than coal. And—small pittance—we may all be involved in helping pay what it costs to write this long delayed postscript to the industrial revolution; the price of bringing miners into the 20th century probably will appear, as we shall see, as pennies on our electric bills.

In the context of technological advancement in nearly every

other area of human enterprise, very little has changed for men who go down to the mines in shafts. Only four months ago, 78 coal miners were trapped and killed below ground in West Virginia in one of the most volcanic eruptions of explosion and fire in the memory of Federal mine inspectors. As at Black Heath, the explosion at the Consolidation Coal Company's 27-square-mile No. 9 mine at Farmington, W. Va., almost certainly was caused by an ignition of methane gas, a volatile, highly flammable, usually odorless and invisible hydrocarbon gas liberated from virgin coal.

At Consol No. 9, a modern, "safe" mine operated by one of the wealthy giants of the industry, the daily methane emission was 8 million cubic feet, enough to supply the heating and cooking needs of a small city if it were captured and sold. The explosion hazard was dealt with there as it is generally in mining today, by only modestly more sophisticated methods than those at Black Heath.

Fresh air is drawn into the mines by giant fans and circulated and directed constantly through the honeycomb of tunnels by means of doors, ducts or sometimes by curtains called brattices (miners call them "braddishes"). The intake air is supposed to dilute and, by law, "render harmless or carry away" the methane and hold the mine atmosphere to less than the legal limit of 1 per cent gas. Unless coal dust is mixed with it—in which case the explosion threshold drops significantly—methane will not ignite or explode in concentrations of less than 5 per cent. Miners live and die today on a margin of 4 percentage points—or less if coal dust is suspended in the air.*

It is known that the giant electric mining machines in use for the last 20 years—machines that chew up and claw coal from the face with rotary bits the size of railroad wheels—churn up an immense amount of dust. The machines have water sprays to settle the dust. But the machines' rapid rate of advance through the seam also liberates much methane.

The first explosion at Consol No. 9 came at 5:25 A.M., Nov. 20, during the cateye shift. It was a day after the passage over

---

* One example of the retarded technology of mine safety is that miners testing for gas still rely today on the Glame safety lamp of Sir Humphrey Davy, perfected more than 150 years ago. The safety lamp is rugged and safe if used properly, but it requires highly skilled operators to read it accurately, and then its accuracy is no more than half a percentage point— or 10 per cent of the margin between survival and explosion.

northern West Virginia of a cold front accompanied by an abrupt drop in barometric pressure. In the primitive mythology of mine safety, these natural events—the arrival of cold, dry air, and a barometric low, which increases the methane liberation in a mine —have been associated for years with disasters. The legendary great mine explosions, from Monongah and Darr in 1907, Rachel & Agnes in 1908 and on up to Orient No. 2 in 1951, have occurred in November and December and in cold, dry weather. The dry air dehumidifies a mine and sets coal dust in motion.

Every fall through 1967, the United Mine Workers Journal had published a fraternal warning to union brothers to observe special precautions in "the explosion season." But, no research having been done in a century of such meteorological coincidences, the industry can and does take no account of what it, therefore, regards as a folklore factor—which might interfere with production. The U.M.W. Journal had not got around to running the 1968 warning when Consol No. 9 blew up. "We figured afterward it would be no use," a Journal editor said later.

No one knows what death befell the 78 men in No. 9. Miners who survive the shock wave, heat and afterdamp (carbon monoxide) of an underground explosion are instructed to barricade themselves in good air, if any, and await rescue. But during the nine days and nights that rescue teams stood by helplessly on the surface at Farmington, there were at least 16 further explosions in the mine. The first blast had burst up 600 feet through the portals and ventilation shafts, blowing the internal works of the mine to atoms and knocking out ventilation circuits. At the top, the main shaft became the muzzle of a mammoth subterranean cannon. The massive headframe, a trestled structure of bridge-size steel I-beams that supported the main hoist, was blown apart. For days, a boiling plume of poisonous black smoke alternately belched from the shaft and then unaccountably reversed its flow and inhaled, bursting forth again with renewed detonations below.

Finally, on Nov. 29, all five shafts and portals at the mine were sealed—capped and made airtight with tons of rock, steel and concrete. Not for months, until engineers are certain that restoring ventilation will not reignite coked embers and trigger the millions of cubic feet of methane collecting in the primordial atmosphere below, will Farmington's dead be disinterred from their gassy grave. The same mine was sealed for more than a year following a less violent explosion in 1954 that killed 16 men (including one, Black Heath–style, topside near the mine mouth), and fires continued to burn in sealed sections of the mine even after production was resumed.

If entombing a mine fire to control it seems primitive in this day of chemical fire fighting agents and automatic deluge sprinkler systems, it is futuristic, compared with the industry's performance in disaster *prevention*. There have been profitable technological advances in the extraction of coal from the seam, and today the industry is on the brink of such a long, secure production boom that big oil companies, with some of the sharpest eyes for markets and profits in the business world, are buying up and merging with coal companies at a rapid rate. But production economies in the past have more often than not been at the expense of human economies, and Big Oil may be surprised to find itself saddled with coal's amazing insensitivity to mayhem and death. It was the fatalistic acceptance of Farmington more than the disaster itself (President Nixon has since criticized this acceptance of death as "as much a part of the job as the tools and the tunnels") that finally started the mine-safety revolution.

At first, at the daily post-explosion news conferences in Consol's cinderblock company store near Farmington (many miners are *still today* in debt to the employers' merchandising subsidiaries for nearly a full paycheck before they are paid), William Poundstone, Consol's executive vice president for mining operations, insisted that the mine was "only technically gassy." W. R. Park, a senior Federal mine inspector familiar for years with the mine, insisted it was "extremely gassy," and John Roberts, a Consol public relations man, called it "excessively gassy." Roberts, a master of malapropism who greeted the news corps before one vigil news conference by asking cheerily, "Are all the bodies here?", also described the No. 9 explosion hazard as "something that we have to live with."

Then came the parade of V.I.P.'s. U.M.W. president W. A. (Tony) Boyle came to the mine head not only to congratulate Consol on being "one of the better companies as far as cooperation and safety are concerned," but to add that if this "safe" mine blew up, "you can imagine what the rest are like." "As long as we mine coal," said Boyle, the philosophical miners' ombudsman, "there is always this inherent danger of explosion." The then assistant Secretary of the Interior, J. Cordell Moore, the department's top minerals man, flew up from Washington to add that "unfortunately—we don't understand why these things happen—but they do happen," and to venture that "the company here has done all in its power to make this a safe mine." (In fact, Moore's own Bureau of Mines had reported substandard rock dusting at Consol No. 9—the most basic of explosion-prevention measures involves rendering coal dust inert with 65 per cent crushed limestone—in all 24 of its inspections there since 1963. The bureau had cited No. 9 for 25 other safety violations since December, 1966. Moore probably saw nothing unusual in that because violations are the norm in most mines.)

Hulett C. Smith, then the Governor of West Virginia, also stood before the television cameras and observed more in sadness than in anger that "we must recognize that this is a hazardous business and what has occurred here is one of the hazards of being a miner."

With that, the fuse, delayed so long, finally blew in Washington. The then Secretary of the Interior, Stewart L. Udall, after eight years of more concern for California redwoods than for miners, denounced the whole system of coal mining—the technological *and* moral systems—as "unacceptable." As an astonished layman, Udall noted that Consol was mining "in an area that really is a low-grade gas field" and that "obviously it is not a solution that is completely adequate to dilute the gas by pumping in air." Within three weeks, Udall summoned a national coal-safety conference which turned out to be one of the most amazing gatherings in bureaucratic history. In a Soviet-style mood of confession, Udall publicly admitted that "we have accepted, even condoned, an attitude of fatalism that belongs to an age darker than the deepest recess of any coal mine. At every level of responsibility, from the individual miner to the highest councils of Government, we have looked with horror on the specters of death and disease that haunt our mines. Then we have shrugged our shoulders and said to ourselves, 'Well, coal mining is an inherently hazardous business' or 'It's too bad, of course, but as long as coal is mined men inevitably will die underground.' These easy rationalizations are no longer acceptable in this time in history."

The stubborn Black Heath syndrome—so costly in human life and so profitable to the industry—finally was broken. Within a week, Bureau of Mines Director John F. O'Leary, on the job one month, issued orders to his inspectors. They were to cease immediately giving prior notification of impending inspections to the operators, a practice known for years to encourage a sudden, temporary kind of mine housecleaning for the benefit of the inspector—"baking a cake," one inspector called it. They were to cease reviewing mine violation reports with owners. Where violations occurred involving imminent danger of explosion, they were no longer merely to write them down as before, they were to close the mine. The list was startling for what it said about past practices.

It is hard to tell which is more gripping—the penny-pinching, corner-cutting and profiteering waste of human life in mines still operated today—Black Heath–style—with bland abandon of what the U. S. Bureau of Mines calls "ordinary regard for safety," or the callous result, the history of human carnage in the mines. The record to date, even the most contemporary chapters of it, is appalling. In the 100 years that partial records of fatal mine accidents have been kept (the early figures are incomplete) more than 120,000 men have died violently in coal mines, an average of 100 every month for a century. The total does not include those who died of what passes for "natural causes" in work that is as notoriously hazardous to health as it is to life and limb. Today, among men aged 60 to 64, the "natural" death rate of miners is eight times that of workers in any other industrial occupation.

Chronic lung disease may, in fact, turn out to be a far worse killer of miners than accidents. The U.S. Public Health Service, in unfinished research that is 25 years behind completed medical findings in British mines, has recently documented that coal dust —not the rock dust associated for decades with miners' silicosis— has become perhaps the pre-eminent threat to survival in the mines.

A prevalence study completed in 1965 found that, conservatively, 100,000 active and retired American coal miners suffered from the progressive, gasping breathlessness associated with prolonged inhalation of fine coal dust, a condition known (from autopsy observation) as "black lung" or pneumoconiosis. The U.M.W. estimates that in the 20 years that electric mining machines have been churning up greater and greater clouds of dust at least one million men have been exposed to an occupational disease whose ravages do not stop with removal to a dust-free environment.

The black-lung hazard—as the coal industry and physicians in its employ constantly point out—is as yet a qualitatively and quantitatively uncertain threat to life. It is real enough, however, to have caused more than 30,000 West Virginia miners, normally among the last in the industry to engage in wildcat strikes, to walk off their jobs for three weeks in February of this year to demand that the State Legislature include black lung in the list of injuries and diseases for which disabled miners are eligible to collect workmen's compensation benefits. Until then, only three coal-producing states—Alabama, Virginia and Pennsylvania—authorized workmen's compensation payments (generally financed by the industry) to black-lung victims, and only Pennsylvania has paid any claims. (In Pennsylvania, the benefits are paid for by the taxpayers, *not* the industry, which may explain how the legislation survived there. Coal has a history of very aggressive lobbying to protect its economic interest.)

In West Virginia's Statehouse last month, a doctor testifying in support of the industry's proposal of further medical studies of black lung before changing the compensation law "in haste," charged that Drs. I. E. Buff, Donald L. Rasmussen and Hawey Wells, the three crusading physicians in that state who had galvanized the miners to strike for health reform, had done more damage as "alarmists" than the disease itself. There was nothing more pathetic, the lachrymose industry witness testified, than a coal miner told to quit the only work he knows just because he is a little breathless. It was a Dickensian performance.

The coal operators, or some of them, have taken the position that pneumoconiosis does not exist. But sudden violence in the mines has been documented monotonously since Black Heath. Last year, alone, 309 miners died in accidents—"needlessly," according to O'Leary, the new and aggressively safety-conscious director of the Bureau of Mines—and the miners' death and injury rates, already the highest of any industry, are on the rise.

The injury *severity* rate in mines, also the highest, is two and a half times that of lumbering, nearly four times that of trucking. Since records of nonfatal accidents began to be archived in 1930, the number of men temporarily or permanently disabled digging coal has risen to 1.5 million. Today, a miner surviving a lifetime in coal (and there is one chance in 12 that he will not) can expect three or four lost-time injuries, not counting one chance in 5 or 10 of serious and eventually fatal lung disease.

Mining, like prostitution, is one of the oldest occupations in the world and is probably as impossible to stop. From the beginning, coal has been a curse on the land from whence it came, blighting the landscape with strip mines and culm banks and polluted streams, extracting for absentee owners vast fortunes from Appalachian states that are today synonymous with poverty, and plunging generations into despair.

But the scandal of gratuitous death and injury in the mines—almost all of it recognized, as the Interior Department report put it recently, as the result of the operators' "tendency to cut safety corners when profits are low and ignore good safety practices when profits are high"—has finally reached the point at which a Republican Administration in Washington is talking about limiting coal production to save lives.

In testimony this month supporting the sudden rush of mine-safety bills in Congress following the explosion at Farmington, this radical notion was put forth by none other than Secretary of the Interior Walter J. Hickel. "It is clear that our society can no longer tolerate the cost in human life and human misery that is exacted in the mining of this essential fuel," Hickel said. "Unless we find ways to eliminate that intolerable cost, we must inevitably limit our mining of coal, which has an almost inexhaustible potential for industrial, economic and social good."

Republican coal barons must have rolled in their graves. Even from Democratic Administrations, this most destructive of industries had never received such a radical warning. In fact, Democrats in Congress have been the protectors of the industry's economic interests over the survival interests of its workers.

In 1941, at the end of three decades during which miners died at an average rate of better than 2,000 a year, a series of terrible disasters which had killed 276 men during the closing months of 1940 finally forced passage of the so-called Coal Mine Inspection and Investigation Act. It was conceded, as the Bureau of Mines timidly put it then, that "speed of operation and demand for maximum tonnage at a minimum cost resulted in a neglect of ordinary safety measures."

In 1941, when technology in the United States had advanced to the threshold of the atomic era, the gross and calculated neglect of ordinary prudence in the powder-house atmosphere of coal mines was evidenced by the fact that barely half the underground coal miners had been equipped with battery-powered electric cap lamps, approved by the Bureau of Mines for the absence of spark hazards. Incredibly, the rest still wore carbide lamps, which gave their light by generating acetylene gas and emitting an open, two-inch jet of flame.

In 1941, half the mines still used unstable black powder for blasting rather than the safer "permissible" explosives recommended for 30 years by the bureau. The carbide lamps were handy for lighting fuses. Some mines had advanced to the employment of "shot firers," solitary men whose job was to shoot down the drilled coal after everyone else had left the mine. It was a concession to modernity. If the mine blew up, only one man was lost.

Everyone knew that disasters could be stopped. "In view of the present knowledge of preventing explosions, disasters are inexcusable and discredit the mining industry," the Bureau of Mines said in 1940. Everyone knew that more improvements in the feeble state mining laws were being blocked than passed. But Congress heeded the industry's states' rights argument. The 1941 act gave the Bureau of Mines for the first time authority to enter and inspect mines and write reports containing noncompulsory safety recommendations, but no powers of enforcement. The states would take care of that.

Since 1910, when the Bureau of Mines was established, its engineers have been testing and recommending to the industry as approved or disapproved—as "permissible" or "nonpermissible" (words that convey more authority than the bureau had then or has today to require their use)—a whole range of mining equipment, including explosives and electric wiring, lights, drills, cutting machines and haulage devices. Such safety-designed machinery is obviously the key to disaster prevention in mines full of a mixture of inflammable methane gas and explosive coal dust.

Yet, nearly half the explosions—835 miners dead—between May, 1941, when the bureau got its authority to inspect and recommend, and July, 1952, when Congress next amended the mine-safety law, were caused by electric arcs from nonpermissible mine machinery. Most of the rest involved nonpermissible —but still not illegal—use of explosives.

Unbelievably, when the misnamed Federal Coal Mine Safety Act of 1952 finally emerged from the coal lobby's permissible cutting machine, it contained a "grandfather clause" which allowed the indefinitely continued use of knowingly dangerous nonpermissible electrical machinery "if, before the effective date of this section . . . the operator of such mine owned such equipment . . . or had ordered such equipment." The law also set up two classes of mines—gassy and nongassy—and it stretched the loophole for nonpermissible equipment even further for the 85 per cent of mine owners lucky enough to meet the nongassy standard.

In effect, Congress told the mine operators that "if you were creating an avoidable explosion hazard before we passed this law, it's all right to go on doing so until the dangerous machinery wears out." Today, this means that spark-hazard machines—some of them rebuilt twice and three times over under the same serial numbers—are still in use in some mines 17 years after the law was passed. A count by the Bureau of Mines in 1967, when the law had been on the books 15 years, showed 1,117 pieces of nonpermissible electrical equipment in use in 159 mines.

The 1952 mine-safety act may have been one of the great legislative mirages of all time. It specifically exempted small mines, those with fewer than 15 employes. Although the small mines were depicted in the industry's testimony as too inefficient and limited in capital resources to bear the cost of retooling for the most basic disaster prevention, their number immediately doubled after the law was passed. Large mines were simply separated into smaller units to evade the law. (In 1966, the small mines were finally brought in—with all "grandfather clauses" still intact.)

Moreover, the law was deliberately written to apply to, and to give Federal mine inspectors jurisdiction over, only certain kinds of "major disasters"—defined by Congress as those killing five or more miners in one stroke. More than 90 per cent of mine deaths then occurred in lonely ones, twos and threes. Far more than half were caused by rock falls from the mine roof, largely at the working face. The 1952 law established roof-control standards, but only for established tunnels used as haulageways where such accidents were least common.

Having extended Federal safety jurisdiction to the kinds of "major disasters" that made the news wires and brought discrediting publicity, Congress emphasized that the new law was *not* to protect the miners from "the lack of, or inadequacy of, guards or protective devices." It was totally silent on hazards to health.

In signing the act into law, former President Truman obviously did not overstate the facts in observing that "I consider it my duty to point out its defects so that the public will not be misled into believing that this is a broad-gauge accident-prevention measure . . . I am advised that loopholes in the law were provided to avoid any economic impact on the coal-mining industry."

Congress has considered mine-safety legislation only three times in the last three decades. But in the years between enactments, there was activity. In 1962, after explosions in the Robena and Compass mines had killed 59 men, President Kennedy commissioned a task force to review the situation. Its report concluded that the industry's continuing disregard of the most basic hazards to life and limb deserved Congressional attention. For one thing, the task force proposed to put a deadline—one year after enactment of an implementing amendment by Congress—on the non-permissible machinery "grandfather clause." It also noted that Britain, producing only a fraction of the coal output of the United States, was spending more than twice as much on mine health research.

But then in a series of private conferences with Bureau of Mines and Interior Department officials, the Bituminous Coal Operators Association, the union-negotiating arm of the coal industry, persuaded them to recommend to Congress a "grand-father clause" deadline of *five* years. Since Congress took no ac-tion on it, the B.C.O.A. had another opportunity last year to persuade the Bureau of Mines to propose an even further exten-sion to *ten* years. The capitulation was so flagrant that the White House, overseeing the draftsmanship of the 1968 mine-safety bill, demanded its exclusion from the bill, which went up to Congress in September. It died without hearings.

Other capitulations to the industry have perpetuated the Bu-reau of Mines's reputation as the submissive captive of the indus-try it is supposed to police. As recently as a year ago, a long-proposed revision of the 1952 law specifically requiring diversion of a minimum flow of dust-and-gas-diluting forced air ventilation to the working face of coal mines—a point beyond the last mov-ing air current in the established workings—was dropped by the bureau upon the B.C.O.A.'s complaint that it would be too costly.

It has been known for years that progressive contamination of mine ventilation air—a pickup of dangerous amounts of methane or coal dust, or both—results from coursing air from one working section of a mine to another before routing it to the surface. The practice is known to have caused explosions and deaths. Yet a year ago the B.C.O.A. was still dickering privately with the bureau, demanding language in the bureau's proposals for tougher mine ventilation standards which would say that if it cost too much to provide a separate "split" of air to each active working place it would not be required until after "a reasonable time"—not, of course, defined.

It is not that any of these proposals were new. The industry could claim no element of surprise—except at the idea of being compelled to adopt them after so long a history of lethal *laissez-faire*. Mine technology has been equal to all of these proposed measures for at least all of this century—for 101,000 mine deaths.

The inclusive almanac of mine disasters published by the Bureau of Mines in 1960 (it is now out of print) says that the violently explosive and unpredictable characteristics of suspended coal dust in mines were known as long ago as 1886. A team of mining engineers which visited all the major coalfields in 1908, a year after the worst mine explosion in American history had killed 362 men at Monongah, W. Va., published a detailed report identifying every source of all the subsequent mine disasters (72,501 deaths—1909 through 1968) and recommending disaster-prevention standards which are *still* not observed.

While lobbying privily against safety, the industry has publicly promoted the idea that the death and mutilation of its workers was a cost of doing business. It got a depletion allowance on its taxes. Its workers got none for their depletion. The industry reaction to disaster was in the brave tradition of "what can you expect in an inherently risky business"—*and* with some of the most effective lobbying in legislative history to perpetuate the trade-off of cheap life for cheap coal. And it has not been alone.

Even on the left in this medieval atmosphere, the miners' union, the United Mine Workers of America, has been so concerned with helping the industry survive its post-war slump and with preserving coal's low-cost competitive advantage over other basic fuels—oil, natural gas and nuclear energy—that it long ago sacrificed what could have been the leadership of a mine-safety crusade for high wages, mechanized high production and the highest accident rate of any industry.

Some of the accidents were no accident. In 1947, the U.M.W. in Illinois was found to have voluntarily signed a labor contract with coal operators in that state whose terms forbade the union from seeking improvements in Illinois' mine-safety law, upon which the industry placed such store in opposing greater Federal control. The Federal law of 1941, then in effect, was no threat to the cheapest production economies; the 1941 act had been so considerate of the industry's faith in state regulation that Federal mine inspectors were denied enforcement powers.

Since 1946, moreover, the U.M.W. had become locked in an embrace with the operators nationally. Through the 1946 coal labor contract, which set up the U.M.W. Welfare and Retirement Fund and financed it by an industry royalty—now 40 cents a ton for all coal taken out of union mines—the U.M.W. also acquired an immense interest in production. The Welfare and Retirement Fund collects income from *operating* mines, not from those harried by mine inspectors or closed down for safety violations.

The U.M.W.'s obvious conflicts of interest are a legacy of John L. Lewis, the 89-year-old former president. Lewis's postwar decision to help the coal industry survive by sacrificing 400,000 miners' jobs to mechanization in return for the company royalties was regarded then as a modernizing act of industrial statesmanship. But it established alliances that obviously are not in the best interest—on mine safety, if nothing else—of the rank-and-file membership. For example, under Lewis the U.M.W. bought control of the National Bank of Washington, a profitable sideline that has furthered the appearance, if not the fact, of shared interests by making loans to coal companies.

Since Congress was no help, in 1946 the Interior Department, which was then operating the mines under President Truman's strike-induced Federal seizure order, negotiated with the unions (as a condition in the contract) safety standards unobtainable by other means. Compliance with the contract's so-called Mine Safety Code, which incorporates many of the reforms talked about since the early nineteen-hundreds, is monitored by Federal mine inspectors. But its enforcement depends on the union, through its contractual right to withdraw men from mines in violation of the code.

Compliance, according to Bureau of Mines Director O'Leary, "leaves much to be desired." The compliance average in 20 of the largest mines is 65 per cent, O'Leary has told Congressional committees, but in some states (depending on coal operator attitudes and union militance) it is as low as 30 per cent and in one state as low as 7 per cent. The U.M.W.'s "safety division" at its headquarters in Washington consists of one man.

The Welfare and Retirement Fund is not the only loser when the men walk out of an unsafe mine. The miners lose wages. When I asked him several months ago whether the U.M.W. had considered negotiating with the companies a requirement that they pay regular wages to men who left a shift while demonstrable code violations were corrected, the U.M.W.'s Boyle, a slight, normally combative Irishman from Montana, told me that that would be impossible because even among miners there were "lazy men"; there would be abuses to get pay for no work. Later, in a safety proposal prepared by the U.M.W., the union finally supported the idea that miners should be paid for time off the job if a *Federal inspector* closed a mine.

But more than any other witnesses on this year's crop of catch-up mine-safety bills, Boyle has agreed with the industry's position.

On the proposed revision that Secretary Hickel and O'Leary have called the reform of "paramount importance," Boyle's stand is significantly less reformist than the industry's. In view of the miserable record of Congressional inaction and protection of the industry, the Administration this year is asking Congress to give the Secretary of the Interior the flexibility of administrative rule-making authority. After hearings, *he* would establish the safety standards. There would be the right of appeal. It is the system in use since 1938 in nearly every other area of Federal regulatory activity, and the coal industry now says it will go along with it if the Secretary's authority is suitably circumscribed to prevent "arbitrary" decisions. Boyle, however, has said he "would rather take our chances with Congress."

Those chances this year are very good indeed, partly because Boyle himself has underlined the unequal forces working for mine safety in the private sector. The U.M.W. is clearly embarrassed by the reformist zeal of what it calls "Johnny-come-lately experts" since Farmington, like Udall, Ralph Nader and Representative Ken Hechler of West Virginia. For suggesting that the union bears some responsibility and that it has compromised and "snuggled up to" management on safety issues, the U.M.W. Journal recently labeled Nader and Hechler as "finks" in a front-page editorial. And the union magazine has engaged in such a Mao Tse-tung glorification of Boyle and his record as a safety crusader —it refers to him as a "union chieftain"—that the U.M.W. has become an embarrassment to its friends in Congress. While fulminating at the charges of collaboration with the industry, the Journal has *not* reported that weeks before the Consol disaster the U.M.W. was convicted along with the Consolidation Coal Company in a Federal court in Lexington, Ky., of conspiring to create a monopoly in the soft coal industry. With the conviction, which is being appealed, went a $7,300,000 damage award, to be paid half by the union and half by the company that Boyle has praised for "cooperation." The case involved Consol's alleged withdrawal of coal marketing services from South-East Coal Company after the company went non-union.

Moreover the coal industry can hardly cry poor this year. Because of its secure grip on a growing share—now more than half —of the fuel market in the surging electric utility business, even the National Coal Association is calling the future "glittering." It turns out that local boosters who, through depression upon depression, have been calling the state of West Virginia "The Billion Dollar Coal Field" were not far from wrong.

As Senator Harrison A. Williams Jr. of New Jersey noted in starting mine-safety hearings, coal has become so profitable that since 1966 the three largest coal producers have been taken over by other giant mineral corporations—Peabody Coal Company by Kennecott Copper, Consolidation by Continental Oil Company and Island Creek Coal Company by Occidental Oil. According to the National Coal Association, the list of oil corporations that have acquired coal-mining companies now includes at least 20 of the major petroleum producers—Gulf, Shell, Humble, Standard of Ohio, Atlantic-Richfield, Sun, Ashland and Kerr-McGee among them. It was a relief to know, Senator Williams noted, that the safety hearings would not be "complicated" by the usual coal claims of imminent bankruptcy. To the oil owners of coal, Williams pointedly observed that the spectacle of oil-well pollution of the Pacific Ocean off Santa Barbara, Calif., and new evidence of "lung pollution" in the mines "may be trying to tell us something." "In both cases," he said, "we find at the top of the ownership structure big oil companies."

Whether or not by corporate edict from these powerful new coal owners, the fact is that the National Coal Association, the largest industry group, is taking a remarkably calm and even welcoming view of the strenuous safety legislation before Congress this year. By enacting the Nixon Administration bill, which is among the strongest of the lot, Congress could close all the old loopholes at once and take—for coal—a daring new step into industrial human ecology. The Nixon bill would require mine operators to attack the black-lung epidemic among miners by reducing coal dust contamination in mine air to 4.5 milligrams of respirable dust per cubic meter of air, as a starter. The standard is a compromise of the U.S. Public Health Service's 1968 recommendation—3 milligrams. It would become effective six months after passage of the law and could be lowered later by decision of the Secretary of the Interior. The dust-control problem is publicly pictured as a cost nightmare by the industry. The Bureau of Mines estimates that the cost will be only pennies per ton.

The economics of mine safety are the one great unknown in this year's reform spree. No one knows what the cost of a century of neglect has been. Lee White, the chairman of the Federal Power Commission, which regulates wholesale electric power rates, opened the door a crack during Secretary Udall's post-Farmington *mea culpa* last December by observing that, as a nation, we have lost money as well as life in the mines, "and we must pay." The F.P.C. is anxious to pass on to consumers "all savings in costs that are properly made," White said. But if it takes an increase in the cost of electricity to indemnify the miners who dig the coal for steam-electric power, "I believe the American people are willing and should be willing to pay that extra cost. . . . For all I know, we are not talking about increased rates but only a smaller decrease in rates."

Some but not all of coal's new 20-year and 30-year contracts to supply the huge fuel demands of electric power contain escalator clauses, which would permit certain price increases to pay for safety. But a share-the-cost program may not be as easy to work out as White made it seem; one reason that the coal industry is so mercilessly cost-conscious has been the strong downward pressure on prices exerted by the electric utilities, including the Government's own Tennessee Valley Authority, the biggest of all coal consumers. The average value per ton of coal at the mine has dropped from $4.99 in 1948 to $4.62 last year.

It may be significant that John Corcoran, the president of Consol—a moderate man to start with, by coal industry standards, and one who has been deeply affected by the Farmington disaster —also is chairman of the National Coal Association and a director of the American Mining Association and the Bituminous Coal Association. The industry does seem to be speaking with a new voice. But the coal industry is still a very loose coalition of new humanists and old buccaneers. And as one of its publicists put it recently, "We are like any association—we reflect the lowest common denominator. We have a few members who think the world is flat, so we have not publicly endorsed the use of globes."

When Big Business Makes Gifts (Tax Deductible)

by Andrew Hacker

EASTERN AIR LINES' recent gift of $500,000 to the Metropolitan Opera for a new production of Wagner's "The Ring" cycle raises an interesting question: What do our major corporations do with their spare cash?

Charitable contributions from corporate treasuries will approach $900-million this year and, if current trends continue, the annual figure will exceed $1-billion before 1970. This is more than simply a great deal of money. For these checks, and the names of the recipients imprinted on them, represent American business's thinking about the social and cultural life of the nation. Moreover, in view of the increasing talk of a new dawn of "industrial statesmanship," an examination of corporate America's philanthropic balance sheet is one way to test the claim that our leading firms are assuming a measure of responsibility for the quality of the country's public life.

One of the first questions that might reasonably be raised is whether companies are giving enough. Under Federal law they are permitted to contribute up to 5 per cent of their pretax profits.

From the *New York Times Magazine,* November 12, 1967, copyright © 1967 by The New York Times Company.

The 1967 figure of $900-million, however, comes to only 1.2 per cent of the permissible total, for annual net corporate profits now exceed $75-billion. In other words, company donations could theoretically reach $3.4-billion, and it is tempting to argue that the business sector of our affluent society can easily afford to give on a more generous scale.

A quite different line of approach can also be taken, however. It can be argued that the entire conception of corporate giving is misplaced, both in principle and in practice, and that the nation loses more than it gains by permitting executives to play the philanthropist. Indeed, I will suggest here that the corporation money which is now earmarked for gifts could and should be going elsewhere: to stockholders (as increased dividends) or to consumers (in reduced prices), to government (as taxes) or even to the general taxpayer (whose own rates might be lower were the business tax yield greater). Hence, it is legitimate to ask whether corporate contributions make the best use of this pool of money or whether other individuals and agencies might deploy these funds more effectively.

One of the unexamined assumptions of our society is that we are a generous people and that our already exemplary record of voluntary giving should be further encouraged—especially by the tax laws. However, corporate cash is rather different in character from personal income. A corporation being what it is, salaried managers have a great deal of discretion when it comes to making donations, even though the money they give away is not really their own. Thus when, say, Metropolitan Life Insurance writes out a check to Radio Free Europe or Yale University, it is not clear just whose generosity is being expressed.

The chief categories of corporate giving are straightforward enough: about 40 cents of every donated dollar goes to health and welfare causes, a like amount to education and the remaining 20 cents largely to civic and cultural activities.

On the health-welfare front, the chief recipients are the thousands of United Funds situated in cities where companies have their plants and offices. These once-a-year omnibus drives have become the most efficient way of raising money for local agencies even though, as one executive put it, "they do take some of the heart out of giving." (All-in-one campaigns also save a lot of administrative bother for corporate givers: "We don't even look at individual diseases," a company contributor said.)

There is a good deal of evidence, however, that United Fund and Red Feather drives have traditionally favored established groups, ranging from the Boy Scouts and the Y.M.C.A. to the Salvation Army and the S.P.C.A. They are particularly chary of supporting new endeavors, especially "community-action" programs that threaten to disrupt existing social patterns. This is not surprising, considering the composition of the committees which preside over these drives.

Usual company practice is to write an annual check and let the locals decide on the distribution of donations. "To refuse to meet your community obligations," a steel executive said, "will create ill-will out of all proportion to the cost of conforming to community sentiment." But what needs to be added is that "community sentiment" is not so much over-all public opinion as it is the attitudes and outlooks of the local gentry. Most large companies are shrewd enough to remain on good terms with Main Street bankers and businessmen, realizing that token displays of deference can pay off when larger issues are at stake.

But local managers of national enterprises have very little discretion about giving. For all the rhetoric about decentralized decision-making within large corporations, philanthropy is still one area where control remains in the head office. Only a very few firms allow their on-the-spot people complete independence when it comes to donations of over a few hundred dollars. "It may seem strange," one headquarters official said, "that we permit a plant manager to use his head when it comes to buying $1-million-worth of chemicals but don't trust him with a $500 contribution." The reason, revealingly, is that while a company may have faith in its supervisors' technical competence, it is not willing to rely on their social or political sophistication.

"There are just too many traps in this giving business," a home-office-based giver explained, "and without the right experience even the most intelligent guy could embarrass the hell out of the company with an ill-advised pledge." For this reason, more than a few firms make a point of automatically referring to the Attorney General's list since, as one executive warned, "the

names of many subversive organizations are highly misleading."
Perhaps they are. Among the 633 cited groups presumed to be
bent on the Government's violent overthrow are such booby-traps
as the Actors' Laboratory, the American Rescue Ship Mission
and the Association of the Interns and Medical Students.

For the past several years, the chief focus and fashion in company giving at the national level has been higher education. In
1964–1965, the last year for which complete figures are available,
businesses gave $175-million to colleges and universities. While
this, as has been indicated, is about 40 per cent of all corporate
contributions, it amounts to less than 15 per cent of the total gifts
received by educational institutions.

One has only to spend a short time in the executive suites of
Park Avenue or Rockefeller Center to see that more and more
corporation executives are getting a good deal of enjoyment out
of seeing themselves as honorary trustees. Eastman Kodak gives
over $2-million each year to education, and the General Motors
scholarship programs pay out more than $5-million annually. U. S.
Steel gives regularly to 250 selected small colleges as well as to
every member of the Association of American Universities.

As might be expected, big corporations prefer the company of
big universities. In a sense, Stanford University (which received
$5.5-million in corporate money) stands in an ambassadorial rela-
tion to Standard Oil of California. Harvard, Columbia, Chicago,
Cornell and M.I.T. get over $2-million each from corporations
each year. (So do less prestigeful Northwestern and N.Y.U.,
which shows the advantages of living next door to corporate
headquarters.)

There is much to be said for supporting the country's leading
institutions, for the entire educational system profits from a hier-
archical arrangement of wealth and quality; but any such hierarchy
must be reasonably strong in its middle reaches, and it is here that
the impact of corporate giving is weakest. There are almost 1,400
private colleges and universities in the United States, and the distribution of business dollars to them is bound to be diffused.

Bennington College's total receipts from corporate coffers, for
instance, amounted to only $5,127 at last reporting, and even a
better known Haverford got less than $35,000. Smith College man-

aged to come away with a little over $100,000, but even that fairly impressive figure amounted to only $42 for each of her 2,400 students—at least a few of whom will end up as corporation wives.

The fact is that corporations cannot be the salvation of private schools. There are just too many of them. What is more, less than a third of corporate contributions are unrestricted funds (and much of this is for matching the gifts of alumni-employes). Company chairmen, no less than the entrepreneurial rich of an earlier day, like to enumerate the ways in which the money will be spent. The Shell Oil Company, for example, by-passes college presidents and distributes $500 to deserving professors for "creative projects." The Esso Education Foundation requires applications for grants, making its own decisions as to which projects warrant support. (These have ranged from "new techniques for theme construction" at Bard College to "group counseling for underachievers" at the Illinois Institute of Technology.)

Companies plainly enjoy their relations with colleges and universities, and not simply on economic grounds. Most corporate donations are not made with any direct *quid pro quo* in mind. Institutions of higher learning still bear some of the stamp of disinterested authority, and corporations seem to think that a portion of that legitimacy may rub off on them if they foot part of the bills. About the closest approximation to gifts-for-services-rendered is Bethlehem Steel's policy of giving $4,000 to colleges for each live management-trainee they supply to the company.

But perhaps the best test of the aristocratic element in corporate giving lies in the amount and proportion of donations going to the arts. For theater, opera, ballet, serious music and the fine arts have only limited appeal among even the middle-class population, and a company runs no great risk of widespread criticism if it declines to support a symphony orchestra or an art museum. Indeed, a recent Rockefeller Brothers report showed that fully half of the corporations they studied gave nothing at all to cultural endeavors.

The 540 large companies reporting to the National Industrial Conference Board last year gave less than $6-million to cultural activities, which averages out to 78 cents for each of their employes. Even the big Pittsburgh enterprises—among them U. S. Steel, Gulf Oil, Westinghouse and Aluminum Corporation of

America—could only manage a $125,000 subvention for their city's orchestra. ("They're all trapshooters," was one characterization of leisure-time preferences among Golden Triangle executives.)

Probably the best touchstone of corporate involvement with high culture is New York's Lincoln Center. It is clearly the most visible enterprise in this area, and it has been as successful in fund-raising as any arts activity can hope to be. On the success side, the center has obtained not only Eastern Air Lines' $500,000 for "The Ring" but also a $450,000 general-purpose grant from Texaco. Another 33 firms have given at least $100,000 apiece—ranging from the predictable I.B.M. to the not-so-predictable Reader's Digest. An inspection of the record shows that Lincoln Center has fared best with what might be called "clean" industries: banking, insurance, investment houses and oil companies. (The last are very antiseptic indeed nowadays: hardly an employe of Shell or Mobil ever sees the stuff any more.) Businesses in which most of the employes do not dirty their hands are apparently more likely to be appreciative of the performing arts.

Yet of the 600 corporations approached by Lincoln Center, more than 200 did not reply with contributions; and a quarter of the 50 largest firms based in the New York area declined to make even token donations. In addition, fewer than 20 firms headquartered outside New York gave gifts. All in all, corporate money amounted to less than 8 per cent of the donations received by the center.

The suspicion arises that only a minority of top management are themselves patrons of the arts. While they are not Philistines or illiterates, they simply live apart from the world of high culture. Hence the occasional impetus to voice the economic argument: "If there are no arts in cities where plants are located," one vice president recently claimed, "engineering and scientific people won't come."

Whether a company-subsidized little theater in Bartlesville, Okla., would actually attract a mathematician who might otherwise have got away cannot really be proved (corporate computers have yet to spell out the factors that induce one man to sign on while another goes elsewhere). Not much more convincing were American Export Lines' announced reasons for financing a Metropolitan production of "Aida" several years ago: "Our line carries opera stars and other artists who spend a great part of their time in travel."

The day has apparently yet to arrive when hard-headed executives can underwrite cultural endeavors without feeling obliged to devise theories about how ballet and opera will sell more electric blankets or attract elusive electrical engineers.

Opera, theater and the fine arts probably mark the farthest frontiers of business generosity. No one expects General Motors to emulate the Ford Foundation by giving $175,000 to the Detroit branch of C.O.R.E., and it would be surprising were Du Pont to be found on S.N.C.C.'s list of contributors. Corporations even shy away from the tax-deductible Legal Defense Fund of the N.A.A.C.P. But in light of all the recent talk about the growing sophistication—indeed, the enhanced social awareness—of corporate thinking, it might be presumed that an agency such as the Urban League would be a ready-made recipient for business money. It is, after all, terribly respectable (too much so for many Negroes, who call it "lily-black") and it makes every effort to accept the facts and values of the economic status quo.

But apparently not. Of the 750 largest companies, only 180 have given $1,000 or more to the Urban League. Another 140 have given less than $1,000; but the majority of the 750 contribute nothing at all. There is some bitterness in Urban League circles about this less than token performance. "Companies will send a man to a dinner to hear Whitney Young," one fund-raiser remarked, "but his firm gives you the run-around when you follow it up with a request for a contribution." Total corporate gifts to the league in 1966 were under $900,000—less than a fifth of what companies gave to Harvard University.

If even an agency such as the Urban League is "controversial," it is instructive, then, to examine the directions that are taken when some corporations channel their contributions in less orthodox ways.

Several million dollars go each year to organizations that devote themselves to "economic education" or to groups dedicated to the elimination of internal and international subversion. These range from the Foundation for Economic Education (which has doubts about the propriety of a Government-owned post office) to the

American Security Council (which urges unalloyed opposition to all shades of Communism). Richfield Oil and Schick Razor have aided Dr. Fred Schwarz's crusades, and various companies underwrite the hyperpatriotic programs of Clarence Manion and Facts Forum.

What needs to be said here is that most blue-chip companies shy away from the ultraconservative organizations. The most generous givers are firms where the top man has a special affinity for ideological causes. A notable example is Patrick Frawley Jr., Eversharp and Technicolor, who recently financed a $100,000 essay contest to muster ideas on how businesses might "meet their responsibilities in the world conflict with Communism." Other firms whose chief executives have shown similar concerns are Motorola, Stewart-Warner and the Illinois Central and Louisville & Nashville Railroads.

A fact requiring some emphasis is that if businessmen feel called upon to assume statesmanlike responsibilities, then the rest of us will have to accept their personal conceptions of what constitutes the public good. The essence of statesmanship, after all, requires turning a deaf ear to the clamor of criticism; it calls for the courage and vision to do the right thing—as you see it— even if the public is against you. If statesmanlike power is what is wanted, whether in the corporate or the political world, then outsiders cannot properly ask to have a say in how it is exercised.

Those who want to give three cheers to Texaco's support for Lincoln Center should not cavil when Richfield Oil subsidizes Dr. Schwarz's Americanism crusades in the Hollywood Bowl. To ask for some kind of "democracy" here is not only self-contradictory but also ill-advised. Were the shareholders of Eastern Air Lines to be consulted on whether they preferred higher dividends or grand opera, there is little doubt as to how most of them would vote.

When all is said and done, the great majority of firms have no real policy, let alone a philosophy, on corporate philanthropy. Companies give because they have money available, and the common approach is to play the game fairly quietly rather than as a full-blown public relations effort. No corporation actually publishes a full list of the amounts it has donated to various causes. "Letting people find out indirectly is the best way," a Koppers vice president remarked. "It is better not to toot your own horn."

Not the least reason for this reticence is that no corporation wants to get the reputation of being a bottomless cornucopia. As matters now stand, companies like International Harvester and Standard Oil of New Jersey get over 5,000 requests for funds every year, and in Jersey's case, more than 700 supplicants annually make personal visits to Rockefeller Center. Hence the comment of an American Cyanamid official: "Any broad publicity is an extremely dangerous thing because it would open the floodgates with appeals."

The problem has come to such a head that a Chicago management consultant advises his clients on how to say no, even supplying sample turn-down letters. ("Your request has been carefully considered by our Committee on Contributions and we regret . . ."; "Priority is given to local projects . . ."; "Current policies of our Board of Directors force us to restrict. . . .")

Whether corporations should be called generous is a matter of interpretation and opinion. Each year the people of America donate about 2.5 per cent of their personal incomes to charities. (Whether *that* percentage constitutes "generosity" is also a matter for some thought.) Corporations give 1.2 per cent of their disposable income, or less than half the rate for the general citizenry. While it is difficult to draw comparisons between business firms and individual households, both do attempt to live within budgets and both are customarily expected to employ at least a portion of their spare cash in charitable directions.

Nor is it easy to decide whether companies can "afford" to give more. The key question is how much of current corporate budgets is going for luxuries that serve no discernible business purpose. It has been argued that jet travel and expense-account entertaining, prestige office buildings and conferences at distant resorts are all costly amenities having no real effects on sales or efficiency. Many corporations do indeed have quite a bit of money in their tills, and they spend much of it in making life pleasant and comfortable for those who inhabit their precincts. Yet even if this is so, it is not clear whether the general public—or even an informed special public—should demand that our business enterprises cut down on their high living so that more money will be available for philanthropic causes.

It should be obvious that all of us are helping to foot the bills. A New York–Washington shuttle flight costs just a little bit more because Eastern supports the opera, and Kodak's dividends are somewhat less than they would be were the company not helping to underwrite the University of Rochester. Indeed, were no business philanthropy to be permitted at all, then 48 per cent of the money now going for gifts would automatically be taken by the Federal Government in corporation taxes. Were that percentage, which will exceed $400-million this year, to be sent to Washington then taxpayers might expect—or at least make a claim for—a lightening of their own April 15 load.

The point is that corporate donations are independent decisions of management supported by both fiscal and legal blessings. It is assumed that company executives will make as good (or perhaps better) use of these funds than would either the consumers of their goods or the holders of their stock or even the Government itself. Indeed, the implicit theory behind the 5 per cent allowance is that corporations should be encouraged to give away several billions of dollars each year to causes their managers deem worthy.

The charm of this theory is that it rests on none of the major ideological premises of our time. Conservatives who adhere to the strictures of a free marketplace have always been wary of corporate benevolence; better to distribute the enterprises' earnings to its owners and let *them* make their own choices about the relative merits of personal comfort and public charity. Those of a more social frame of mind wonder about a Government's willful decision to deprive itself of much-needed tax revenues by permitting businessmen to play the philanthropist: better to have the elected representatives of the people decide on the priorities and problems of our time.

At issue is not whether our corporations' choices of charities are imaginative or inspired; for the most part, they are not. The committees that decide on donations are composed of cautious career men, and it is idle to expect them to enter areas that threaten to be disruptive or controversial. At the same time it is impossible to claim that the conventional targets of corporate gifts are actually undeserving. Even respectable, established and middle-class recipients like Lincoln Center, Cornell University and the Lenox Hill Hospital continue to perform useful services.

What can be predicted, however, is that even if business giving were to undergo an appreciable rise the same sorts of agencies as are now being supported would continue to be the major beneficiaries.

The dilemma we face is that personal philanthropy and government programs are either not willing or not able to cope with the most pressing domestic problems of American society. Most citizens are reluctant to lower their own standards of life to alleviate the suffering of individuals who have been left out or behind in an otherwise affluent generation. Not the least consequence of tax-free business giving is the preservation of the popular illusion that needy causes are taken care of through corporate generosity.

Conservatives are clearly correct in protesting that individuals are ceasing to feel themselves responsible for the condition of the society of which they are a part. One way to test this conservative indictment would be to pay out full dividends to stockholders—just to see what they did with the extra money. If individuals made more charitable contributions and took fewer Caribbean vacations, then the theory would be shown to have some validity. If they didn't, then at least we would have learned some interesting facts about ourselves.

At the same time, it is clear that more and more government agencies are showing themselves to be surprisingly venturesome. It may well be that 50 cents in tax money spent in a birth-control clinic in Bedford-Stuyvesant will do the nation far more good than a whole tax-free dollar that a corporation contributes to Williams College. Given the record thus far, there is reason to question whether business philanthropy has been doing much more than subsidizing primarily middle-class agencies and organizations which could well be made to find alternative sources of support.

No matter how much they may protest their comparative poverty, most opera-lovers and the parents of most college students are quite well off and can afford to pay substantially more than they now do for tickets and tuition. Calls for education and culture at subsidized rates ill become individuals who cheerfully pay the full price for color television sets and air-conditioned automobiles. It is simply a matter of getting one's priorities in order.

The critical and pressing fact is that only well-financed programs on the part of government agencies will begin to make effective inroads into the tensions and deprivations that scar the part of America not blessed with middle-class incomes. The absence of any significant business contribution in this area, coupled with the apparent paucity of tax revenues, suggests the need for a serious review of just how the nation's discretionary dollars are being spent and who ought to be spending them.

Unwritten Constitution
for Our Economy
by Adolf A. Berle, Jr.

THE BRIEF but violent political struggle between the steel industry
and President Kennedy brought three facts to public conscious-
ness: first, that there is an economic community of the United
States in which all of the United States has a stake; second, that
within that community the economic power both of big labor and
of corporate management exists under an unwritten "social contract," holding both to certain responsibilities as well as granting
both the privileges that make this power possible; third, that under
this social contract the Government can—and perhaps must—
intervene when economic power in private hands threatens the
economic community of the United States. As the dust dies down,
these three considerations stand out.

Winning the steel battle solved an immediate situation. But it
also posed a problem. The power of a big union to dictate wages
has been obvious for years. Nominally, a union negotiates through
"collective bargaining." Actually, its negotiating position is backed
by its power to cripple not only the employers but the public
and the country by tying up production and service.

Equally, the power of big industry to "administer" a price has
been known to students for years. (Big Steel's ability to do so

From the *New York Times Magazine,* April 29, 1962, copyright © 1962 by
The New York Times Company.

has just been analyzed in a book by a well-known economist, Dr. Gardiner C. Means.) Here prices are supposedly set by the "open market"; in reality, they are set up by the decisions of large companies, whose example is usually followed promptly by the smaller companies. True, both the unions' and the companies' actions are somewhat limited by market conditions. But such limitations establish only a nebulous maximum.

Since 1946, in fact, Big Steel and big labor have, at more or less regular intervals, raised both wages and prices—until the next-to-last time around. Then, the steel workers obtained higher wages, but President Eisenhower stepped in and induced Big Steel not to raise its prices lest inflation result. This, perhaps, accounts for the present bitter feeling of Big Steel in the battle they have just lost.

"We were rooked last time with a wage increase and no price increase," one United States Steel man said to me during the engagement. "This time, we can't let ourselves be rooked again."

In their view, they had acted, to their cost, like economic statesmen on the urging of President Eisenhower and Vice President Nixon. They had absorbed a substantial increase in labor costs at the expense of profit. Now they were asked to do the same thing again.

The results of the battle made it clear that wage levels, up to now set by union power, and prices, up to now set by management power, will hereafter have to be set in the light of possible Government intervention. Now the nation squarely faces the questions: How is this power of intervention to be handled from here on out? What are the real relations of big business, big labor and the Federal Government?

Traditionally, the problem was supposed not to exist. Bargaining between employers and labor, on more or less equal terms, was supposed to set a fair, or at least a viable, wage level. The open market was supposed to set the price of steel, and of other commodities. Corporate managements would seek and get the best price the market would let them charge, while competition would assure its fairness.

Government, according to this thinking, had no right to stick its nose into either process. If it tried to tell the union what it should or should not ask, it was out of order. It had still less right to expect businessmen to discuss with Government what prices they should charge (this turn in the recent battle angered some steel executives as much as the supposed "doublecross" angered the President).

Neither labor nor management likes to accept loss of power. The "hate Roosevelt" bitterness really resulted from the modifications imposed by his Government on the power of the banking and financial community over credit—even though this group prospered under the modification. Now, in the industrial field, similar modification is appearing and a new relationship between industry and Government is necessarily being forged.

Briefly stated, the emerging relationship is this: When the wage and price levels markedly affect, or threaten to upset, the economy of the country, the Government claims (indeed, has successfully claimed) power to step in on behalf of the "public interest."

Here is the difficulty. Anyone who uses the phrase "public interest" must be prepared to say what he thinks it means, on pain of being intellectually shot at the next academic sunrise. The words themselves tell nothing. There are no defined criteria where wages and industrial prices are concerned—nothing like the rules setting "reasonable rates" or "reasonable return on investment" in regulated businesses such as the electric light companies. Nor can there be.

Public utilities are given monopoly franchises by Government; in return, they accept Government regulation of their rates and profits. But regulation of wages and prices in most other areas of industry is obviously a last resort except in time of war or national emergency. Private enterprise, by setting its own prices, and unions by setting wage rates, insulate the Government from an endless series of economic shocks, any one of which might otherwise stir messy political issues, sometimes of major severity.

And yet there has always been recognition that the Government had a reserve power and responsibility for keeping the economic peace. It has done so repeatedly. This theory is sometimes called the doctrine of impact. When the exercise of management power "impacts" unfavorably on the public welfare and consequently on public opinion a political process is set up which causes the Government to intervene. The result in the United States has frequently been the setting up of formal or informal, long-range or short-range economic plans for the industry concerned.

Oil, sugar, much of coal, most of agriculture have for years operated under such plans emerging from such crises. They may grow out of unduly low prices or wages—or out of unduly high prices or short supply. In 1947, in this same steel industry, under the leadership of the late Senator Robert Taft, a short-range plan (called "voluntary allocation") was enacted by Congress to apply to the steel plants, with their participation and, in part, at the urging of the companies themselves.

Now, of course, it is becoming plain that the major industries are not disconnected businesses, but are all involved with the economy. This is nothing new to scholars: it comes as a surprise only to a generation too young to remember the Blue Eagle of the National Recovery Act. The Government's power to intervene has long been a settled fact and the most recent incident over steel is merely a revealing illustration.

As to the method of intervention, I suggest that the President's Council of Economic Advisers may well become the key agency in the next phase.

The council's job is "to formulate and recommend national economic policy, to promote employment, production, and purchasing power under free competitive enterprise." It has the best statistical service in Washington—and American statistics are among the most complete in the world. It reports to the President and has an opposite number in Congress known as the Joint Economic Committee, whose chairman is Senator Paul Douglas of Illinois.

The council is supposed to coordinate economic policy throughout the Government. It works particularly closely with the Federal Reserve Board, the Treasury and the Department of Labor. It knows all about wages and prices and profit levels in all major industries. It knows, better than most of us, that jobs and prosperity depend in great measure on a steady investment of capital, accumulated out of profits and depreciation, in new facilities and plants for heavy industry. And it can make excellent estimates of the quantities of industrial output which will be consumed this year—and next. Its views, therefore, on acceptable wage and price levels are, and should be, extremely important.

The council can advise the President—and through his authority advise both big labor and big corporations—about where the peril points are. It can advise the President when the Government should intervene to modify private decisions based on power, either of labor to tie up plants by strike, or of management to set prices by administration. It can and indeed does keep a very close check on these allegedly private decisions, taken in company offices or union headquarters. It could communicate to either or both when it sees a peril point approaching. And it can advise the President when intervention is needed in the "public interest" —that is, when employment, production and purchasing power under free competitive enterprise are likely to be weakened, when inflation becomes a danger, when economic stability generally is likely to be threatened.

I think there may have to be another battle no less dramatic than the steel-price fight before the full relationship is clear. The President has demonstrated that big business does not act isolated from political factors and that the Government can control when necessary. It is no less true, but not yet as clear—and it must become so—that in an equivalent case the Government can do the same thing with big labor.

We have had spectacular cases where labor unions relied solely on their power to take and hold, irrespective of the effect on the economic community.

Some weeks ago the electric workers' union tied up construction in New York with a demand for a twenty-hour work week. A couple of years ago, the airline pilots (whose salaries began at around $15,000 a year) demanded pay running up to $40,000 a year and struck, wrecking the Christmas holidays for millions of Americans. We have had instances of a railroad workers' strike paralyzing the country, though these are fortunately rare.

In all these cases, damages to the economy and cost to the public was incalculably greater than losses to employers or gains to the workers.

If, in an emergency, the Government can intervene with a decision affecting the prices of commodities, in like emergency it can intervene to act on labor's decisions on wage levels. The two go together; if the Government's power can be invoked in the first case, it must also be applicable to the second. Unions, like corporations, are members of, and indeed get their power from, the economic community whose outlines are now emerging.

If a conflict involving labor is presented, the President has powers and ammunition comparable to those he used in the steel price battle. They are, of course, different. His greatest weapon is the ability of the White House to mobilize public opinion; this can be decisive in many situations. He can energize immediate investigation by committees of Congress and can make information available to them. While anti-trust laws do not ordinarily apply to labor unions, the unions are not totally immune. They can be named co-conspirators with others where price-fixing is involved.

Where the industry is essential to defense (as most basic industries are) the President has the power to take over the plants or facilities affected and have the Government run them. He can move into the hazy area of so-called secondary boycotts of sympathetic strikes. He can recommend to the Congress changes in labor legislation. Big unions know—and say so frankly—that the organization work of years can be destroyed with a stroke of the Congressional pen.

In any struggle with management, the Government powers are limited, but specific; therein lies their force. In dealing with labor, they are less specific but potentially far more powerful. There are, of course, strong reasons for not using them save in crisis, but they are there—as the passage of the Taft Hartley Act over the solid opposition of organized labor effectively proved.

The social contract under which big corporations and big unions operate is more formal than the political-social contract imagined by Rousseau. The law gives corporations their right to exist, to move in interstate commerce and to accumulate, over unlimited time and in unlimited amount, the earnings that build their capital. The tax and depreciation laws can increase or diminish that privilege.

Big labor exists because Federal legislation grants and protects its power to organize and to bargain collectively. It sanctions and enforces its wage contracts. Without these legal privileges, it would almost certainly wither—which few Americans desire.

In both cases, the powers were given, and are acquiesced to and continued, because the public interest (however indefinite that phrase may be) certainly includes maintaining high employment, high production, fair distribution of wages, an acceptable price level and an economy as free as possible from inflation, booms and busts.

Attainment of economic power in both groups and its continued enjoyment depend on assumption by the powerholders, both in management and in labor, of responsibility to foster, or in any event not to work against, these interests. The peaceful life of the entire American economic community depends on them. When, therefore, the exercise of power threatens these functions or is exercised in disregard of the responsibilities accepted, the Government not only may, but must, intervene.

As matters stand at present, the method of that intervention is determined by circumstances. The Executive Branch of the Government has many diverse powers—some of which were exhibited by President Kennedy in the seventy-two hour battle. And if the Executive power is not enough, the Congress is always there. Meanwhile, the Council of Economic Advisers can estimate the interests, the economic considerations and the perils. It can make clear to all parties the dangers involved in the abuse of power.

In my judgment, an evolution of governmental intervention was, and is, inevitable. The steel battle did not create, but rather revealed, the reality of the economic community we have created and of the social contract under which its power elements exist. In our Anglo-Saxon way, we have built and are building an unwritten economic "constitution," bit by bit, but with great strength, covering all essential elements.

If Big Steel had a duty to use its price power with great moderation, it likewise has a right to demand proper consideration of its need for capital and of the part prices play in building that capital. If big labor has a right to use its power to secure continued employment and equitable wages, it has a corresponding obligation not to use that power so that the result is interruption of the functioning of the economy.

The Government must assure that such responsibilities are met. For they have become conditions of life in the vast, intricate, integrated, interconnected, interdependent economic machinery of the United States. Under them 185,000,000 Americans have to live.

Part 5

CORPORATE SIZE, PERFORMANCE, AND PUBLIC POLICY

ANY DISCUSSION of the corporation must eventually address itself to the question of the rationale for big business. The basic controversy centers around the presence or absence of a meaningful correlation between the giant corporation and superior performance. As might be expected, opinions tend to be polarized. There are those who believe that big business is a prerequisite for the realization of the benefits inherent in modern technology and mass production. At the other extreme are those who regard bigness as a major threat to competitive markets, consumer sovereignty, and a liberal democracy.

Powerful arguments have been marshalled on both sides, and, perhaps not unexpectedly, recommendations for public policy tend to reflect an implicit or explicit acceptance of one side or the other. To the advocates of bigness, vigorous anti-trust policy is either irrelevant or a positive barrier to the attainment of economies of scale and high levels of innovation. In contrast, the critics of bigness hail vigorous anti-trust enforcement as a safeguard against the evils of monopoly power associated with excessive concentration.

Unfortunately, attempts to determine the merits of these con-
flicting views have been something less than successful. Economists working in the field of industrial organization have tried
to examine the relationship between size of plant, size of firm,
levels of concentration, and measures of performance. The results often tend to founder on problems of definition, the need
to develop more precise techniques for quantification, and the
dearth of adequate data. At best, the findings cast reasonable
doubt on our ability to accept out-of-hand the proposition that
bigness and concentration are requisites for high levels of efficiency and research and development in the manufacturing sector. In the absence of more conclusive findings, the controversy
can hardly be expected to subside.

In this section, Adolf A. Berle and Sumner H. Slichter present
the case for bigness, hedged by appropriate caveats. The critical
response comes from Emanuel Celler, long-time chairman of the
House Committee on the Judiciary. (Celler's response appeared
as letters to the editor.) Some insight into the business community's thinking on the subject of size and efficiency is supplied
by W. D. Smith's report on the reaction of competitors in the
IBM anti-trust case. Finally, Raymond J. Saulnier's review of
John Kenneth Galbraith's *New Industrial State* is particularly
appropriate at this point. More than any other contemporary economist, Galbraith has argued that bigness has rendered obsolete
the roles traditionally ascribed to the marketplace and anti-trust
action, and that new public policies are in order. Saulnier's
critique should whet the reader's desire to read the original work
and formulate his own conclusions.

Bigness: Curse
or Opportunity?

by Adolf A. Berle, Jr.

"THE CURSE OF BIGNESS" was Louis D. Brandeis' fighting phrase fifty years ago. Bigness was tyrannical, inefficient, a threat to democracy. "Nobody," he stated tersely, "can understand a billion dollars." His writings sparked an era of reform that President Woodrow Wilson named "The New Freedom." Now, in 1962, bigness is familiar. And more of it seems inevitable, as new consolidations make regular, and not unsympathetic, headlines throughout the country.

The New York Central and the Pennsylvania, largest of the Eastern railroads, vote to merge, creating a multi-billion-dollar system dominating the northeast quarter of the United States. Two airline giants, American and Eastern, do the same. In Washington, Congress passes tax legislation cleaning up an anti-trust suit which forced du Pont to get rid of its stockholdings in General Motors. This is a step backward from bigness—but du Pont is still a billion-dollar (and growing) concern, while General Motors ($8 billion in assets) reports with satisfaction that it sells half the cars in the country. The only competitor in its class is Ford, which sells the lion's share of the other half.

Unchallenged is American Telephone and Telegraph Company,

largest corporation in the world (more than two million stock-holders, $17 billion assets). In New York, the Morgan-Guaranty interests propose—and intend to consummate—a bank-holding operation to rival California's $10-billion Bank of America–Trans-America chain overshadowing the Pacific Coast and Mountain states.

The "bigness" that worried Brandeis and Wilson in 1912 involved corporations owning a few hundred million dollars in assets. A half-century later, we live, more or less comfortably, with corporations twenty times that size. Merger announcements like those in the news today would, in Brandeis' time, have exploded land mines of public resentment. War cries would have been raised against rule by plutocracy from corporate board rooms, against "trusts exploiting the people," against the wiping out of individual enterprise, against threats to small business.

Today only one serious voice is raised. It is that of the labor unions. And they, if you please, have not the foggiest objection to mergers or bigness as such. They only want guarantees that there will be no lay-offs and that the merger will not diminish the number of jobs available. The general public enjoys a mild spasm of apathy. If anything, it likes the idea: the companies' stock may go up.

The most spectacular fact about today's mergers and bigness is that they set up economic facts quite different from those of 1912. Then, they meant more than mere concentration of business operation and production. They meant that a few titans—named Carnegie or Rockefeller, perhaps, or Vanderbilt or Harriman, or Jay Gould or Collis Huntington, or J. P. Morgan or Jacob Schiff—and their respective lieutenants became vastly richer and personally more powerful. Their private wealth leaped from hundreds of millions to billions. In fact, these and a handful of others like them then "owned" the huge enterprises. Their word was law. Their goodwill meant everything; their enmity was deadly.

These men are gone. There is now no remotely equivalent group. The wealth represented by the big corporations is no longer held by a tiny, dictatorial oligarchy. It is held by millions of American shareholders. These may own, but do not manage. They have property without power. The New York Stock Exchange estimates that there are 12,000,000. (I should guess 9,000,000

might be nearer.) There are also the mutual funds in which 3,-
000,000 Americans share. This last figure overlaps the Stock
Exchange figure somewhat.

Stock is still not well distributed. Too few hold too many shares.
Yet distribution continues to split up big holdings. Most big corporations are not—indeed cannot be—"controlled" by any shareholder.

Pension trust funds, almost entirely for the benefit of labor,
have grown. Their dividends and profits are destined to pay old-
age and similar allowances. Foundations, universities and other
institutions also hold blocks of stock, large and small. The "widow
and orphan" holders—the classic tear-jerker beneficiaries pulled
out for public-relations purposes in former times—have multiplied.

Making these individuals and these interests richer is not considered a political crime; it is, rather, looked on as a positive
benefit. Mergers and bigness obviously do mean higher concentration of professional management and power. But they no longer
mean a greater concentration of personal wealth.

As for the operation of a business, bigness means more efficient
production and service—up to a point. No one knows quite
where that point is. Yet in many, perhaps most, industries the
"optimum size" of an enterprise—the size of greatest efficiency—
would seem to be big indeed by Brandeis' standards.

The calculation is technical. It stems from two economic facts.
First, the operation has to be large enough to make mass-produc-
tion service and distribution possible. Second, the public needs,
or at least wants, uniformity in certain matters. If I own an automobile, I want gasoline of standard quality available to me every-
where in the United States, distributed at convenient points. I
want to be able to buy necessary spare parts in New York, in
Los Angeles and at way-stations in between.

The 1962 American migrates as readily as a Canada goose. As
he becomes increasingly dependent on household machinery like
washing machines and refrigerators he wants familiar models and
convenient servicing. Whether he knows it or not (I think he
does), he wants an organization big enough to provide these
things. This involves pretty big concerns. Americans accept the
fact.

Does all this mean that some companies become too big for

the jobs they undertake? It would be nice if we could say that businesses tend to limit themselves to "optimum size"—that is, to get as big as they should, for highest efficiency, and then stop.

This optimum size differs, of course, from industry to industry. To make and sell steel requires a business kit costing around half a billion dollars. A cement or nylon business would need less. The "right" size today can change overnight if a new technique is developed. So far, new technical processes seem to have favored bigness. Science, however, keeps moving. Tomorrow, newly invented pocket-edition plants may perhaps put the behemoths out of business. But this is not now on the horizon.

The art also of "organization"—making many men scattered all over the country work together effectively—has never been defined with clear rules. According to Parkinson's Law, a big organization will keep on growing long after growth is no longer justified. Yet a first-rate management and new methods seem steadily to increase the number of men capable of being managed.

Optimum size, at present, is determined not by knowledge but by profit experience. The size of the concern that makes the most money is considered, if not optimum, at least pretty satisfactory. And here bigness seems to win. The big ones do make higher profits.

The Federal Trade Commission and the Securities and Exchange Commission put out, jointly, a magazine called "The Quarterly Financial Report for Manufacturing Corporations." It classifies companies by bigness—billion-dollar corporations and up; those with $250 million to a billion assets; with $100 million to $250 million; pygmies with $5 million or less, and so forth. Almost invariably the concerns having a quarter of a billion of assets or more show the highest rates of profit on stockholders' equity. The net profit take of the "bigs" usually runs from 10 to 15 per cent better than those of the "smalls" (less than $250 million).

Yet one odd twist offers food for thought. The really "small" concerns—$5 million or less—in many fields average out better than their bigger brothers. The little specialty companies equipped with topflight brains do about as well as the billionaires. This is not, of course, true in all areas. In the so-called durable-goods trades, for example, you cannot manufacture automobiles or aircraft or the like on $5 million or less investment. The over-all picture then shows that, if money-making is the test, the "bigs" win by a substantial margin.

One comes on a teasing question here. Are these behemoths good at making goods—or merely good at making money? Do they come out better because they manufacture more efficiently— or because they "control the market" and collect unduly high prices from the long-suffering American consumer?

Again, no one quite knows. It is pretty clear that most prices are established only partly by competition, and partly by administration. Economists are just beginning to wrestle with the problem of "administered" prices. The three or four "bigs" in any particular line are happy to stay with a good price level for their product. If the price gets too high, some smart vice president in charge of sales may see a chance to take a fat slice of business away from his competitors.

But while any one of the two or three bigs knows he can reduce prices and start taking all the business there is, he knows, too, that one or all of his associates will soon drop the price below that. In the ensuing price war, nobody will make money for quite a while.

So, an uneasy balance is struck, and everyone's price remains about the same. Shop around for an automobile and you will see how this works. Economists call it "imperfect competition"—a tacitly accepted price that is not necessarily the price a stiff competitive free market would create. Only big concerns can swing this sort of competition effectively.

We do not really know whether bigs make more money because they are efficient or because, through their size, they can "administer" prices. They may not, under the anti-trust laws, agree or conspire or cook up arrangements with one another to "administer" the price or split up territory between themselves. If they do that, they are likely to be in for a rough session with the Department of Justice or the Federal Trade Commission—as some very prominent companies have recently found out. But even without such malpractices, prices can be stabilized.

One thing is clear. The public draws the line when bigness becomes monopoly. Opinion is clearly defined on that point. It is not merely because monopoly is a bad word; the semantics of the situation have been fortified by experience. If an American gets mad at his car when designers go crazy, and a salesman pushes him to pay for chromium he doesn't want, he likes to change to another make. If fed up with a refrigerator company that makes him buy a new machine when all he needs is a ten-dollar replacement for an old part, he wants a different dealer. If he has difficulty at his bank, he feels safer when there is another bank available.

He is reconciled to "natural monopolies" like telephone systems and electric light companies—but only because (after a long and now-forgotten fight) he has the Federal Communications Commission and local Public Service Commissions to protect his rights. If bigness means monopoly, he doesn't want it, but he will go along with it—as in the latter examples—if he knows there is Government supervision and regulation.

In former days it was said that the public wanted a "competitive free market." This was nineteenth-century economic language. I doubt whether very many Americans know the difference between a competitive free market and a follow-the-leader market today. Or would care much if they did. They want prices kept "reasonable" (meaning a figure they can pay without too much pain). They believe, rightly, that two or three concerns looking for business will police each other. The actual bigness of the concerns does not seem to worry them. If anything, they rather like it.

The pattern of American business shows this. In most industries —in addition to the regulated transport, communication and public-utility companies, which are large, anyhow—there is bigness. In each industry, two, three, four or five companies account for from two-thirds to five-sixths of all production and sales in the field. Behind them trail some dozens of smaller companies who are, in the language of the bigs, "allowed to live."

Outside the service and fashion trades, where individuality counts for everything, this is the normal situation. There are some exceptions: real estate, for example, where anyone can get into the game, and banking, where the law does not allow country-wide branch banking and the Federal Reserve really controls the show.

In fact, though not yet in law, the Department of Justice is allergic to bigness carried beyond a certain point. Legally, the anti-trust acts forbid only "monopoly" and conspiracy or agreements "in restraint of competition or trade." Unless it violates these strictures, any corporation can, in theory, be as big as it likes. But when it becomes really big, as some of the automobile and electronics and bank holding companies are big, the Anti-trust Division starts paying attention.

The company's next move—say, a merger with a smaller corporation—prompts immediate investigation. The technical question, of course, is whether the new acquisition appreciably restrains or eliminates competition. But behind this there is an emotional attitude: ought this corporation be allowed to own as much as it does?

I have, unworthily, wondered whether the Supreme Court's decision requiring du Pont to get rid of its stockholdings in General Motors did not reflect some of this emotion. Technically, of course, the Supreme Court held that because of du Pont's stockholdings, General Motors was likely to buy paint and supplies only from du Pont, thus cutting out du Pont's competitors. But the memory of Louis Brandeis' attitude is still strong in the court.

My own thinking, for whatever it is worth, is a trifle unfashionable, but I think justified by facts. Bigness is here to stay because it is needed. The United States is bigger and can take it. The population of the United States has doubled since Brandeis wrote his famous article. The gross national product (after allowing for depreciation of the dollar) is at least six times as large.

And the shape of the economy has changed. It is now, besides being tremendous, more mobile, more complex, enormously mechanized and intricately tied together. Its basic services, such as transport and communications, must go on, uniformly and without interruption. Production, manufacture and distribution of basic natural resources—oil, steel, copper, chemicals—must be continuous. Living standards, for better or for worse, have become more uniform and Americans want about the same products in Portland, Ore., as in Boulder or Bayonne.

Mass markets mean mass enterprise and uniform service means huge organization. Preferably these enterprises will work out at, or near, "optimum size." In many, perhaps most, lines, this means bigness. There are additional advantages: big concerns regularly (perhaps under compulsion) provide better pay and working conditions and are moving toward more continuous employment. And they can take chances in developing new products and processes that smaller concerns cannot.

But, as the Government figures show, there is a stratum of small enterprise, comprising about one-third of all private business. No herd of behemoths has yet occupied, or ought ever to occupy, the whole living-space of new ideas and new possibilities. There is now, and should always be, opportunity for a Henry Ford tinkering with a horseless carriage in a barn; for a trio of young engineers working on a sun-powered battery; for a zealot cooking up an electric generator that anyone can put in his cellar and use to illuminate his house.

If the American system ever puts a stop to this sort of effort, its growth rate will slow down. Its "bigs" will grow torpid. Worse yet, it will lose its most priceless asset—a steady supply of men who buck the system, establish their right to manage and become available to direct the biggest—or the smallest—enterprise. We do moderately well in using bigness. But we have, and must maintain, our respectable areas of smallness.

The results are not bad, and not perfect. Better financial support should be made available to the "smalls," especially when they begin to grow. The Federal Government is beginning to recognize this need. I think more can be done toward liberalizing patent laws, too, so that small concerns can have as ready access to the technical heritage of the country as do the big corporations, with their huge research laboratories. Mergers are not objectionable if they do not unduly narrow this creative economic belt. They become deadly dangerous when they do.

These are, I think, the tests to apply when one reads that the Central has merged with the Pennsy, or Eastern Airlines with American. Not size, but results, dictate the answer.

The Threat of Bigness

LETTER TO THE EDITOR:

A. A. Berle's interesting article, "Bigness: Curse or Opportunity?" which appeared in a recent issue of your magazine, may be answered by pointing out that mass production is not necessarily associated with great size. Thus, for many years a single so-called "ribbon" machine was capable of producing 800,000 light bulbs a day, or more than one-third of the nation's needs for a year. The acceptance by the American public of varied types of foreign cars attests to the fact that the American consumer is receptive to variety as well as to uniformity.

I think that this country does need big companies as well as small ones. The trouble arises when we forget that the reason for the existence of many large companies is not necessarily a justification for the gargantuan size of our more enormous business behemoths.

It is hardly public apathy that has spurred the activities of the Small Business Committees of both the House and the Senate. It has not been public apathy which, in the last eight years, has led to an intensified effort by Government agencies to utilize the anti-merger statutes, or which prompted Congress to enact the two major anti-merger statutes in the banking field in 1956 and 1960.

Efficiency does not necessarily increase with the size of a company. Thus Prof. Joe S. Bain, in the March, 1954, issue of American Economic Review, made a study of twenty manufacturing industries and concluded that economies "of the scale of firm beyond the size of a single optimum plant were either negligible or totally absent."

Mr. Berle feels that bigness makes for innovation and research. But the risk of cost of change in monolithic companies is often so great that many prefer to remain in status quo, until forced to change by the proven success of smaller competitors. Thus, it took the American motor industry a number of years to get around to compact cars—after the invasion of the market by the foreign manufacturers. Even though imitators, the capital resources of the big fellows are such that the general public associates a particular product with them rather than with the smaller originator.

The simple truth is that kudos for innovation and research cannot be confined to either large or small companies.

Convincing proof has yet to be presented to warrant accepting the danger of bigness with complacency.

EMANUEL CELLER,
Chairman, Committee on the Judiciary,
House of Representatives,
Washington, D.C.

A Defense of Bigness in Business

by Sumner H. Slichter

THE RECENT DECISION of the Supreme Court in the du Pont–General Motors case suggests the desirability of a review and an appraisal of American policy toward competition, monopoly, and bigness in business. The decision reveals the strong determination of the court to prevent competition from being weakened and the court's willingness to resort to controversial interpretations of the law in order to implement the public policy of preventing restraints on competition.

But the decision also reminds us that much thinking on the relation of bigness to competition is out of date and unrealistic. Hence, the adaptation of traditional American anti-trust policy to the facts of modern industry requires that we take a fresh look at the role of large enterprises in American business—particularly the role of large enterprises as a source of vigorous and dynamic competition.

When one compares the economy of the United States with the economies of other advanced industrial countries, four characteristics stand out conspicuously.

(1) The Government of the United States endeavors through broad and drastic laws to prevent restraints on competition and

From the *New York Times Magazine,* August 4, 1957, copyright © 1957 by The New York Times Company.

to forestall the growth of monopoly. Most other advanced industrial countries either tolerate considerable restraint on competition or even encourage organizations of businessmen that are designed to control competition.

(2) Competition in American industry is far more vigorous and pervasive than in the industries of any other advanced industrial country. Indeed, the vigor of competition in the United States almost invariably attracted comment from the European productivity teams that visited this country in the years following the war.

(3) The United States has many more huge business enterprises than any other country. Several years ago this country had more than 100 corporations (exclusive of purely financial ones) with assets of more than $250 million each. General Motors produces far more cars than the combined British, German and French automobile industries, and the United States Steel Corporation produces more steel than the entire British steel industry.

(4) Production in many American industries (especially those requiring large capital investment) is highly concentrated in the hands of a few large concerns. As a general rule, the concentration of production in other industrial countries is far less than here.

These four characteristics of the American economy are not unrelated. It would be wrong to ascribe the widespread and intense competition in American industry *solely* to the strong public policy against restraint of trade, monopolization and interference with competition. Conditions in the United States—the absence of class lines, the abundance of opportunity, the weakness of tradition—have long made life here highly competitive in all its aspects, and competition in business is just one manifestation of this general competitive spirit. But America's unique and firm public policy against restraints on competition has undoubtedly helped greatly to keep industry here strongly competitive.

This strong policy, however, has paradoxically encouraged the development of giant industrial corporations and the concentration of production in many industries among a few large concerns. The growth of enterprises in Europe has been limited by the practice of forming cartels—a practice which governments have tolerated and even encouraged. The cartel or trade association divides markets among its members, limits the growth of the most efficient concerns, and assures the weak, high-cost concern a share of the market.

In the United States, where cartels are illegal, each concern is pretty completely exposed to competition from all other firms, and business goes to the firms that can get it. This means that in many industries production is gradually concentrated in the hands of a few industrial giants, and only a small part of the business is left for small firms.

The trend toward corporate bigness in industry has led many students of anti-monopoly policy to believe that the American policy of encouraging competition and discouraging monopoly is turning out to be a failure and to conclude that steps need to be taken to limit the influences of large enterprises in American industry. Of many proposals that have been made, two principal ones are of particular interest.

One proposal is that new restrictions be placed on mergers. Some have urged that no merger be permitted which cannot be justified by technological reasons. Some have proposed that mergers involving a corporation above a given size be prohibited unless found by the Federal Trade Commission to be in the public interest.

The second proposal deals with the concentration of production in various industries into a few enterprises. It is urged that the Government undertake a comprehensive survey of American industry to determine whether enterprises exceed the size required by modern technology and that the Government be authorized to break up large firms that are unnecessarily large.

Both of these proposals are based on fallacy. They rest upon a mistaken conception of the role of large corporations in American business and particularly upon the relation of large corporations to competition. Each, if put into effect, would weaken rather than strengthen competition. In fact, in order to stimulate competition, existing restrictions on mergers should be relaxed, not tightened, and large enterprises, instead of being threatened with break-up, should be given a clear mandate to grow, provided they use fair means. Let us examine more completely each of these two proposals to restrict the growth of enterprises.

I.

The proposal that new restrictions be placed on mergers arises from the fact that the United States in recent years has been experiencing a great wave of mergers. But recent mergers have not weakened competition. On the contrary, they have indirectly strengthened it because they have enabled managements to build more diversified and better-integrated enterprises—enterprises which are more capable of reaching all parts of the vast domestic market, of adapting themselves to market shifts and changes in technology, of riding out the ups and downs of business, and of supporting technological research and development. Many large firms and firms of moderate size have acquired small firms, but the acquisitions by the very largest firms have not been numerous.

The specific circumstances surrounding each merger are unique, but a case-by-case examination shows how mergers are helping to build stronger enterprises, better able to compete and to hold their own in competition.

Let us consider a few examples. A maker of cans bought a concern manufacturing plastic pipe in order to get a foothold in the plastic pipe business. A maker of railroad freight cars bought companies making electrical equipment, truck trailers and dairy supplies in order to shift from a declining business to expanding businesses. A food manufacturer bought a West Coast manufacturer of salad seasoning in order to give nation-wide distribution to its product. A maker of household ware bought a supplier in order to have a source of pressed wood handles for its appliances.

Unusually competent managements often buy other concerns so that they can spread good administrative methods to less efficiently operated enterprises.

The many advantages produced by mergers show that the proposal that mergers be prohibited unless they can be justified by technological reasons does not make sense. There are good reasons for mergers that have nothing to do with technology.

Moreover, it would be unwise to require Government approval of all mergers involving an enterprise above a specified size. That would be substituting the decision of Government officials for the decision of businessmen on matters that the businessmen are better able to understand. The public interest is amply protected by the present drastic provision of Section 7 of the Clayton Act.

Indeed, the fact that mergers often make for more vigorous competition by helping managements build stronger and more efficient business enterprises indicates the need for relaxing the present severe restrictions on mergers contained in Section 7 of the Clayton Act. This section prohibits any merger which is likely to lessen competition substantially in *any* line of commerce. The fact that the merger may increase the intensity of competition in *other* lines of commerce makes no difference. As Section 7 now reads, the *total effect* of the merger on competition is irrelevant. If it is likely to lessen competition substantially in any one line of commerce, it is illegal.

Obviously, the section as it now reads conflicts with the national policy of encouraging competition. It should be rewritten to make the legality of mergers depend upon the *total* effect on competition, thus permitting any merger that has the net effect of increasing competition.

II.

The second proposal—to remake the structure of American industry by breaking up the largest enterprises—rests upon the mistaken view that, where output is concentrated among a few concerns, effective competition does not occur. The error of this view is shown by the vigorous competition in various industries in which most of the output is made by a few firms—in such industries as the automobile, tire, refrigerator, soap, cigarette, paper products, television and many others.

There are two principal reasons why competition tends to be vigorous when production is concentrated among a few large concerns. One is that such enterprises keep close track of their rank in sales and fight hard to move ahead of rivals or to avoid being surpassed by rivals. The second reason, and one that is rapidly gaining in importance, is the fact that competition among large firms is being stimulated by the growth of technological research.

It is only within the last several decades that managements have generally discovered the big returns yielded by technological research. As a result, the outlays by private industry on research and development increased nearly six-fold between 1940 and 1953. In 1957, the total research and development expenditures of private industry, exclusive of the aircraft industry, which is a special case, are running about 71 per cent greater than they were in 1953. By 1960 outlays on research are expected to be 21 per cent above 1957.

No expenditures are more competitive than outlays on research, for the purpose of these expenditures is to improve products, develop new products and cut costs. More than 70 per cent of the outlays on research and development are made by firms with 5,000 or more employes because concerns with large sales can best afford this overhead expense. Hence the rapidly mounting outlays on research indicate both the growing competitiveness of American industry and the increasingly important role large enterprises are playing in making competition more intense.

Incidentally, competition among large firms is superior in quality to competition among small firms and serves consumers more effectively. This is because the greater research by the large firms gives the consumers a wider range of choice over a period of years than competition among a much larger number of small firms that can afford little or no research. The large firms are constantly experimenting with new features in their products which they hope will win the favor of consumers. Sometimes consumers like the new features, sometimes they do not, but at any rate they have been given a choice. In general, the wider the range of choice open to consumers, the more effectively is the welfare of consumers advanced.

In view of the growing importance of large enterprises as a source of competition and the superior quality of this competition, a move to break up large concerns would be a blunder. There is much to be said, however, in favor of incentives for enterprises to split themselves voluntarily, if the managements consider a split desirable. The resulting increase in the number of top managements with independent authority to make policies and to try experiments would be favorable to technological progress—provided the concerns are large enough to support extensive research. A good incentive for voluntary splits would be created by relieving stockholders from liability for the capital gains tax on the appreciation in their holdings from the time they purchased the stock up to the date of the split.

But enforced splitting of enterprises, except as a remedy for flagrant monopolizing of trade by unscrupulous methods, would be another matter. It would be demoralizing to managements to be penalized for winning customers by having to submit to an enforced disruption of their organizations.

In fact, the present law needs to be clarified in order to encourage a few of the very largest concerns to strive harder for a bigger share of the market. The Sherman Act forbids monopolization of commerce or attempts to monopolize it. In general, successful growth, due to superior efficiency and not aided by illegal practices, does not violate the law provided there is no deliberate attempt to acquire monopoly power. But what practices are evidence of "deliberate attempts" to achieve monopoly power?

The managements of a few very large and efficient concerns apparently fear that efforts to get more business by cutting prices will be held to be attempts to monopolize. There is need to make clear that efforts to win business by giving consumers the benefits of low costs will not be regarded as monopolistic.

Americans should hold fast to their traditional views of the importance of vigorous competition in industry. This philosophy and the actual practice of vigorous competition have been unique and invaluable national assets which have contributed immensely to the progressiveness and efficiency of industry in the United States.

But Americans need to discard some widely held but out-of-date views concerning the relationship between bigness and competition. They need to grasp the fact that when production is concentrated among a few large concerns rivalries become peculiarly intense and the additional fact that in an age of technological research the large enterprise is an increasingly important source of competition.

Americans need to understand that a variety of conditions— rapidly changing technology, the growing importance of industrial research, the growing strength of trade unions—tends to increase in many industries the size of the enterprise that is able both to compete and to survive in competition. Hence, we are likely to see a spread of the tendency for production to be concentrated in a few large or fairly large firms.

But this trend, if it occurs, should not disturb us. It will simply represent an adaptation of industry to the conditions of the time.

The strength of competition in American industry will to an increasing extent be determined by the scale of technological research and development. Research will grow as rapidly as engineers and scientists can be found to man the laboratories. Hence, one can predict with confidence that competition in American industry will continue to gain in intensity. And large enterprises, far from being a menace, will, to a growing extent, be the instruments by which the country is given the benefit of large-scale technological research and of increasingly vigorous competition.

On Bigness in Business

LETTER TO THE EDITOR:

In his article, "A Defense of Bigness in Business," (Aug. 4) Sumner H. Slichter recognizes the many positive values contributed to the United States economy by competition under America's unique antitrust policy. Mr. Slichter accurately points out that this competition has contributed to the development in the United States of huge business enterprises that alone account for more production than do entire industries in other free countries.

None the less, despite his recognition of these benefits, in a puzzling course of reasoning Mr. Slichter arrives at the strange conclusion that the best way for the American people to assure continuation of the benefits from competition is to relax the antitrust laws that prohibit mergers and to relax existing prohibitions against monopolization.

Mr. Slichter would have us believe that some mysterious alchemy provided by the economic planning and technological research of the leaders of our largest corporations would convert his proposed antitrust relaxations into stimuli for increased competition. My own experience from Congressional investigations into the activities of corporate executives brings me to sharply different conclusions. For a number of years I have been privileged to serve as chairman of special committees with jurisdiction to investigate antitrust subjects. Investigations into the operations of a number of industries has convinced me that to preserve the competition that is so essential to American economic well-being we must have, indeed, a more vigilant application of our antitrust standards. A selective strengthening, not a relaxation, of our antitrust laws is required to remove deficiencies as they are disclosed by our antitrust enforcement officials.

The course of action Mr. Slichter recommends not only would fail to preserve the competitive values he praises, but, on the contrary, I believe would do much to destroy competition.

One of the primary reasons Mr. Slichter fails to recognize any danger from the growth of the "concentrate" pattern in American industry, and which underlies his plea for relaxation of our antitrust safeguards, is the competition he foresees in the fields of research and development. This type of competition, I believe, does not afford sufficient protection to the public.

There is unanswered as yet the question of the optimum size that is needed to support an aggressive and productive research laboratory. It cannot for example, be contended successfully that, had the Government in its antitrust case against A. T. & T. been able to secure a separation of Western Electric from A. T. & T. and the Bell Laboratories, either entity would have lacked ample resources for independent research. Had such a separation occurred and independent research organizations been established, it seems probable that Western Electric would have been in a position to give effective competition to R. C. A. and Westinghouse in many electronic fields. Interjection of independent rivalry in these fields could not but have been of benefit to the public.

Mr. Slichter also holds that the current wave of industrial mergers has not weakened industrial rivalry. On the contrary, he is of the opinion that mergers have strengthened competition. His views are not shared by most of the Government officials who have had occasion to examine this problem.

Mr. Slichter expresses concern over the Supreme Court's ruling in the duPont case. It must be borne in mind however, that the court there found: ". . . that duPont purposely employed its stock to pry open the General Motors market to entrench itself as the primary supplier of General Motors' requirements for automotive finishes and fabrics."

And, particularly, the Court further found: "The fire that was kindled in 1917 continues to smolder. It burned briskly to forge the ties that bind the General Motors market to duPont, and if it has quieted down, it remains hot, and, from past performance, is likely at any time to blaze and make the fusion complete."

Surely, if any effect at all is to be given to the policy for competition expressed in our antitrust laws, combinations of the magnitude involved in General Motors-duPont must be reached and stricken down. There should be no relaxation in our antitrust laws which would enable such combinations to be consummated legally.

EMANUEL CELLER

Competitors Unsure I.B.M. Should Be Split

by William D. Smith

SUPERSTITION HOLDS that births and deaths come in threes. For the International Business Machines Corporation, anti-trust suits have just arrived in threes.

The first was filed on Dec. 11 by the Control Data Corporation, a major I.B.M. competitor in the large-scale end of the computer business. Shortly afterward, the Data Processing and Financial General Corporation, a leasing company, filed an action.

The final bomb, which fell on Jan. 17 as the last gasp of the Justice Department under President Johnson, was an anti-trust move against I.B.M.

None of the suits was entirely unexpected, although I.B.M. had done its best to avoid them. Doing its best included hiring Burke Marshall, a former top Justice Department anti-truster, as general counsel. Mr. Marshall has moved to the company's management committee and has been replaced by Nicholas deB. Katzenbach, another former Justice Department luminary.

The cry is "break up I.B.M.," but many of the complaining voices are not so sure the giant computer company can be effectively and fairly dismembered.

A number of others are not so sure they want to see it happen anyway.

I.B.M. is already a giant company but some day in the future it may be the largest commercial enterprise in the world. That is, unless the present anti-trust suits take a serious toll of the corporation's vitality.

The computer business is presently the world's fastest growing industry and some day in the not distant future it may be the largest as well.

Above these facts floats the I.B.M. mystique, a reputation of near-invincibility that has been earned by hard work, hard sell and, some say, hard-heartedness.

If one were asked to identify the company that represented the best in American business techniques, I.B.M. would probably be the overwhelming pick by serious students of the free-enterprise system.

Isaac Auerbach, president of Auerbach Associates and a former president of the International Federation of Information Processing Societies, has commented, "The Control Data suit is the greatest paean of praise to I.B.M. I have ever read. It accuses them of doing everything so damned well that other companies just can't keep up."

"Doing everything so damned well" has enabled I.B.M. to dominate the computer business in a way no other company dominates any other major market. General Motors has slightly more than 50 per cent of the United States auto business and about one-third of the non-Communist world's car trade. United States Steel has less than 25 per cent of the domestic steel market. The Standard Oil Company (New Jersey) has about 15 per cent of the non-Communist crude production.

I.B.M. shipped 76 per cent of the value of all general-purpose computers in the United States in 1967, according to the Justice Department suit. Overseas, it has more than two-thirds of the market.

The Justice Department suit asks the court for divorcement, divestiture and reorganization of I.B.M. to alleviate what the Government believes are illegal practices.

How to do this without hampering the industry's growth and

without unjustly crippling I.B.M. is a major question presently being batted around data processing circles.

"Remember, I.B.M. is not General Motors where the Chevrolet division could probably be broken out with very little trouble. Computer software is tied up with hardware, peripheral devices must interface with the central computer and be capable of being driven by the software. It is all part of a whole fabric that can't be broken apart very easily."

The Government has also asked that I.B.M. be made to separate its pricing for computer hardware, peripheral equipment, software and customer support or maintenance.

I.B.M. presently sells or leases a computer for a fixed fee that covers all costs.

Its competitors, especially leasing companies and software concerns, charge that this practice has prevented their growth. "Who is going to pay for something when they think they are getting it free?" they ask.

Jim Arachtingi, a vice president of Auerbach Pollach & Richardson, Inc., a Wall Street investment house specializing in technological issues, commented, "Some people think that the antitrust action is great for the independents and bad for I.B.M. I think this is wrong."

"I.B.M. was probably moving toward separate pricing for inside economic reasons anyway. The great cost in the computer business is the price you pay for skilled people. Separate pricing may enable I.B.M. to make the present people costs of software and maintenance profit centers in their own right."

Mr. Arachtingi disagrees with the contention that separate pricing will be great for the independents because it will enable them to sell toe to toe with I.B.M. He commented, "The Justice Department probably is running a more serious risk of doing damage to other companies rather than I.B.M. by requesting separate pricing."

He asks, "Who in the industry will be able to compete with I.B.M. on a price basis if I.B.M. wants to bear down?" He pointed out that I.B.M.'s hard-sell tactics have never included price cutting and that I.B.M. equipment has usually sold at between 10 and 20 per cent above competitor's products.

"This created an umbrella under which other companies could sell and still make a profit. Take this umbrella away and some companies will suffer."

Nonetheless, Mr. Arachtingi thinks that separate pricing could be a shot in the arm to the software business, but only for the strong companies. A profit-conscious I.B.M. software operation could push the industry to greater heights, creating a bigger pie in which all the solid companies could share.

The decision on the case will be far in the future. The implications will be even farther.

The Shape of Things

by Raymond J. Saulnier

THE NEW INDUSTRIAL STATE. By John Kenneth Galbraith. 427 pp.
Boston: Houghton Mifflin Company. $6.95.

Of his new book, John K. Galbraith says that it stands in relation to "The Affluent Society" as a house to a window, an apt and
useful contrast. The 1958 volume afforded a view of consumption
as one aspect of American life; "The New Industrial State," on
the other hand, deals with the whole structure of American society,
centering on its economic institutions, and Mr. Galbraith argues
a theory of how it has come to be what it is.

This is a tightly organized, closely reasoned book, notable for
what it says about the dynamics of institutional change and for certain qualities of its author: a sardonic wit, exercised liberally at the
expense of conservatives, and unusual perception. That the latter
in fact produces slightly out-of-focus images of reality (the key to
understanding Mr. Galbraith) makes it, in a way, all the more
interesting.

Although the book's theoretical structure is formidable, its
architecture is not particularly novel. It is strongly reminiscent of,
among American writings, Thorstein Veblen's "The Engineers and
the Price System" (1921); among contemporary writers, Robert
Heilbroner and Daniel Bell come to mind as social scientists ex-
ploring the same range of problems and coming to broadly similar
conclusions.

From the *New York Times Book Review,* June 25, 1967, copyright © 1967
by The New York Times Company.

But novelty isn't everything: one can make a decent case for the proposition that it is more important to be right than different. The critical question is whether Galbraith's building-blocks are sufficiently strong to support his structure. This reader thinks they are not. It is not that what he says on specific issues is completely wrong. Rather, what he says is just true enough to be plausible, but not true enough to make a convincing case. In the end, what Mr. Galbraith presents is a shaky edifice.

Briefly, his theory of social change is technological determinism. As he sees it, modern technology has two principal effects. First, it is so intricate as a process that it can be practiced only by highly specialized professionals operating primarily in groups, their individuality largely submerged in a world of committees within committees. They constitute what he calls the "technostructure" and have a counterpart in government. After the technostructure, the second major creation of modern technology is the "mature corporation," which comes into being because it is the only entity able to supply the organization of effort and the large amounts of capital required to make technology work. In this context, the anti-trust laws lose their meaning. Such commitments of specialized professional personnel and capital make planning by industry an absolute requirement of survival; because so much is at stake, the mature corporation can take no chances. The security of the technostructure, made increasingly precarious by specialization, requires that things be arranged in advance.

What remains for Galbraith to explain—and this constitutes the major part of his book—is how the mature corporation, in an increasingly intimate alliance with government, arranges things so they come out as the technostructure wants and needs them to come out. It will be no surprise to those familiar with his views that Galbraith sees not the slightest chance of accomplishing this by the simple expedient of being informed of consumer wants and organizing to supply them. The market is not reliable: demand and supply must be managed. Advertising takes care very nicely of the consumer's specific choices in spending income; and the possibility that over-all purchasing power might be inadequate—a calamity the technostructure, as such, would be powerless to prevent —is eliminated by fiscal and monetary policies under which government maintains aggregate demand at all times at appropriate levels.

Next, the mature corporation has achieved security against two additional industrial risks: the need to rely on capital markets for financing, with all that that means in accountability to outsiders, and the pressure of trade union demands. As Galbraith sees it, internally generated funds free the mature corporation from dependency on bankers; and a benign state, more and more seen by industry as a partner in its affairs, has largely neutralized trade union power through wage guideposts. Whatever remains of what Galbraith once regarded as the countervailing power of trade unionism is being eliminated by technology, which tends to ally the worker more and more with the technostructure.

Finally, through large military and space expenditures—also useful for maintaining aggregate demand—government underwrites research and development that goes beyond the resources of even the mature corporation, e.g., the supersonic transport, but which is essential to the full flowering of the technostructure. All in all, a pretty tidy world.

Galbraith gives relatively little attention to the question of where this is leading us, but from what he says, and from what is implied by his dialectic, I judge that what might emerge is a kind of "corporative state." In any case, he sees the technostructure of business and government tending to merge into a single technocratic class and pretty much taking charge of things. The one group capable of humanizing the institutional change technology is propelling, and of keeping it on a democratic path, is the "educational and scientific estate." If Galbraith has heroes, they are here.

So much for the essentials of the theory. The crucial question in evaluating it is whether corporate enterprise and government have in fact achieved the degree of control he attributes to them. It is not enough to say they have achieved important control; the question is whether the process has gone far enough to have produced the institutional transformation his theory implies.

In the first place, is the consumer the manipulated, accurately forecastable, somehow faceless figure he is pictured as being, buying what he is told to buy at prices and in amounts that suit the convenience and security of the technostructure? Without meaning to underrate the adman's successes, I suggest that there is little in experience or logic to support this view. If advertising had the power here alleged, would a product ever lose its market position, let alone fall altogether? But the record is full of fatalities; indeed it is rare that a product, design or style, no matter how much advertising money is spent, does not at some point fall from favor. By some beneficent law of nature, admen consume admen.

Second, there is no evidence that corporate enterprise has achieved meaningful financial independence. In the years 1960–65, corporations went to the market for one-third of their capital requirements; and last summer a good many treasurers got a quick course of instruction in the virtues of liquidity.

Third, the familiar concept of separation of corporate ownership from control, a piece of now-conventional wisdom that is a key building-block in Galbraith's structure, is actually quite obsolete. It misses entirely the hawk-eye surveillance of corporate management by institutional investors and security analysts, all surrogates of the individual shareholder and, Galbraith notwithstanding, still very much interested in profit maximization. As for comfortable independence, it would be difficult to name a figure on the American scene, political personages not excepted, more closely monitored than the head of a large corporation.

Fourth, contrary to what Galbraith states or implies, there is no convincing empirical evidence of a trend toward greater concentration in markets (for example, in the findings of the Senate Judiciary subcommittee that recently studied this question); there is no basis for asserting that a market with only a few large suppliers (an oligopoly) cannot be intensely competitive, and no *a priori* reason why oligopoly cannot be economically efficient.

Finally, is the technostructure, through its alliance with government, protected against cost increases, and assured of never-failing aggregate demand? Was not 1966 the year the wage guideposts collapsed? And has it not been demonstrated in the past nine months that even with military expenditures approaching $75-billion a year, there is still a risk of recession? It is part of the now-conventional wisdom that the state can prevent such mishaps, but there they are—accompanied, moreover, by budget deficits that could exceed $25 billion a year and a payments imbalance that threatens both the international monetary system and the nation's gold supply.

What it all comes to is that the U. S. economy is not as neatly buttoned-up as Mr. Galbraith's book would lead one to believe. He disarms potential critics with occasional displays of modesty: "Truth is never strengthened by exaggeration" (p. 165) and "I argue only for a complex two-way flow of influence" (p. 317). But his argument is basically dogmatic. Its elements are sufficiently out of focus to produce a distorted over-all picture.

This is not to deny there is a risk that our economy, in its relation to government, will evolve into the near-monolithic shape implied by Galbraith's theory. But if it does, I doubt it will do so by the route he has sketched. Unfortunately, there is more than one road to the monolithic society. A possibility altogether too likely is that basically inflationary fiscal and monetary policies will be persisted in, will invite more and more pervasive regulation of prices and profits and will in the end amount to a suppression of private undertakings.

There is an extremely important difference between these two possible roads to statism: there is a certain inevitability implied in Galbraith's (basically, the evolution is propelled by the invisible hand of modern technology) but no parallel inevitability about the second (in which man-made decisions are decisive). Moreover, as a theory of institutional change, the second has three notable merits: it is a better fit to the facts; it places responsibility where responsibility belongs; and it provides more basis for hope that genuinely democratic institutions can be preserved.

But this is another story; for the moment, it is pertinent only to repeat one's admiration for Mr. Galbraith's considerable intellectual achievement. "The New Industrial State" deserves the widest possible attention and discussion. It will provoke much argument among economists; it may well inspire graduate schools of business to ask new questions about what they are doing; and, hopefully, it will provide a conversation-piece in executive dining rooms. All in all, a constructive result.

Part 6

MERGERS AND CONGLOMERATE COMBINATIONS

MERGERS PROVIDE a convenient means for corporate expansion and growth. Generally, there are three kinds: horizontal, vertical, and conglomerate. Horizontal mergers refer to the absorption of firms in the same line of business (for example, one automobile manufacturer acquires another automobile manufacturer). Vertical mergers refer to expansion backward to the source of supply, or forward to sales and distribution outlets (for example, an automobile manufacturer buys a steel mill or a series of retail sales outlets). Conglomerate mergers refer to the acquisition of unlike product lines (for example, an automobile company purchases a computer manufacturer).

The effects of mergers have long been a matter of concern for public policy. Growth by horizontal merger results in an increase in concentration in a given market, and, therefore, an increase in monopoly or oligopoly power. Vertical mergers pose problems in the sense that the vertically integrated firm may be able to squeeze nonintegrated competitors. The conglomerate is the newest form of merger, and in some ways the most mystifying. It is not clear that the conglomerate will always weaken competition. Indeed, it may introduce innovative pressures in the short run, depending on the market structures involved. The increased hostility of many managers to conglomerate takeovers attests to this fact. In addition, the conglomerate firm holds a special attractiveness for prospective buyers and sellers of corporate properties. Diversification, risk minimization, increased efficiency, improved earnings, and financial manipulation all have a unique appeal to the parties involved. Nevertheless, the conglomerate, like all forms of mergers, suffers when viewed from the standpoint of the public interest, because it tends to foster a hardening of market structures in the long run and increased overall corporate concentration.

The collection of articles in this section relates primarily to the merger wave of the late sixties which involved the meteoric rise of the "new" generation of conglomerates. J. J. Abele's essay serves as an introduction by recounting some of the more bizarre mergers and the diverse reasons for them. In the second article, Harvey H. Segal presents an overview of the logic of the conglomerate as a means for growth and expansion, the forces checking this growth, and the implications for competition and public policy. In the third article, R. D. Hershey examines the intriguing role of the large banks in promoting mergers. In the fourth article, Abele focuses attention on the fact that the recent wave of mergers is an assault on the corporate establishment that has led to much anxiety among corporate managements that previously felt immune to takeover. Finally, Isadore Barmash raises a valuable point by calling attention to those factors, including the prompt full disclosure of merger negotiations, which cause merger plans to collapse. Such factors deserve more attention.

Analysts Look for the Logic in Multi-Industry Mergers

by John J. Abele

SOME CORPORATE mergers don't make sense—or do they?

That is a question bobbing around in the wake of a new rash of conglomerate or multi-industry mergers in which a company in one field weds with another in a completely different field.

In the last two weeks, the whirl of the merger-go-round has involved proposed unions of companies through exchanges of securities with an aggregate value of about $2-billion.

It has produced such startling combinations as these:

¶A leading electronics company (Radio Corporation of America) and a major paper producer (St. Regis Paper).

¶An insurance company (I.N.A. Corporation) and an airline (World Airways).

¶An electronics company (Teledyne, Inc.) and an insurance company (Argonaut Insurance Company).

¶A finance company (Transamerica Corporation) and a broadcasting company (Metromedia, Inc.).

¶A carpet maker (Mohasco, Inc) and a manufacturer of plumbing equipment (American-Standard, Inc.).

¶A producer of communications equipment (International Telephone and Telegraph Corporation) and a vending machine and food-service organization (Canteen Corporation).

Cross-industry mergers are old stuff for I.T.T., which in the past has acquired such diverse companies as Avis, Inc., the car rental company; Levitt & Sons, the home builders; Rayonier, Inc., a woodpulp manufacturer; and Sheraton Corporation, the hotel chain. Currently pending for I.T.T. are acquisitions of the Continental Baking Company and the Thorp Finance Company.

The seeming incongruity of these crazy-quilt moves frequently puzzles observers of the financial scene, including stockholders of the companies involved. It also has produced some cross-fire between security analysts accustomed to judging companies on a one-industry basis.

The proposed union of R.C.A. and St. Regis, for example, has drawn a cool reception from analysts in the electronics and paper fields.

The electronics analysts question how St. Regis, which has had an erratic earnings record despite a steady rise in sales to last year's record of $722-million, will be able to help R.C.A., whose profits have marched upward for the last seven years. They also take a dim view of the addition of a cyclical, commodity-type business such as paper to the glamorous world of electronics.

Analysts of the paper industry, on the other hand, concede that the industry does have some Plain Jane aspects, but they are also aware of the value of St. Regis's extensive reserves of timber and land and the profit potential of new production facilities. They question whether the company is letting itself go at a rather cheap price.

A problem that frequently confronts the management of an acquired company, however, is that the value of its assets and earnings power may not be recognized in the stock market.

R.C.A.'s willingness to buy St. Regis, for example, pushed the paper company's stock as high as $43.50 a share, a level it has not seen for seven years.

The management of R.C.A., it would appear, sees something in St. Regis that other investors have not. And St. Regis, for its part, apparently believes its stockholders would receive a price for their shares from R.C.A. that other investors were not willing to give them.

Conceivably, R.C.A. could dress up St. Regis's earnings a bit by selling off some of its landholdings, reaping a capital gains profit, or by increasing cutting of the company's timber, bringing in more capital gains and some favorable tax considerations as well.

The R.C.A.–St. Regis situation points up the two key ingredients an acquiring company is seeking to achieve through an acquisition: assets and earnings.

The assets can either be liquidated in whole or in part, providing the acquirer with additional funds, or they can be used as part of a broader financial base that the acquiring company can use to borrow funds to carry out other expansion and diversification moves.

Part of the earnings can be used to pay off the costs of the acquisition, whether in the form of dividends on common or preferred stock or debt interest on money borrowed to make the acquisition, and the balance can be added to the profits of the acquiring company, making its stock more valuable.

"A company can buy earnings for a while, but it eventually gets to a point where it needs assets to provide a broader borrowing base," declares Roland B. Williams, a security analyst who follows conglomerate companies for E. F. Hutton & Co., Inc.

Mr. Williams sees two principal reasons why companies in glamorous fields are interested in buying companies in more prosaic activities.

First, he says, is the possibility of what the new management can do with the acquired company's assets, either in the form of increased borrowing power or through adjustments in earnings that can result from conversion of some assets into cash.

Second, he says, is that the stocks of the less glamorous companies usually sell at reasonable levels in relation to their assets and earnings and can be acquired more cheaply than rapid-growth companies whose stocks are selling at loftier price-earnings multiples.

Other examples of what Wall Street calls an "asset play" abound in recent cross-industry mergers.

The acquisition of assets to increase borrowing power apparently was the major factor behind the recent proposal to combine the Xerox Corporation, the leading manufacturer of office copying equipment, and the C.I.T. Financial Corporation, a major sales financing concern.

The addition of slow-growing C.I.T. to fast-growing Xerox dismayed many adherents of Xerox, a feeling reflected in the persistent weakness of Xerox stock since the news was announced.

Those with more faith in Xerox, however, contend that the company must be planning a major expansion move in the future, one that would require far more financial resources than it would be able to muster on its own. The acquisition of C.I.T., which had assets of $3.4-billion at the end of last year, presumably would go a long way toward supplying that capability.

At the same time, Xerox will realize a significant addition to its profits by combining the earnings of C.I.T. with its own. (In 1967, Xerox earned $97-million and C.I.T.-$60-million.)

A similar move involved the combination of cash-shy Control Data Corporation, a major computer producer, with cash-rich Commercial Credit Corporation, a finance company that earlier had been sought by Loew's Theatres, a fast-growing hotel and theater chain.

Finance companies have been particular targets of many leading conglomerate companies. Gulf and Western Industries last week moved to complete the acquisition of Associates Investment Company, in which it already has a 92 per cent interest.

The Avco Corporation, another highly diversified company, has agreed to acquire the Seaboard Finance Company. Avco entered the financing field several years ago through the acquisition of the Delta Acceptance Corporation, a move that eventually set the stage for Avco's merger last year with the Paul Revere Corporation, an insurance organization.

Insurance companies also have become prime targets of conglomerate-oriented companies, many of whom regard insurance companies as "sleeping giants" with vast amounts of assets that can be gainfully employed in other pursuits.

Typically, insurance companies do not make much money on their insurance business—many write their underwriting results in red ink—but they do receive a large and steady flow of cash from their policy holders.

Insurance companies also have huge amounts of money invested in their portfolios of stocks and bonds. Profits from the investment side of the business often defray losses from the insurance side.

The investment portfolios present a tempting target for would-be acquirers. The City Investing Company, for example, recently acquired control of the Home Insurance Company, whose portfolio includes some $200-million in unrealized capital gains.

Conversion of part of those gains into cash would give City Investing substantial funds to expand its growing list of profitable manufacturing companies.

Two other conglomerates, National General Corporation and A.M.K. Corporation, have been waging a running fight for control of another insurance organization, the Great American Holding Corporation.

Great American, whose assets at the end of 1967 were $587-million, has agreed to a merger with A.M.K., a meat-packing and machinery company. But this deal appears to have been foiled by National General, which claims to have won 75 per cent of the insurance company's stock through a tender offer.

Some of the insurance companies have begun to turn the tables on the conglomerates by starting off on their own aggressive acquisition programs.

I.N.A. Corporation, formerly the Insurance Company of North America," has become something of an "instant conglomerate" through its plans to purchase World Airways; Winfield & Co., a mutual fund manager, and the Star Sprinkler Corporation, a maker of fire-prevention equipment.

The Urge to Merge — the Time of the Conglomerates

by Harvey H. Segal

AN ENCHANTMENT with innovation embraces all facets of contemporary society: the new writing, the new sound, the new politics. Micro-skirts and Nehru jackets, hirsute males and close-cropped females are conspicuous symbols of changing fashion. Computers and lasers, organ transplantation and space exploration foreshadow radical changes in the basis of physical life, while in business, the revolution is heralded by the rise of the conglomerate, the corporation that grows rapidly by moving into unrelated markets through mergers.

To the geologist, a conglomerate is a rock composed of stone fragments held together by hardened clay or some other cement. Analogously, the conglomerate corporation is a group of companies which operate in separate markets and are held together by bonds of financial and administrative authority.

Last month, the world of finance was agog with the announce-

From the *New York Times Magazine,* October 27, 1968, copyright © 1968 by The New York Times Company.

ment of what could be one of the largest mergers on record, the offer by the Xerox Corporation to buy control of the C.I.T. Financial Corporation. Xerox dominates the photocopying market and is moving into the fields of education, health and peripheral computer equipment. C.I.T., in addition to being the second largest commercial credit company, has moved into baking. X-ray equipment, insurance, office furniture and greeting cards. Clearly, a Xerox-C.I.T. union would be of the conglomerate type. But despite the size of the merger—C.I.T. has $3.4-billion in assets on its books, more than those of any company ever acquired by another—the merged corporation would not be nearly so diversified as some other conglomerates.

As an example of spectacular diversification consider the International Telephone and Telegraph Corporation. With $2.96-billion in assets at the end of 1967, I.T.T. ranked 17th among the nation's industrial companies. Originally an international communications company that still operates telephone systems and other enterprises in 123 countries, I.T.T. branched out first into the manufacture of telephonic equipment, a natural enough development. But in recent years, under highly efficient and aggressive management, it has come to rent cars (Avis), operate hotels and motor inns (Sheraton), build homes (Levitt & Sons), bake bread (Continental), produce glass and sand, make consumer loans, manage mutual funds and process data.

But if diversity were the only criterion for distinguishing a conglomerate, General Motors, Ford and General Electric would each outrank I.T.T. G.M. makes locomotives, refrigerators and washing machines. Ford produces a line of radios and household durables. G.E. produces jet engines, computers and synthetic diamonds in addition to its traditional lines of electrical equipment. But none of these is a true conglomerate.

What distinguishes I.T.T. is the source of its recent growth. Its assets grew by more than $2-billion in the period 1960–1967, and mergers accounted for more than a third of that total. In the same period, mergers made no contribution at all to the asset growth of G.M. or G.E. and accounted for a little more than 6 per cent of Ford's. Xerox's spectacular progress is the product of internal growth rather than expansion through merger.

In perusing the list of the 200 largest manufacturing corporations, conglomerates can almost invariably be distinguished by the high contribution of mergers to their asset growth. In 1966–1967, mergers accounted for nearly 46 per cent of Litton Industries' growth, and for others, the figures were as follows: F.M.C., 80 per cent; General Dynamics, 69 per cent; Gulf & Western, 47 per cent; Textron, 69 per cent; Martin Marietta, nearly 100 per cent, and Glen Alden, 94 per cent.

Only eight conglomerates ranked among the 200 last year, but they accounted for all the exciting merger action. Ling-Temco-Vought, which ranked 92d, bought control of the 63d-ranking Jones & Laughlin Steel Corporation with assets of $1.1-billion. P. Lorillard, the tobacco company that ranked 184th was acquired by Loew's Theatres, a dazzling conglomerate that couldn't even qualify for the 200 club in 1967.

Mergers and rumors of merger are the daily grist of the financial press. The Radio Corporation of America plans to acquire control of the St. Regis Paper Company through an exchange of stock valued at $700-million. Glen Alden wants to take over Schenley distillers. Gulf & Western is accumulating stock in Pan American World Airways, and Ling-Temco-Vought is negotiating to acquire Ryan Aeronautical.

What accounts for this corporate acquisitiveness, this frenzied urge to merge? Is the driving force biogenetic in origin, a vestigial survival of prowess from man's primitive past? The evidence points to dollars, rather than chromosomes.

About 50 years ago, E. I. du Pont de Nemours, which now ranks 16th among the industrial corporations, was on its way to becoming a massive conglomerate. It acquired nearly 23 per cent of General Motors stock during and after the First World War, and in the nineteen-twenties accumulated huge holdings of U.S. Steel stock which it sold when the Federal Trade Commission began an anti-monopoly investigation.

Du Pont was seeking profitable outlets for its rapidly accumulating earnings. But a distinguishing characteristic of today's conglomerates is they are not giants surfeited with cash, but growing boys who aspire toward giantism. Why do they strive to grow ever larger? The explanations that are readily offered by the new conglomerate entrepreneurs are noteworthy for their novelty if not sophistication. One could hardly expect less from the hardworking corps of public relations men who serve them.

In the horse-and-buggy era, firms diversified in order to lessen risks of failure and more fully utilize their resources. The classic case is that of the coal-yard operator who delivered ice in the summertime. But in the age of "management science," synergism is the byword. In its corporate context, synergism implies that the total capabilities of a large organization far exceed those of the sum of its divisions taken separately. Crudely stated, it is the proposition that two plus two are equal to at least five.

If a group of applied physicists is joined with an electronic-equipment manufacturer, it's reasonable to suppose that the merged company will be able to take on new business—research and development contracts—which neither could have handled before the union. And with a greater capability for taking on larger contracts, it becomes easier for the company to borrow the money that may be needed to finance work in progress.

But in the move from simple examples to corporate realities, synergism loses its force as an explanation of conglomerate mergers. In the case of Litton Industries and other conglomerates that reshape the managements of acquired companies and guide them through systems of centralized controls, some synergistic benefits might be realized. But the elements of the Ling-Temco-Vought complex function independently of one another and presumably the C.I.T.'s management would also remain intact after the proposed merger with Xerox. In such instances, therefore, especially when conglomerates are as widely diversified as I.T.T. or L.T.V., it's difficult to attach much weight to synergism.

The more decentralized the conglomerate becomes, the more it resembles a mutual fund or a pension trust account in a bank. Neither play active roles in the management of companies in which they hold stock.

Synergism implies greater efficiency in the production of goods and services, but it is doubtful whether such considerations weigh heavily in merger decisions. Yet there is no doubting the fact that managements which pursue aggressive merger policies can persuade investors to pay more for their stock. Thus, it is to the stock market rather than the production line that one must look for an explanation of the conglomerate corporation.

Conglomerates vary widely in size and maturity. Textron, which achieved success a decade ago in moving from textiles into optical instruments, electronic equipment, paper machinery, aircraft and a host of other fields, doesn't make news so often with announcements of acquisitions as Gulf & Western. Some conglomerate rockets have burned out (Merritt-Chapman & Scott) and others (Olin Mathieson, for one) have failed to reach their earnings targets. But the underlying strategy of conglomeration is essentially the same in every case: It consists in making investors willing, if not eager, to pay higher prices for shares in the company's stock, more in relation to each dollar that the conglomerate earns.

The relationship between the market price of a share of stock and the company's earnings is the price-earnings ratio—in the parlance of Wall Street, the P/E. Suppose that two companies, A and B, each have one million shares of common stock outstanding and net earnings of $2-million, or $2 a share. Yet A's stock sells in the market for $80 a share, or 40 times earnings, and B's sells for only $30, or 15 times earnings. Why the disparity? Why does the market—the investors—believe that A's future is rosier than B's, that over time its price will rise faster and farther?

Many factors make for differences in price-earnings ratios, but two which attract much attention are growth and risk.

If A's earnings have been growing at an average rate of 10 per cent a year and B's at only 6 per cent, the investor who assumes that both trends will continue into the future can draw a clear inference. A's earnings will double in a little more than seven years, but nearly 12 years will elapse before B makes the same progress. Hence, A's stock will command the higher P/E so long as the market expects it to move along the same growth path. But that expectation can easily collapse. A decline in a quarter's earnings, a failure to get a fat defense contract or a completely baseless rumor about managerial friction can result in an abrupt decline in A's P/E.

The other element is risk. If investors believe that there is one chance in 10 that A's earnings will fall below $2 a share as against one chance in five for B's, they will pay more for each dollar of A's earnings. High rates of earnings growth may not in fact be accompanied by low risks. Companies with high average rates of growth can suffer setbacks from year to year. But investors in forming their subjective judgments associate rapid growth with low risk; they assume that per share earnings can only move in one direction—up. They see in the conglomerates a means of reducing risk through size and rapid growth.

Conglomerate entrepreneurs—or conglomerators—must raise the price-earnings ratios of their stock if they are to expand, for unless it's loaded with cash, the rising conglomerate must depend on loans to acquire new companies. The higher the price of its common stock, the more it can borrow by pledging stock as collateral or the more it can raise by selling bonds that are convertible into common stock at a prearranged price. Where the merger is consummated through the exchange of stock, the higher the market price of the conglomerate's stock, the fewer shares it must give up in exchange and the smaller the dilution in the earnings per share.

The need for maintaining a rising P/E never ceases so long as the conglomerate continues to make acquisitions. And in order to avoid a decline or a slowdown in its earnings per share, it should seek to merge with companies whose P/E's are lower than its own.

It's not necessary for conglomerators actually to demonstrate that they can diminish risks and raise earnings per share through diversification. The mere intention to embark on the path of conglomeration may be sufficient to raise expectations. Franc Ricciardi, an alumnus of Litton Industries, who helped to turn Walter Kidde & Co. into a successful conglomerate, explains that the "stock market was very generous" with the new management from the start. As soon as they "threw their hats in the door," Kidde stock "went up 60 or 70 per cent, in the expectation that something might happen."

There are many stars in the conglomerate firmament, but none shines so brightly as that of James Joseph Ling, a 45-year-old high-school dropout who was born in Hugo, Okla. (population 6,287). In 22 years he has parlayed an investment of $3,000 in an electrical contracting shop into a diversified empire with more than $2-billion of assets and $3-billion in sales. A financial Archimedes, he has demonstrated what can be done with the leverage of rising P/E's.

After scoring a success as an electrical contractor—his skills were acquired in the Navy—Ling was able to go public when a Dallas investment banker agreed to underwrite stocks and bonds in Ling Electronics. That venture prospered, and in 1960, Temco Electronics and Missiles was acquired along with Altec, a major producer of sound equipment, and other companies. Two years later, in 1961, the Vought was added to Ling-Temco when Ling borrowed $10-million to gain control of Chance Vought, an aircraft, missile and electronics company with sales of $195-million. He was assisted by Troy Victor Post, a friend of Lyndon Johnson's. Post's own conglomerate, Greatamerica, which controlled insurance companies, a large bank and Braniff Airways, was merged into L.T.V. in 1967.

Texas tycoons are not noted for modesty in their personal tastes, and Ling is no exception to the rule. The cost of his home—a Palace of Versailles in the style of a Holiday Inn—is variously placed at figures in excess of $1.5-million, inclusive of a guest house, now under construction. "People don't live like that in the Northeast," a New York banker remarked, "even when they can afford it."

Ling once proclaimed that his goal was a combined sales total of $10-billion a year, and he took a giant step toward achieving it when he acquired control of Wilson & Co. in 1967. It was a performance that combined exquisite financial insight with perfect timing, one that made Ling the Lorenzo of the conglomerators.

Wilson was itself a conglomerate, producing sporting goods, meats and chemicals. Its sales were then nearly $1-billion, as against $468-million for L.T.V. Yet the python swallowed the pig.

In the spring of 1967, Ling was able to borrow $80-million from New York brokers, London merchant bankers, insurance companies and university trust funds in order to buy a controlling interest in Wilson stock. He paid a premium of 25 per cent over the market price to get it. The remaining Wilson stock was acquired by offering the owners a special L.T.V. convertible preferred stock.

Then he embarked on "Operation Redeployment," a tactic pursued in 1965 to reduce L.T.V.'s debts. He broke Wilson up into three independent companies, listed them on the exchange and sold blocks of stock to the public which in no case amounted to more than 25 per cent of L.T.V.'s holdings. Intrigued brokers referred to the new issues as "golf balls," "meat balls" and "goof balls."

The sale of Wilson stock brought in $44.4-million, enough to retire more than half of L.T.V.'s debt. But the real pay-off came a short time later when the market had an opportunity to appraise the prospects of the new Wilson companies and boost their P/E's. The happy result was that L.T.V.'s remaining holdings of Wilson stock were valued at a cool $250-million. With his highly appreciated bag of assets, Ling was in a position to offer collateral for bigger loans for bigger acquisitions. The opportunity came in May this year when he raised $425-million in cash to gain control of the Jones & Laughlin Steel Corporation. L.T.V. put in about $200-million from its own kitty and borrowed the rest, principally by tapping the Eurodollar market—U.S. dollars held on deposit in European banks.

Other conglomerators play variations on the same pecuniary theme. Meshulam Riklis, the scholarly chief of Glen Alden, accomplished less spectacular feats by selling convertible debentures, bondlike instruments that can be swapped for common stock. He once referred to them as "Castro [convertibles] pesos," and again, the ease with which they can be sold hinges on the crucial P/E of his common stock.

What the accomplishments of Ling, Riklis and other imaginative entrepreneurs suggest is that the process of conglomeration can be self-sustaining and self-financing. So long as the skies are blue, higher earnings beget higher share prices; bigger loans mean bigger mergers.

The delightful author of "The Money Game," who writes under the pseudonym of Adam Smith, ended his survey of the cool world of conglomerates with a query: "If the Federal Reserve is printing money like a banana republic, why shouldn't some private citizens try it?" One searching question leads to others. Is conglomeration, with its reliance on rising P/E's and ever larger loans, a source of economic instability? And if conglomerates don't cause the collapse of the economic system, won't they destroy competition by vesting more and more power in fewer and fewer companies?

The first question must be answered with a certain diffidence by anyone old enough to remember the 1929 crash. Yet it seems unlikely that a failure of the conglomerate to perform according to expectations could in itself lead to a re-enactment of that tragic scenario. For that to happen, the monetary policy of the Federal Reserve System would have to be as perversely deflationary as it was between 1929 and 1933.

Several of the high-flying conglomerates have already failed to maintain their growth trajectories without causing chaos. Litton Industries, partly because of managerial difficulties and partly because of the softening of demand in the 1966–1967 mini-recession, suffered a setback in per-share earnings. So did several other conglomerates. And the market, as is its wont, promptly knocked down their P/E's.

Some conglomerates, as J. Howard Laeri of the First National City Bank remarked, are "lured to bigness by the siren of leverage" and "may prove to have more ambition than talent." Investors who buy their stock can be badly burned, victims of the cult of instant earnings growth and the willful suspension of disbelief. Even those who attempt to exercise care by investigating the earnings records may be gulled. At least two highly respected accountants have charged that conglomerate accounting practices create an illusion of growth that may be anchored only in arithmetic.

One practice under strong attack is the indiscriminate lumping together of the earnings of a new acquisition with those of the parent company. XY, a conglomerate, acquires Z in 1966, a year in which its earnings were $2-million. In 1967, the Z division's earnings of $1-million are added to XY's earnings of $2.2-million, and the result is that the XYZ Corporation proudly proclaims a gain of $1.2-million or a 60 per cent increase in its earnings.

But is it really a gain? It may well be that Z's profits fell from $1.5-million in 1966 to $1-million in 1967, a case of reverse synergy that is not uncommon. Restating the earnings for both years on a comparable basis gives $3.5-million for 1966 and $3.2-million for 1967. Thus the gain of $1.2-million was in fact a decline of $300,000.

Another objectionable practice is the pooling of merged assets—

"dirty pooling," in the words of an irate accountant. Suppose that XY buys Z for $20-million in cash, but enters the assets on the merged balance sheet at Z's "book" value, or historical cost, which is only $15-million. The suppression of the $5-million under pooling-of-interest accounting raises XYZ's earnings by dint of the lower depreciation charges against Z's scaled-down assets. Another distortion occurs if XYZ later sells Z's assets for $19-million and records a $4-million "profit."

Such hanky-panky can mislead the investor who reads only the glowing prose of the president's letter and not the statistical tables of the annual reports. Reforms are being pressed by the Securities and Exchange Commission and the accounting societies. One that would provide much more relevant information would compel companies to report both sales and earnings by divisions rather than as lump sums.

Contrary to what might be suspected, conglomeration confers no clear tax advantage. Where the stocks exchanged are of equal market value, the merger is tax-free. Where cash premiums are paid for the stock of the acquired company or where higher priced debentures are exchanged, taxes must be paid on the basis of the spread between market shares.

But none of the problems raised by the emergence of the conglomerate corporation are so complex—or politically explosive—as those relating to their impact on competition. Mergers once posed relatively simple anti-trust problems. For the most part they were horizontal (one retail food store taking over another in the same market) or vertical (the acquisition of a slaughter-house by a retail food chain). Legality hinged on whether the mergers would lessen competition in the affected markets—not an easy judgment to make, but conceptually manageable. But conglomerates, which account for about 90 per cent of the assets acquired by merger—or for about $10-billion in 1968, according to preliminary estimates by the Federal Trade Commission—can't be fitted into a neat analytical scheme.

Conglomerates raise the issue of political power in a new and disquieting fashion. Litton, L.T.V., General Dynamics—to name only a few—owe their rise to defense contracts and a continuing relationship with the Federal Government. The "military-industrial complex," of which President Eisenhower warned before leaving the White House, is very much a reality.

But hard evidence of enhanced political power through conglomeration has not been assembled. There were grumblings when Ling's acquisition of Jones & Laughlin was not challenged on anti-trust grounds. One executive, whose prospective merger collapsed because of an unfavorable reaction from the Justice Department, remarked bitterly: "We're not from Texas."

The Ripon Forum, the serious organ of a society of liberal Republicans, has carried an analysis of the S.M.I.C.—Southwest Military Industrial Complex—in which it was suggested that the Johnson family may be linked to L.T.V. through shareholdings in the Greatamerica Corporation, on whose board Justice Abe Fortas once sat. But the links, to say nothing of the implied influence, have not been demonstrated.

Critics sometimes charge that conglomerates result in over-centralization, the deadening hand of managerial bureaucracy. But conglomeration and centralization needn't go hand in hand. When Ling took over Wilson, he decentralized its management by breaking it up into three companies. L.T.V.'s acquisition, in short, resulted in a measure of *de*conglomeration, the object of which was to persuade the market that Wilson's P/E's should be higher. (It would be fascinating from several vantage points if General Motors were to tear a page from Ling's book and reconstruct its divisions as independent corporations.) So there is the possibility that conglomeration will have little impact on the concentration of economic power if divisions have autonomy in the management of their affairs.

Conglomerators often boast of intensifying competition by reviving dormant companies, especially those which are closely held by families anxious to disengage themselves and delighted to exchange their equity interests for shares in rapidly appreciating stock. Many of such claims must be regarded with skepticism. But there are instances in which conglomerates *have* contributed to the intensification of competition. By providing Sweda with financial and managerial resources, for instance, Litton Industries mounted a competitive threat in a market dominated by National Cash Register.

Little light has yet been cast, however, on most of the anti-trust issues. Veteran antitrust economists, whose survival in Washington's lobby jungle is a tribute to their courage, argue that conglomerates pose several clear threats to competition, and their contentions are mirrored in recent F.T.C. and Supreme Court decisions.

The first threat is from price subsidization—the use of profits, earned in a market where the position of the conglomerate is strong, to drive out the competition in another market by cutting prices below costs and subsequently raising them. If entry into the market is easy, the conglomerate's higher profits will soon attract competition. But if there are substantial barriers to entry, the gambit could pay off.

Second, if the conglomerate is very large and commands great financial resources, its move into a highly competitive market of small sellers could discourage potential entrants.

Third, there is reciprocity—the fear that the conglomerate will use its power to effect tie-in sales. Conglomerate X buys ball bearings from Company Y which in turn gets its steel from Company Z. If X acquires Z, it may then put pressure on Y to buy X-Z steel at an unfavorable price by threatening to patronize another manufacturer of ball bearings.

There are sharp disagreements among economists and lawyers as to whether these threats to competition are palpable. Nonetheless, the F.T.C., at the behest of Senator Philip Hart of Michigan, the chairman of the Anti-trust and Monopoly Subcommittee, agreed to undertake a broad fact-finding investigation of conglomerates.

That decision elicited a loud blast from James J. Ling. He warned insurance company executives in Chicago of "the bureaucrats who would democratize and socialize all business and thus pave the way for the ultimate demise of the enterprise system. . . ." But several body blows later, he cryptically remarked that: "I don't want to be in a position of condemning all bureaucrats because it's not unlikely that I'll wind up being one myself one of these days." Ling is a generous contributor to a business group that is backing Hubert Humphrey, so it is to be wondered which Cabinet post is being coveted in whose Administration.

The one certainty that emerges from the web of controversy is that the conglomerate issue isn't going to be resolved by Ling's rhetoric, the F.T.C.'s fact findings or the interpretations of the courts. A new, or at least novel, style of entrepreneurship is evolving, one based on raising expectations of rapid growth. It might disappear when the conglomerators, like Alexander, weep because there are no more worlds to conquer—but that isn't likely to happen for a very long time.

Banks Add Role as Marriage Brokers

by Robert D. Hershey, Jr.

MANY OF THE nation's largest banks—moving beyond "friendliness" themes to build business—have now institutionalized courtship and marriage.

The banks in recent years have set up departments to make matches for their corporate customers, hoping that one plus one makes almost two. In this sector of the banking business, it never makes more.

Mergers and acquisitions form a field where the banks have long been involved, if only on an informal basis. But recent activity has swelled to such an extent that, according to one estimate, there are about 25 banks with departments specifically organized to search out partners for customers or prospects and to advise them in such matters as setting the terms.

Basically, the banks are out to help their customers grow in size so that they have greater need for bank services and more money to keep on deposit.

"We look primarily for improved banking business," said H. Eric Schmidt, a vice president of the First National City Bank, in a recent interview. He noted that potential trust department business is often considered a key factor.

One problem the matchmakers face is a shortage of brides, companies that wish to be acquired. New York's two largest banks—Chase Manhattan and First National City—have lists of well over 1,000 companies that are anxious to make acquisitions, while their lists of sellers consist of only a few hundred, not all of them desirable.

"Generally, the things actively on the block for sale are not as attractive as you would hope. It's really refreshing when you find a good one," declared Chase's Harry P. Abplanalp, a vice president in the bank's corporate finance and research division.

Mr. Schmidt acknowledged this shortage. "This has always been true," he said but added, "There are plenty of sellers around if you know where to look for them."

The banks also face the hazard of losing business instead of gaining it. "We're not anxious to see our customers acquired," Mr. Abplanalp said.

Large regional banks, especially those in New England, Philadelphia and the Midwest, seem to have suffered most in this regard as local companies lost their identities through merger with bigger concerns who often use the facilities of the giant New York banks. New York has six of the seven largest banks in the nation.

If it is a bank customer who makes the acquisition the bank stands to come out ahead. Nonetheless, according to the Chase banker, "one and one are always less than two in these situations. The name of the game is to keep a major share of the business."

Over the last 10 years or so the merger and acquisition game has changed dramatically, the bankers said. First of all, since there are many more companies looking for acquisitions, the price of partners has gone up and even second-rate companies receive bids.

"Only a few companies have not been approached," Mr. Abplanalp declared. "There are no virgins left as far as acquisitions are concerned."

It was also noted that no longer is there a stigma attached to being receptive to bids. Moreover, even reluctant companies have become more willing to consider offers because of obligations to do the best they can for their increasingly astute and demanding shareholders.

Looking over their shoulders are the regulatory authorities and the stock exchanges, who demand full and prompt disclosure of company developments.

Just last week, the Securities and Exchange Commission won a victory in its fight to establish a precedent governing the stock market trading of corporate insiders privy to confidential information. A United States Court of Appeals upheld the S.E.C.'s appeal of a lower court's decision that had cleared 10 defendants in the well-known Texas Gulf Sulphur Company case.

Last month the New York Stock Exchange announced a broadly expanded disclosure policy that requires its companies to divulge information about major steps, whether under negotiation or in the planning stage, as soon as they extend beyond a company's top management.

These pressures have caused another phenomenon—a large increase in the number of mergers that are announced, then broken off.

Companies these days are often "bought on the numbers" and an agreement in principle to merge is announced. Only then are the buyer's personnel sent to examine the plant and inventories to determine the final price, a procedure that in many cases causes disagreement serious enough for the plans to fall through.

Another change in the business over the last decade has been a growing sophistication of corporate financial officers. They expect the banks to advise them about acquisitions or financing arrangements in greater detail.

Chase's corporate finance and research department, which acts as a clearing house for mergers and acquisitions, works closely with two others—financing development and technical services, both of which add their expertise to corporate planning.

And the banks have turned to computers to make projections assuming this or that merger or various interest rate levels, components that may determine a company's performance. Mr. Schmidt called this function "computer-assisted financial forecasting."

How do the bankers feel about what often emerges from the results of their work—conglomerate companies?

Mr. Abplanalp said he had no strong feelings one way or another about conglomerates, but he did point out that many such companies, as do others, contain "a lot of fluff."

The Chase banker says that first should come the investment decision and then when it is proved sound the best way to finance it should be taken up.

Competition for matchmaking business, described by the bankers as "fierce," comes from the investment bankers, who have always counted this a major part of their business, from business brokers (including those sometimes called finders) and most recently from accounting firms.

Accountants usually have an even more intimate relationship with corporate clients than do banks, since most large companies have several banks but only one accountant and, as a defensive measure, they have become very much more active in arranging mergers. Sometimes they are the first ones a company will consult in the preliminary stages of a merger or acquisition.

The banks receive a fee for their work when a merger is consummated, but they shy away for legal reasons from putting it on a percentage basis.

Take-Overs Shake Business

by John J. Abele

IN THE WORLD of business, as in other areas of American life, the Establishment is under fire.

The flood tide of corporate mergers that has swept over the business world in recent years has begun to lap against some members of the industrial elite once considered impervious to outside bids for control.

It also has begun to affect leading companies in the fields of insurance, banking and finance.

The situation has reached the point where some financial observers have begun to pose the possibility that not even the nation's largest corporations—General Motors and United States Steel among them—are immune from take-over bids.

W. T. Grimm & Co., a Chicago consulting firm that specializes in mergers and acquisitions, has estimated that some 4,400 merger proposals were made last year.

That was an increase of 50 per cent over the 1967 figure, which, in turn, was 25 per cent higher than in 1966. Grimm expects merger proposals in 1969 to top 5,400.

The lightning pace of mergers has begun to produce thunderclaps of reaction in Washington and Wall Street:

¶Representative Wilbur D. Mills, the powerful chairman of the tax-writing House Ways and Means Committee, has introduced a bill that would sharply limit the tax advantages of debt securities issued in mergers.

¶Richard W. McLaren, the new head of the Justice Department's Anti-trust Division, has served notice that he plans to move "promptly" against some conglomerate mergers—those involving unions of companies in different fields.

Robert W. Haack, president of the New York Stock Exchange, has warned that the dubious quality of some debt securities issued in mergers makes them unfit for listing on the exchange and could impair the common-stock listings of the issuers.

Other aspects of mergers are now under study by a variety of Government investigators, including the Federal Trade Commission, the Securities and Exchange Commission and committees of the House and Senate.

The proliferation of merger activity has affected the lives of millions of Americans who work for, do business with and invest in the securities of companies involved in mergers.

For some, it has meant lost jobs. For others, it has provided new opportunities for success. Long-standing relationships between suppliers and customers have been disrupted by changes in control of once independent companies. The business lives of scores of communities throughout the nation have been drastically affected by mergers.

The problems that can arise from the merger boom are amply illustrated by the Allis-Chalmers Manufacturing Company, a large but ailing producer of farm, construction and electrical machinery that has alternately embraced and rebuffed a half-dozen corporate suitors in the last two years.

In a last-ditch effort to revamp its operations so that it would be more resistant to take-over attempts, Allis-Chalmers last year brought in a new president, 52-year-old David C. Scott, who began a program of "major surgery" to build a "new" company.

Last week, in a progress report of sorts, Mr. Scott gave the results to date of his "Operation Turnaround":

¶Allis-Chalmers had a net loss of $54-million in 1968, including special charges of $33-million related to plant closings and other major changes.

¶The company reduced its corporate staff from 1,510 persons to 132 in six months. By the end of 1969, it expects to "release" 5,000 nonproduction workers.

¶Twenty-two changes were made in the company's top management. Among the executives who left the company were its chairman and its chief financial officer.

Despite all these changes, Allis-Chalmers still faces a take-over bid by White Consolidated Industries, a one-time sewing machine manufacturer that now is a highly diversified conglomerate.

Allis-Chalmers hopes to deflect the White bid on anti-trust grounds, contending that the two companies are in similar lines of business.

The applicability of anti-trust laws to the welter of corporate consolidations is a growing source of controversy in the business world.

To some observers, the merger boom is seen as an increase in economic concentration and a threat to competition. To others, it is instilling new vitality into companies who have lagged competitively because their managements have failed to utilize fully their resources of production, financing and people.

Many recent mergers and acquisitions do not fit into traditional anti-trust concepts. A large number, for example, have been carried out by conglomerate companies expanding into fields in which they have not been represented previously.

The conglomerates have adopted the use of mergers and acquisitions as a principal mode of producing rapid growth that gives them massive manufacturing and financial resources.

They have been highly successful. More than a dozen companies generally recognized as conglomerates now rank among the largest industrial corporations in the nation with sales and revenues of more than $1-billion a year.

The merger boom is rapidly changing the face of American industry. About 80 companies that were in Fortune magazine's 1962 listing of the nation's 500 largest industrial companies are now part of, or controlled by, other corporations.

A score of additional companies in the fields of finance, transportation and merchandising also have been absorbed by other companies.

More than 30 of the companies in Fortune's 1968 listing of

largest companies will not appear on next year's list because they will have been merged into companies. A dozen more are currently involved in merger discussions or contests.

B. F. Goodrich, one of the nation's largest rubber companies, currently is waging a major battle to prevent a take-over by Northwest Industries, a holding company that controls the Chicago & North Western Railway.

The General Host Corporation, a tourist services and food company, has won control of a majority of the stock of Armour & Co., one of the largest meat packers. The Youngstown Sheet and Tube Company, a major steel producer, has agreed to a merger with the Lykes Corporation, a shipping company that had been rebuffed by Youngstown in two earlier bids.

The ranks of independent sales finance companies, among the most asset-rich corporations in the country, have been decimated by the recent acquisitions of the Commercial Credit Corporation, the Associates Investment Company and the Seaboard Finance Company.

In the field of insurance, the Home Insurance Company, the Reliance Insurance Company and the Hartford Fire Insurance Company have been, or are about to be, taken over.

On Wall Street, the merger boom has produced a land-office business for the investment bankers, commercial bankers and lawyers who help arrange mergers or conduct the proxy and tender fights that accompany contested merger bids.

And stocks of merger prospects have been a fruitful source of business for the financial community.

Although many stock market analysts look askance at the feverish trading in merger stocks, stockbrokers and investors have greeted the deluge of merger announcements with wild abandon, gleefully bidding upward the stocks of the companies involved.

Among the eager participants in this bidding spree have been many institutional investors, a category that includes mutual funds, pension funds, insurance companies and banks.

Investment institutions of this type used to buy and hold stocks for the long term. But the increasing emphasis on stock market "performance" in recent years has made many of these institutions as eager to cash in on a quick profit as the most speculation-minded brokerage-house board-room trader.

The merger fever also has spread to many of the nation's 26 million stockholders.

In addition to trading profits, merger situations have given stockholders a new source of power at the expense of a corporation's management and directors.

Long relegated to the role of interested but quiet bystanders in the affairs of major corporations, stockholders now have come to represent the balance of power when a company is fighting a take-over bid.

By their decision to accept or reject the blandishments of a premium price for their shares from a company bent on a take-over, the stockholders can decide whether the company in which they have invested will continue on its own way or be merged into another company.

The merger boom has produced substantial profits for many investors. It also has produced risks and losses for many others.

Shares of the United Fruit Company, for example, soared from a price of $52 a share early last fall to a high of $88 under the impact of a series of competing bids that ended with the A.M.K. Corporation's acquiring more than 80 per cent of the stock of the company once considered a prime example of "Yankee Imperialism" in Latin America.

Shares of the Sinclair Oil Corporation soared from $76 a share to $138 as the company, eager to turn back a bid for control by Gulf and Western Industries, quickly arranged a merger with the Atlantic Richfield Company, another major oil concern.

Sinclair stock plunged $17 a share, to $94, on Feb. 18 after a Federal judge temporarily blocked the merger, then rebounded to $127 when the merger finally took place.

Last September, shares of the C.I.T. Financial Corporation zoomed from $46 a share to $60 on news of a proposed merger with the Xerox Corporation. They fell back to $46 in November, when the agreement was canceled as abruptly as it had been made.

Before making its bid for Sinclair, Gulf and Western had accumulated a large block of the oil company's stock. It later agreed to sell the stock to Atlantic Richfield at a price that reportedly gave Gulf and Western a pre-tax profit of some $50-million, almost as much as Gulf and Western earned from its own operations in 1968.

These and similar situations have prompted some financial observers to suggest some supposedly merger-minded companies appeared to be more interested in stock market profits than in running their own businesses.

Critics also have charged that, knowing of the tendency of investors to bid upward the prices of stocks involved in possible merger situations, some companies have used merger proposals to stimulate stock price increases that bring substantial profits on stock they purchased before disclosing their interest in another company.

Some observers even suggest that some companies appear to be acting in collusion in concocting merger proposals that have little chance of actually being successful. The proposals, however, do bring immediate publicity to the offer maker and frequently result in large price increases for its stock.

Other critics decry the various types of "funny money" used by many merger-minded companies. A typical merger "package" being offered in exchange for the stock of a company, for example, consists of a small amount of cash, a large amount of debentures, and warrants to buy the acquirer's stock at some future date.

In this sort of transaction, a stockholder is exchanging his equity ownership in a company for the debt of the acquiring company. To many small stockholders, a "convertible subordinated debenture" sounds impressive; actually it is little more than a glorified I.O.U. And the interest payments on the debentures will come out of the earnings of the acquired company.

In many cases, the actual market value of a debenture is far less interesting than its stated face value.

Warrants can be similarly deceptive because they derive their value from the difference between the price at which they allow the holder to buy stock of the issuer and the actual market price of the issuer's stock.

A warrant, for example, may allow the holder to buy the issuer's stock at $20 a share. If the stock is selling at $25 a share, the warrant has an immediate value of about $5. If the stock is selling at $18 a share, $2 below the exercise price, the warrant has no actual value except for those investors willing to pay a premium in hopes of a future rise in the price of the stock.

Disclosure Rules Affecting Mergers

by Isadore Barmash

HEAVY PRESSURE for full, prompt disclosure of merger negotiations is being cited in the financial community as the cause for a current rash of "unmergers"—corporate marriages being called off before they are even consummated.

Urging by the Securities and Exchange Commission and the New York Stock Exchange not to delay public disclosure of merger talks is held by numerous observers on Wall Street, in banking and in business to be leading to premature disclosures.

Often, they said, announcements are being made before the principals in the companies involved have had a chance to explore the marriage's real potential and even before they have generally agreed on terms.

The result, in too many cases, these sources said, is that once those involved have had a chance to probe into the apparent benefits of a merger or acquisition, they find there is little validity in the talks that they have already announced.

But Donald F. Turner, a former United States Assistant Attorney General in charge of the anti-trust division of the Department of Justice, said that he doubted the early disclosures of merger negotiations were causing a rise in the number of merger cancellations. Since last May, Mr. Turner has been a professor of law at Harvard Law School.

"I'm sure that it is causing some," he said, "but generally, I would say that a merger that is invalid is invalid anyway, regardless of whether it is announced in its early stages." Interviewed after making a speech on antitrust practices before the New York Bar Association, he added, "I am in favor of early disclosure. I think it is in the public interest."

The disclosure element is, however, not the only basis for the "unmerger" tendency that has arisen in the midst of the booming merger trend.

During the first nine months of 1968, business merger announcements rose 37 per cent to a total of 3,158, over last year's level of 2,304, according to W. T. Grimm & Co., a financial consulting concern specializing in mergers and acquisitions.

But, in the same period, the cancellation trend almost doubled, running 96 per cent over the same period of 1967. A total of 229 cancellations occurred against 117 in the comparable 1967 period.

That, however, is hardly the whole story. Within the last 10 days, the "unmerger" trend hit perhaps its greatest stride. One of the biggest merger proposals in history, that of the Xerox Corporation and the C.I.T. Financial Corporation, was killed in a terse announcement Wednesday afternoon, ending a proposed marriage that promised a dowry of some $1.5-billion.

Several days before, the Penn Central–Kayser-Roth merger, involving $230-million in stock, was terminated. The following day, another merger, involving $173-million in stock, was ended before it reached fruition, that of the American Express Company and the California–Western State Life Insurance Company, Sacramento.

There were others in that short, recent period, too.

Among the larger announced mergers that were cancelled were those of American Standard, Inc., and Mohasco Industries, Inc.; the Clevite Corporation and Gould–National Batteries; Sperry and Hutchinson, Inc., and Western Girl, Inc.; the Southern Industries Corporation and the Jim Walter Corporation; and the Allstate Investment Corporation and the Shared Data Corporation.

Almost all sources checked concur in the causative effect on the trend of early disclosure, as well as on these other basic reasons:

¶Poorly conceived combinations, with no marketing or product fit or "synergistic" potential for the companies involved.

¶Companies with high stock multiples overly anxious to acquire others with lower multiples so that the surviving concern's earnings would be enhanced.

¶More stringent scrutiny and restriction from Government agencies, sometimes after they have given an initial go-ahead to the merger or acquisition.

¶Adverse shareholder reaction in the case of one of the merger partners.

¶A sharp decline in the value of the shares of one partner, leading to disillusionment on the part of the other to go ahead with the deal.

¶Personality clashes among the principals, which seemed to intensify as they got more deeply involved in planning the wedding.

¶An internal erosion of enthusiasm as important executives begin to fear for their jobs when the merger nears completion.

Walter Jeffers, vice president of the First National City Bank here, said late last week that "we are all being told about mergers early in the game these days.

"I would say that the batting average of mergers consummated among those announced is, however, no greater than it has been, but the fact is that the number of mergers is up. We're seeing more of them, and since business is getting more adventurous, we're seeing bigger ones. And they're hitting the front pages as a result."

While early disclosure may be leading to potential cancellations, said Mr. Jeffers, he is convinced that there are no distinct changes in the marketplace that might lead to merger terminations, as there were in 1966. Then, he said, the stockmarket decline and the tightness of money formed a combination that spelled the end of numerous pending affiliations.

Xerox and C.I.T. Quiet

Why did Xerox-C.I.T.'s marriage founder? Neither company would give a reason. But Wall Street analysts suggest that the marriage was not "made in heaven"—the companies were not suited for each other, in other words. In addition, it was said,

Xerox shareholders vocally made known their objections to the combination of their company, widely hailed as a growth company, with C.I.T., which has followed a more conservative path.

Some sources liken the situation to the merger proposed more than a year ago between the Consolidated Foods Corporation and the American Tobacco Company. Shareholders of Consolidated Foods communicated their displeasure to management, which helped to "pre-annul" that marriage.

Why the cancellation of the Penn Central–Kayser-Roth deal? Again, neither company is talking, but analysts are. Said one: "They are two completely incompatible companies, and that didn't much change in the months they were talking. Railroads haven't shown any skill at merchandising, so why the tie-up with a merchandising company? Tank cars, truck trailers, metal fabrication, yes—but hosiery? It was impossible to put together."

Conglomerate Concerns?

If that is the case, what about conglomerates?

Several analysts replied that most of the larger conglomerate concerns have developed an over-all management skill at operating diverse companies, but those with the greatest potential seem to be the technology-oriented ones, such as Litton Industries and the Teledyne Corporation. But others, such as Ling-Temco-Vought and Gulf & Western Industries, which seemingly want to run the gamut from industrial to consumer-oriented companies, do not have the same degree of confidence on Wall Street, as yet, because of their very diversity.

Howard Suslak, president of MacDonald & Co., financial consultants specializing in mergers, is one who strongly believes that the influence of the Texas Gulf Sulphur situation, involving disclosure of corporate developments, has caused many company heads to interpret too literally the new disclosure regulations.

"Actually, many chief executives feel overly obligated to disclose that they are discussing the possibility of getting together on a corporate marriage," he said. "This leads to too many premature disclosures, which can be just as misleading, or more so, than no disclosure at all at that point in time."

Many early discussions between company principals are "flirtations" rather than marriage proposals, Mr. Suslak suggested.

"Therefore, most announcements to the effect that two companies are holding conversations are meaningless, since the conversations must be of an exploratory nature in order to find out if there is a compatibility between the companies, and, more important, between the two chief executives," he said.

Mr. Suslak said that often merger proposals are formulated by "share-oriented" people. As a result, the proposals look "great statistically, but they have no *raison d'être* because they lack operating synergism." As a result, he said, when the two principals begin to explore the merger plan, they find that the combination results in making the companies to be combined "bigger and weaker, rather than bigger and stronger."

A spokesman for Merrill Lynch, Pierce, Fenner and Smith, the largest brokerage concern, suggested that perhaps the major reason for mergers coming "unstuck" is that many large proposed mergers offer little in the way of mutual objectives, particularly in relation to marketing, product or manufacturing similarities.

Often, he said, the search for such mutual benefits continues to be elusive until the deal simply folds up.

Part 7

THE MULTI-NATIONAL CORPORATION

MANY OF THE largest U.S. corporations are in the process of becoming multi-national enterprises. Of course, American firms in industries such as copper and oil have had foreign operations for many years in order to take advantage of resource deposits scattered throughout the world. But now foreign subsidiaries have taken on a new attractiveness in Europe, Canada, Asia, and elsewhere, where they are a particularly effective means for realizing comparative production advantages or gaining entry into rapidly growing markets. American corporate entry into the European Common Market is a good illustration of the latter. The lowering of tariff barriers among the nations of the Common Market encouraged a rush to establish European subsidiaries by the purchase of existing firms or by direct investment in new facilities.

Entry by American firms into foreign markets has generated significant criticism. In less developed economies, individual firms and joint ventures by several corporations have been met with charges of neo-colonialism. Of course, critics are inclined to overlook the higher risk associated with unstable political institutions in these nations. In Western Europe there is apprehension over the allegedly widening technology gap between the capabilities of the American firm and local industry, as well as concern over the economic power of U.S. corporations. J. J. Servan-Schreiber expressed this view cogently in *The American Challenge:* "In fifteen years the world's third industrial power, after the United States and the U.S.S.R., could well be not Europe, but *American industry in Europe.*" In particular, Europeans are troubled by American corporate dominance in areas that hold the promise of greatest future growth—such as the computer, electronics, space, and aircraft industries.

A full appreciation of the role and place of the multi-national corporation requires that it be viewed within a broader political-economic context. Edwin L. Dale's article in this section takes America's high economic base and growth rate, relative to other nations, as a point of departure for considering a series of problems relating to American foreign expansion. The multi-national corporation plays a central role in this setting, and Dale proceeds to delineate a variety of political and institutional factors bearing upon such firms. Both Dale and Servan-Schreiber raise appropriate questions; satisfactory solutions will await further investigation and the passage of time.

The U.S. Economic Giant Keeps Growing

by Edwin L. Dale, Jr.

A NEW Government statistical series has just disclosed the astonishing fact that United States manufacturing capacity has doubled
since 1951. We added as much in the way of new plant and machinery in the last 15 years as we built in the first 150 years of
the nation's industrial history. And we may well double capacity
—and actual output—again in another 15 or 20 years.

All of this would be interesting enough by itself, but it becomes
awesome when we recall that 15 years ago the United States
already had far and away the world's largest economy. Now it is
nearly twice as big, and simple arithmetic shows that it is widening the gap over the rest of the world all the time. Even if some
other nations, such as Japan and the Soviet Union, show larger
percentage growth than we in many years, the absolute margin
of the United States increases, even allowing for the normal short-
lived dips that our economy occasionally experiences. (Suppose
the size of the Soviet economy is put at 50 and that of the United
States at 100, and suppose the Soviets grow at an unlikely 8 per
cent a year and the United States at 5 per cent; after five years
the United States would be about 125 and the Soviets 70, for a
gap of 55 instead of 50 today.)

From the *New York Times Magazine,* March 19, 1967, copyright © 1967
by The New York Times Company.

The world is becoming increasingly aware of the sheer giantism of the American economy—and of some of the business firms that make it up. Much of the world does not like what it sees. A Belgian is not overjoyed to learn that General Motors sales in a year are more than his nation's entire gross national product; an Englishman or Frenchman, used to a long history of power and influence, is likely to be resentful at the discovery that United States economic growth in one year is equal to half the British or French G.N.P. or the whole of Canada's. And as for the poor countries, their sense of impotence and frustration can only be increased by their awareness of the wealth enjoyed by the vast majority of Americans.

In a future that is foreseeable—not so far down the road as to be beyond imagination—some other countries will get where we are now, in terms of the standard of living of their people. Nearly all German and British and Japanese families will own cars, for example, probably within a generation. A little farther down the road, it is possible that most Russian families will own cars, too.

There is nothing unique, or unrepeatable, about our American experience. A combination of education, technology and reasonably sophisticated government policy to avoid calamitous inflation or depression can eventually bring other industrial countries to our present level of per-capita income, and perhaps even poor countries in a distant future. The evidence suggests rather strongly that a relatively free market economy, with strong personal incentives, probably will get other countries there faster, but there is no point in arguing that issue. Most industrial countries are trying it the free-market way in any event.

For present purposes, however, the fact that other countries can become "rich," too, does not matter. We are not only rich but big and growing. History has given us a large territory and a fairly large population. When Germans live as well as we do today, they will produce only a quarter as much steel as we do now, not to mention what we shall be producing when they get to that point. Our new investment in plant and equipment last year alone was equal to almost two-thirds of the British, French or German G.N.P. When they get where we are now, we shall have three cars a family, figuratively speaking, and factory workers will be buying custom-made suits. More important, our total productive power will be further ahead than ever.

In any case, it is rightly said and universally known that the United States has almost unbelievable "economic strength." But those two words, now so casually a part of our discourse, do not have self-evident meaning.

Just what does our wealth, our economic power—and its continuing growth—mean for the United States as a nation in the world? Does it enable us to throw our weight around? Does it enable us to achieve our foreign-policy objectives? Does it enable us, assuming we so desired, to "dominate" other nations? Or does it mean little more than that the United States has the highest standard of living for its own citizens ever known to man?

Let's try to define the meaning of our economic power. The story, as will be seen, is mixed and full of shadings. We cannot begin to think intelligently about our world role until we know the implications, and the limits, of our economic strength.

The first item on the list is of profound, if obvious, importance: Our economic size and strength enable us to have as much military might as we desire without significant strain or sacrifice of our living standards.

Not only have we been able to build a nuclear deterrent of awesome magnitude, but we have proved ourselves able to fight a major war—the war in Vietnam—with amazingly little economic strain. The cost of the war, at $23-billion in the coming fiscal year 1968, is large, but it is only 3 per cent of the G.N.P. There have been no shortages to speak of, and surprisingly little inflation, and we have even been able to expand nondefense public expenditures. Economic strain at home was one of the reasons that finally induced France to give up Vietnam; that will not happen to us. If we quit, it will be for other reasons.

In a sense, then, our economic strength has made it possible for us to have a military strength that only a Soviet Union can approach and no other nation can even contemplate (though in the distant future China might also enter the big leagues). To be blunt about it, we could conquer or defeat in war any nation in the world. By the terms of history, this is the essence of power.

But there is another side to this picture. Given our nature and our traditions—and our wealth—we have no wish to conquer. Our military might is defensive, not offensive. Even when it is used, or threatened, as in Vietnam, Cuba or the Dominican Republic, our Government conceives of that use as defensive. Some Asians may think we want to "occupy" Vietnam in the old imperialist tradition, but they are clearly mistaken.

In addition, Vietnam itself shows the limits of even limitless military power. For reasons unconnected with our power, it is proving a war very difficult to "win." While our economic strength helps to give us the military capacity to be as invulnerable as it is possible to be in the age of missiles and atomic weapons, it does not give us the power or ability to order the world as we want it. Nations, rich and poor, do not hesitate to vote against us in the United Nations, for example, even though we could, figuratively speaking, blow them off the face of the earth.

The next item concerns what has come to be known as "economic domination," which agitates Europeans and Canadians particularly. This stems entirely from an almost mindless, unplanned penetration of other economies not by our Government but by our private firms.

There is no doubt, as a starter, that scores of our largest companies have the resources, as a result of their sheer size, to build or buy plants in other countries. And there is no doubt they have been doing so. Our direct productive investments abroad now exceed $50-billion, compared with only $12-billion 15 years ago.

The American "big three" auto companies now dominate the British auto industry. International Business Machines and General Electric together dominate the computer industry in France. And as for Canada, we are all familiar with the fact that the bulk of major manufacturing and mining is under American control.

But once again, the picture is not all one-sided. Several points must be made.

First, with the single exception of Canada, American-controlled output remains a tiny fraction of total production in foreign countries. The same is true of annual new investment. Germans still control German industry and Englishmen control British industry, taken as a whole. Much of our investment is in oil and minerals, not industry.

Second, any country that does not want American investment can simply keep it out. Most countries already have controls that can be exercised, and often are exercised, at will. Japan, as one example, has chosen to keep American investment out. Granted that an occasional frustrating situation can arise, such as the recent one involving the British Rootes automobile firm; the British Government did not want Chrysler to take over, but only Chrysler had the money to prevent Rootes from going bankrupt. The same happened with General Electric and Machines Bull in the computer field in France. But these are the exceptions.

Third, American-owned establishments abroad are subject to the laws of the country concerned. Even if our Government had some hidden and nefarious design, and even if the private companies wanted to follow our Government's dictates, they would be largely powerless.

The fact is, of course, that our Government is of mixed mind about direct corporate investment abroad. For the time being, at least, these investments, to the extent that they are paid for by dollars sent from the United States, are contributing to the deficit in our balance of international payments. This, the measure of the total flow of dollars to other countries—for imports, for tourism, for troops we keep abroad, for foreign aid, and for private investment—against foreign expenditures here, has been in serious deficit since 1958. The deficit has recently been reduced, but some part of it is still being settled annually through a loss of our gold, which cannot continue indefinitely.

And so the Government, far from wanting to "dominate" other economies, has invoked a complex voluntary program to slow the amount of investment abroad, over the protest of much of the business community (though it is complying). And even if the balance of payments were not a problem, and the Government put no limits on investment abroad, the aim would not and could not be to "dominate" anybody.

Britain's Prime Minister Harold Wilson expressed European fears in unusually "Gaullist" terms recently in a speech to the Council of Europe in Strasbourg. Said Mr. Wilson:

"Loyalty [to the Atlantic Alliance] must never mean subservience. Still less must it mean an industrial helotry under which we in Europe produce only the conventional apparatus of a modern economy, while becoming increasingly dependent on American business for the sophisticated apparatus which will call the industrial tune in the seventies and eighties."

Mr. Wilson is talking here of what it is now intellectually fashionable in Europe to call the "technology gap." Based largely on American achievements in a few fields—computers, space, to a lesser extent airplanes—the "gap" is believed in heartily by politicians, somewhat by businessmen and scarcely at all by economists. It is true, of course, that giant American corporations can afford to spend more on research than typically smaller European corporations, but after that truism the argument becomes fuzzy.

British stereophonic equipment is rapidly breaching the American market, as are Japanese miniature television sets. A new American synthetic fiber plant is going up at this moment in North Carolina with largely German equipment. The new European color television system is, on early evidence, a bit better than ours. European cars and steel are doing very well in our market, as anyone can see, and last year our imports of sophisticated machine tools reached a record.

Nonetheless, Mr. Wilson's concern is understandable. He and others hope to solve the alleged problem by enlarging the European Common Market and creating huge European-scale industrial firms that would have resources to match those of the Americans. Already Britain and France are collaborating on a supersonic passenger airplane. But whether the general idea of larger European companies and mergers across frontiers proves practicable or not, the fact remains that there is no American *political* intention to dominate others through either private investment or technological superiority.

If there were, it is failing miserably. Writing recently about Italy in The New Republic, Philip Ben noted that that country "has drawn her own conclusions from the spectacular decline of American influence and prestige in Europe." Our diplomats, speaking frankly, would probably concur, at least part way.

In general, our direct private foreign investments seem to be causing us more political trouble than influence. They are constantly exacerbating our relations with Canada and have begun to arouse hostility in Europe. The investments cause difficulty, real or imagined, for others but they add nothing to the power and influence of the United States. And they are something that other countries can shut off at any time—perhaps at some economic and technological cost to themselves, but that is their privilege.

We come next to an area of great irony. Can and does the United States use its economic power to gain its own ends in purely economic international negotiations? The almost fantastic answer is that in the crucial areas of trade and international finance we are in a position closely resembling that of a beggar.

Nearly five years ago we held open to the world, through the Trade Expansion Act of 1962, the supposedly dazzling prospect of a reduction of 50 per cent in nearly all our tariffs. It would be inaccurate to say that the world yawned, but it hardly jumped for joy. We have spent the intervening time cajoling the European Common Market and such nations as Japan and Canada to reduce their own tariffs enough to make it a fair bargain—and so far without success. The most we can do is threaten to withdraw our tariff-reducing offers, and this does not seem to frighten the others all that much.

One reason is that, while we are the world's largest single importer, our imports make up only 14 per cent of the world total. Our market is attractive, but not absolutely essential, to the world's trading nations, who trade more with each other than with us. We appear to be getting a poor bargain out of the "Kennedy Round" of tariff negotiations because others insist on keeping protection against our exports in some key sectors, above all in agriculture, and our threat to limit our own tariff reductions is not enough, by itself, to make them change their minds.

As for international finance, here, as most Americans and foreigners concerned with the problem see it, we are in a position of positive weakness, despite our unbounded "economic strength." A tiny tail, the balance-of-payments deficit, wags the huge dog. The loss of a ton of gold, worth $30-million, is more important than the addition of many billions to our gross national product. Not only has our bargaining position in negotiations for international monetary reform been greatly weakened, but we may even have to seek this year our first international loan, from the International Monetary Fund, to avert still larger loss of gold.

There are some economists and others who argue that this posture of international pauperism on the part of the United States is ridiculous and needlessly humiliating. They say that the United States could, by a unilateral act, transform the present world monetary system, dethrone gold and crown the dollar as king.

The question is far too complicated, and its elements far too uncertain, to be discussed here. It is barely possible that our Government might one day try the bold moves that have been suggested. But that is certainly not likely now. Officials are far from convinced that such a stroke would work. Instead, we are struggling to eliminate the balance-of-payments deficit lest the dollar turn dangerously "weak"—and unwanted—in international transactions. The day could theoretically even arise, if our payments deficits persist long enough, when American tourists would find other countries not wanting, or taking, their dollars.

All of this may be a reflection on the flaws of the international monetary system rather than on the "strength" of the United States. But the fact remains that a payments deficit running between $1-billion and $3-billion annually—or well under half of 1 per cent of our gross national product—has put us in the embarrassing position of begging such a country as Germany for money to offset the cost of our troops there and of having to await the wishes of the Europeans before we can achieve our aim of monetary reform.

Finally, there is the question of direct relations with other nations, chiefly through our use of foreign aid.

Here again, our economic strength gives us, on paper, great leverage. This includes, of course, the wondrous capacity of our agriculture in a hungry world. There is no doubt, too, that we can use, and have used, our money to exact certain changes and decisions in foreign countries, and our money can make an important difference in some "emergency" situations, such as in the Congo a few years ago. But the limits turn out to be more impressive than the strength.

The first, and somewhat ironic, limit is that our Congress and people do not much like the idea of foreign aid. We simply do not give a great deal—the total is well under 1 per cent of our G.N.P., even including food give-aways.

The second is that there are great dangers and obstacles involved in bluntly using our money as a bribe to win desirable changes in policy in other countries. The great majority would simply say, "Keep your money, and we'll keep our pride—and our policy." Thus there has been no effort at all on our part during the current partial famine in India to win the support of the Indian Government for our policy in Vietnam. Besides, with very few exceptions our aid is only a tiny fraction of even a poor country's total resources—hardly enough to give us great leverage over what they do.

The principal leverage we have been able to exert—frequently with the help of the World Bank and International Monetary Fund —is on internal economic policies of recipient countries. Such changes, when we can bring them about, are deemed to be in the best interest of development of the country itself, not our best interest.

It is true that aid can be and is used subtly in small amounts to maintain American or Western "influence" in given situations where a government may be teetering toward Communism. Thus we may train the police force in one country or give weapons to the army in another. But this is a game that any Western nation can play. France plays it, chiefly in Africa, as well as or better than we do. It does not depend on our economic strength, for the amounts involved are invariably small.

Perhaps the supreme irony is in the discovery that, even if we gave a great deal more foreign aid, we could not achieve the partially idealistic and partially selfish purpose of orderly economic development in the poor countries. After more than a decade in the great and frustrating effort to achieve economic development, the world is sadder and wiser; it has found, among other things, that outside capital, while helpful, is not nearly enough to bring about the desired result. There are grave limits to what money can accomplish.

Where then, after this examination, do we stand? What does our economic power really mean?

It means, first and foremost, a high standard of living for our citizens. Our polluted air and crowded highways notwithstanding, this is a blessing that none of us should overlook. Our wealth has created problems and we certainly have not achieved "the good life"; but our high money incomes have opened up for the great majority of us opportunities for enjoyment and enrichment undreamed of in all history.

It means, second, a relatively painless military power of such dimensions as to make us as safe as a modern nation can be. But perhaps the key words are "relatively painless." The Soviet Union also has enormous military power with only half the economic strength; it was willing to make the sacrifice.

It means, third, a penetration of other countries by our private corporations that is viewed by both us and those nations with mixed feelings, can be cut off by others at any time and appears to have no relevance at all to the achievement of American diplomatic and political goals.

It may mean, fourth, something in the way of "power of example." Most unbiased people in the world, probably even including the Russians, can now see that modern capitalism works pretty well—from the example of postwar Western Europe as much as from ours. Many of the Communist countries are even groping toward a form of the profit motive and a more market-oriented price system.

This does not mean, however, that the Nassers, let alone the Castros, or the Indira Gandhis, all follow the example. Nor does it mean that broadly following the economic example says anything about a nation's foreign policy. Ask de Gaulle.

Beyond those four things—only the second of which has major relevance to the pursuit of our world goals—our economic strength means astonishingly little. If our economy doubles its size again by 1980 or 1985, and further widens its lead over all the rest, this will not make us any better able than we are now to prevent revolutions and aggressions and general waywardness in the rest of the world. Nor will it enhance our ability to achieve constructive goals such as freer world trade, monetary reform or economic development of the poor countries.

Perhaps this should not disturb us. Ours is not a tradition of conquest, nor even one of throwing our weight around. But it is well in any event that we recognize and reflect upon the irony of how little help our enormous wealth, apart from our military strength, is in the game of international politics.

We are a giant, to be sure. But the pygmies all about us will not do our bidding—even when we tell them it is for their own good.

Suggested Reading

I. The Corporation in Modern Capitalism

Adolf A. Berle, *The American Economic Republic,* New York, Harcourt, Brace and World, 1964 (Harvest paperback).

Milton Friedman, *Capitalism and Freedom,* Chicago, University of Chicago Press, 1962 (Phoenix paperback).

John Kenneth Galbraith, *The New Industrial State,* Boston, Houghton Mifflin, 1967 (Signet paperback).

Eli Ginzberg, D. L. Hiestand, and Beatrice G. Reubens, *The Pluralistic Economy,* New York, McGraw-Hill, 1965.

Edward S. Mason, ed., *The Corporation in Modern Society,* Cambridge, Mass., Harvard University Press, 1959 (Atheneum paperback).

J. J. Servan-Schreiber, *The American Challenge,* New York, Atheneum, 1968 (Avon paperback).

II. Behavioral Studies of the Corporation and Corporate Management

Chester I. Barnard, *The Functions of the Executive,* Cambridge, Mass., Harvard University Press, 1938.

Richard M. Cyert and James G. March, *A Behavioral Theory of the Firm,* Englewood Cliffs, Prentice-Hall, 1963.

Peter F. Drucker, *Concept of the Corporation,* New York, John Day, 1946 (Mentor paperback).

John G. Fuller, *The Gentlemen Conspirators,* New York, Grove Press, 1962.

W. Lloyd Warner and James Abegglen, *Big Business Leaders in America,* New York, Harper, 1955 (Atheneum paperback).

III. Corporate Ownership and Control

Adolf A. Berle, *Power Without Property,* New York, Harcourt, Brace, 1959 (Harvest paperback).

Adolf A. Berle and Gardiner C. Means, *The Modern Corporation and Private Property,* revised edition, New York, Harcourt, Brace and World, 1968 (Harvest paperback).

Joseph A. Livingston, *The American Stockholder,* Philadelphia, J. B. Lippincott, 1958 (Collier paperback).

IV. Industrial Organization and the Corporation—The Interrelationship Between Market Structure, Conduct, and Performance

Joe S. Bain, *Industrial Organization,* 2nd edition, New York, Wiley, 1968.

John Maurice Clark, *Competition as a Dynamic Process,* Washington, D.C., Brookings Institution, 1961.

A. D. H. Kaplan, Joel B. Dirlam, and R. F. Lanzillotti, *Pricing in Big Business: A Case Approach,* Washington, D.C., Brookings Institution, 1958 (paperback).

Douglas Needham, *Economic Analysis and Industrial Structure,* New York, Holt, Rinehart and Winston, 1969.

V. Public Policy and the Maintenance of Competition

William L. Baldwin, *Antitrust and the Changing Corporation,* Durham, N.C., Duke University Press, 1961.

John Kenneth Galbraith, *American Capitalism: The Concept of Countervailing Power,* Boston, Houghton Mifflin, 1956 (Sentry paperback).

Carl Kaysen and Donald F. Turner, *Antitrust Policy: An Economic and Legal Analysis,* Cambridge, Mass., Harvard University Press, 1959.

Martin L. Lindahl and William A. Carter, *Corporate Concentration and Public Policy,* 3rd edition, Englewood Cliffs, Prentice-Hall, 1959.

Mark S. Massel, *Competition and Monopoly,* New York, Doubleday, 1964.

Gardiner C. Means, *Pricing Power and the Public Interest,* New York, Harper, 1962.

Henry C. Simons, *Economic Policy for a Free Society,* Chicago, University of Chicago Press, 1948.

VI. Direct Regulation of Business as Public Utilities

Henry J. Friendly, *The Federal Administrative Agencies: The Need for Better Definition of Standards,* Cambridge, Mass., Harvard University Press, 1962.

Martin G. Glaeser, *Public Utilities in American Capitalism,* New York, Macmillan, 1957.

Harry M. Trebing, ed., *Performance Under Regulation,* East Lansing, Mich., Michigan State University Press, 1968.

Index

A Note on the Editor

Harry M. Trebing is Professor of Economics and Director of the Institute of Public Utilities at Michigan State University. He has served with the Federal Communications Commission and in 1968–1969 was a consultant to the President's Council of Economic Advisers and to the President's Task Force on Communications Policy. He is the author of *Performance Under Regulation* (with R. Hayden Howard) and *Rate of Return Under Regulation*.